The Thief of Happiness

Also by Bonnie Friedman

Writing Past Dark: Envy, Fear, Distraction,
and Other Dilemmas in the Writer's Life

The Thief of Happiness

The Story of an Extraordinary Psychotherapy

Bonnie Friedman

Beacon Press ■ Boston

Beacon Press
25 Beacon Street
Boston, Massachusetts 02108-2892
www.beacon.org

Beacon Press books
are published under the auspices of
the Unitarian Universalist Association of Congregations.

07 06 05 04 03   8 7 6 5 4 3 2 1

"My Gertrude Stein" first appeared, in slightly different form, in *Sister to Sister:
Women Write about the Unbreakable Bond,* edited by Patricia Foster (Doubleday,
1995).

This book is printed on acid-free paper that meets the
uncoated paper ANSI/NISO specifications for permanence
as revised in 1992.

Text design by Dean Bornstein
Composition by Wilsted & Taylor Publishing Services

Library of Congress Cataloging-in-Publication Data
Friedman, Bonnie.
The thief of happiness : the story of an extraordinary psychotherapy /
Bonnie Friedman.
   p.   cm.
ISBN 0-8070-7242-7 (cloth)
ISBN 0-8070-7247-8 (pbk.)
1. Friedman, Bonnie.   2. Analysands—United States—
Biography.   3. Psychotherapy—Case studies.   I. Title.
RC464.F75 A3 2000
616.89'14'092—dc21
2001002562

Contents

Introduction

"Enter treatment with me and you will write your book," said the woman with the molasses-edged Virginia accent on the other end of the phone, and so I did. I'd been unable to write for four months. I'd cursed, wept, stared out the window at tall boys banging basketballs as they went striding to Collins Cove at the end of my street and then, lazily scratching their arms from sunburn, came loping back; watched the yellow leaves twirl down from the London plane trees and the sky go lard white, holding back snow; scoured books by experts, even chanted affirmations, and nothing, nothing. The page stayed blank.

Two weeks after I began treatment, I was writing my book.

And addicted.

Dr. Harriet Sing was a tall woman with sardonic blue eyes and a ballerina's posture. She wore glossy black boots from which occasionally emanated a horsey scent, and dangling silver-and-turquoise earrings that framed a shrewd but welcoming face, and she had a sort of wry Andie MacDowell merriment although her hand when she shook mine was always firm and dry as a wood paddle, even after we'd sat for hours in her overheated office. She was finishing her doctorate while working at the Princeton mental health clinic when I first met her, a woman of about thirty-seven with a cello voice, her hand scratching notes into a yellow notebook.

At the start I sat on a gray fabric bench opposite her inquisitive gaze. Most of the treatment, though, I lay on a hard vanilla couch and stared into a Picasso room that opened onto a plank of Mediterranean. Sometimes the blue of that high sea was a wall of water rising, about to cut off the air supply. Usually, however, it was the very shade of bliss itself, and if I could just work my way past the eleven fat white chickens in the painting's foreground (how often I'd counted them!) and the two scrawny crows, if I could only decode the hieroglyphs flourishing up from the unconscious, the bliss would be mine.

Dr. Sing nodded her head. She seemed to be scratching her way into me with her pen and yellow notebook, as if she'd transformed into one of those arsenic chickens with its little red claws.

And from our very first sessions, strange things happened. A switch seemed to have been thrown in my life and the entire electromagnetic field reversed its current. My best girlfriends became terrifying. My husband's parents, too, converted into ogres. My pen flew across my page and I pumped gas into my Civic and raced north every other week, and mice overran my dreams, and my very own glorious sister turned and was revealed to be someone I'd never seen although we'd shared a bedroom growing up and I knew her imprint was on me like a fleur-de-lis seal pressed into warm wax.

"You're so different from how you were!" said my friend Linda, a decade-long reporter for *Newsweek*. We hadn't spoken in four years.

"What do you mean?"

"Well, you're much more confident. You've got your own opinions. No, it's more than that. You just really didn't believe in yourself before. There was always something questioning in your tone of voice. Did you do something?"

"I've been in therapy."

"Honey, whatever that person did, it works!"

I nodded, and Linda's words rang in my mind. No, I hadn't believed in myself. I'd seemed to be make-believe, at any instant liable to collapse back into a Cinderella with scabby knees whose true function was to scrub out ashes. That conviction of being worthwhile that many others had—I'd just never had it. I didn't know it could be acquired. I didn't know that there was a systematic way by which one could acquire it.

The therapy lasted seven years, more than many marriages. The last two I drove four hours in each direction to see her, a Friday pilgrimage. Count up the miles and I circled the earth. I packed peanut butter and banana sandwiches and oranges and wedged my cup of coffee next to the emergency brake, and set off early to ascend to Dr. Sing's hot white attic by one. And I went from being a person obliviously scraped out by envy to being someone who tended to feel okay and often thankful and glad. From being a person who chose spectacular, intimidating friends to being a person who chose friends with whom it was possible to feel interesting, too.

But the biggest effect of the therapy was something incalculable. In so many circumstances I used simply to vanish, as if a trapdoor had flopped open beneath my feet, or as if certain other people represented warps in the air, heat miasmas, the sight of which fixated and jinxed me, converting me into something inanimate. Now I could stay alive in far more situations. No, the effect of this therapy seemed bigger than even that: it acquainted me with something quite good and enduring, a tribe of downy chickens that thrive despite the persistence of two gaunt morbid crows, a feeling that life itself is good, and that most people are good, and a relief from a certain melancholia and hypervigilance.

"Leaving therapy is like stepping through a circle of fire," a great novelist once wrote. This proved accurate in my case.

Dr. Sing said I shouldn't stop. Her outright disapproval of my decision frightened me. I was afraid to leave without her blessing, afraid that without it I'd lose my writing again, and my equanimity. She had a mortgage on me, although it had been I paying her all those years. Still, she was the mistress of my soul, the queen of my unconscious. I worshipped—but how could I know this?—Dr. Sing. She possessed magic when everything else in life was dull and degraded; she set the magic in my hands, in my pen. She infused with meaning experiences that up until then had the blandness of Styrofoam, the bulk and screech of Styrofoam—the shadow of a tall brother slicing like a scissors up the pavement, a sister squat as a pasha at her desk, licking her finger, flipping an endless page in *The Father Brown Omnibus*, the part in her hair a perfect bisection of her head in the night window, ruler-straight and frighteningly pale.

Leaving Dr. Sing after a session was a protracted descent down Jacob's ladder through Maine, through Massachusetts, down to lower Connecticut and my own tan ranch house. The trip south was so long that by the time my garage door started to hoist I had the sensation I'd consumed the highway itself, and was full of grit, soot, pebbles—everything that Dr. Sing had for a shining moment transfig-ured. The disparity between the road under my wheels and the pagoda-esque height she occupied always seemed proof I must keep returning to her until no disparity existed and the shining pagoda had somehow become my world. She charted me; she formulated me. How could I ever go? She truly seemed the conquistador of the unbounded country inside, as if by naming my rivers and mountain-tops she'd staked an indelible claim and, if I left her, everything would be reduced to ink on a map, rendezvous points I couldn't reach alone.

Oh, fine for others to say go, leave, you'll be perfectly all right, don't worry a thing about it. I didn't know how to leave intact. And that was the way I wanted to go.

I was sitting in an apartment in Brooklyn half a year after I termi-nated, sipping from a big cool glass of pineapple juice and watching a TV balanced on a new, uninstalled boxed Sears dishwasher, when suddenly I put down my glass. A man was being interviewed whose wife had left her earthly "vessel." She was one of the Heaven's Gate people who synchronized their suicide to coincide with the Hale-Bopp comet, on which they believed they would fly off. This man himself had been a member of Heaven's Gate until just last year, when he'd left.

"Do you ever wish you'd just kidnapped her back to society?" the interviewer asked.

"No." The man shook his head firmly. "It would have done no good. She'd have been miserable and run back."

"What do you think of the leader, who went by the name of Do?"

"The thing you have to understand about him," said the man, "is that he bled sincerity."

I nodded. For my therapy had taught me a great deal about cults. It taught me what it feels like to think you know things lots of ordi-nary people never will and to believe you've been lucky enough to be taken up into the ranks of the elite. I'd discovered, too, what it means to be in the thrall of another person, to believe this other per-son has unique access to mystical information, and to have connection with her be synonymous with well-being and any division from her at all cause for racing anxiety. The entire rest of the world constituted outsiders. The words she said had an ecstatic effect on me whether or not I understood them. I couldn't imagine happiness in a life without Dr. Sing: How to stop missing her? I didn't know—despite the most excellent practical advice from those who wanted the best for me—how to gain release.

"You're wrecking your health!" screamed my mother when I got sick with a fever for the fourth time running after my eight-hour drive. "Wake up, honey! The coffee is burning. Look," she said desperately, "if you go up to her this week, I really don't want to talk to you again!"

I laughed. "It's okay, Mom."

"It's *not* okay," she said.

And it wasn't.

Still, it was imperative I find my own way out.

Cults aren't rare. Lots of us surrender our independent thinking surprisingly frequently; many passionate relationships are really a cult of two. And when you get something extraordinary from another person, something long-craved and with repercussions that shimmer through your entire life, something that literally affects your dreams at night and your use of them in the morning, it's probably good not to leave too soon.

I received something supremely useful and in leaving I gained still more. This is the story of a valuable spiritual apprenticeship and a triumphant independence. It starts with a block. As Dr. Sing pointed out, "All blocks are a fulfillment of the wish to say no." I didn't know to what I was saying no or that I was saying no. But no it was.

CHAPTER ONE

The Girl in the Cake

The prize I'd won had transformed into a curse. After a decade's hard work, I'd received validation. A book contract; a door to Oz. But instead of feeling rich, I was desperate. Instead of being handed a key, I'd been locked. I couldn't work on the book. I could scarcely breathe. An alarm rang just on the edge of audibility and something inside me went rigid, quivering, like a dog hearing a whistle that my conscious, human self couldn't detect.

My predicament, from what I could gather, had little to do with writing. It seemed to have to do with being a woman and a daughter. I'd arrived at some outer boundary of my personality and stepped past. I'd walked through a force field, unbeknownst. Activities that had been as easy as breathing now presented irresolvable complica-tions—pointing out to the woman at the dry cleaner's a shattered button caused by her pressing machine and asking that the button be fixed, deciding whether or not to meet a friend for supper in Har-vard Square. My very thoughts fled me as if fearing contamination. I felt trapped in a fairy tale where gold spins backward into hay, and the damsel, kissed at last, climbs into a block of ice.

I was thirty-two, happily married, and living on the ground floor of a sunny Victorian house in Salem, Massachusetts, with a scrap of beach at the end of the block and a big pink flourishing rosebush in the yard. I couldn't understand what had gone wrong.

Hadn't I been trained for success? I'd spent my girlhood sledding face-first down the hills of Van Cortlandt Park and reading *The Hardy Boys* and then *Ms.* When I was in seventh grade my sister mailed away for the Virginia Slims datebook, which, aside from pictures of women dashing from outhouses with cigarettes in their hands, featured a feminist quote for each week. I copied the quotes on orange and purple squares of paper from the chunky, twisting

■ 6

pad I kept in my thing drawer. Gloria Steinem. Betty Friedan. The squares formed a throbbing checkerboard I slept under: a women's lib grid. At thirteen I entered the Bronx High School of Science just as my brothers graduated, marching in every morning beneath the towering mosaic of Madame Curie with her test tube and Ptolemy beside a splayed, glittering compass, and the words EVERY GREAT ADVANCE IN SCIENCE HAS ISSUED FROM A NEW AUDAC-ITY OF IMAGINATION.

One brother became a hematologist/oncologist who directs a blood bank. The other is part of management in a prestigious engineering consulting firm that originated at M.I.T. My sister, unfortunately, succumbed to multiple sclerosis. But I continued to believe heart and soul in the American virtues of hard work and eventual reward. So why did my own yes turn into no? Why did the good thing, once I finally had it, thwart me?

Before I found Harriet Sing I tried and tried to understand, and blindly collected the materials I'd need for the journey ahead.

"If you can't write the book then we'll send the money back," suggested my husband one morning. We were side by side in the car in the driveway. I was wearing a plum, imitation-down coat over the T-shirt I'd slept in and red Dr. Scholl's sandals. He wore a pinstripe suit.

"We will not send the money back!" I said.

The magic money! It seemed like such a great quantity then, although in fact it would scarcely have afforded a diet of macaroni and cheese along a corridor of housemates in Allston.

Yet every box of Stella D'Oro Breakfast Treats it bought was enchanted and the two radial tires it purchased from Cambridge Tire in Malden seemed more beautiful than any others could possibly be. The money vanished fast. But even if I could, I wouldn't return it: that would be handing back the ball gown for rags. Still the spoken words haunted: "Send the money back . . . send it back," like the whisper initiating a dream sequence. How to flee that voice? Or could one annihilate it? The windows chattered and murmured from the trucks pounding their way down Broad Street. A phone

rang in a distant apartment. If only the world would be quiet, then I
could think. But even when I woke in the middle of the night the
streetlamp across Pickman Street buzzed like a cicada, and distant
sounds rushed in, a plane overhead, an ambulance racing.

Each sound seemed to spool toward an answer. Each sound—in-
terruptive, commanding—was something to which I couldn't help
but devote myself. I flew away on the roar of that plane but it dissolved into the thrum of the fridge compressor, the cube of the orange clock whirring on the peach crate beside me. In the morning,
sitting at the desk, I couldn't think a thought through to the end or
even the middle. Brakes screeched, the surface of the world broke
like a pond. Eleven-thirty and the sun was a grinning fool in the sky,
but I crept into my bed. In my ears rang that alarm on the very edge
of audibility, as if God Himself were stroking the hi-hat.

I'd longed to achieve, longed for a sign of acknowledgment. Still,
when it at last came, it upset me—the dash of sugar that throws
everything out of solution. The stuff that had lurked inside, saturated in transparency, became visible at last, crystallizing, cascading.
But what exactly was coming out? I'd always assumed I was basically
invisible. It didn't matter if I wore the same pilled gray sweater three
days in a row at college: no one saw. It didn't matter if I read a book
under my desk in fourth grade: no one could see. I believed quite literally I was mostly transparent; if I kept my glance averted then I was
no more than a mirage shimmer, a warp of air.

Yet with what hunger I had yearned to be "recognized"! As if
someone else's seeing me would endow me with something that
deserved to be seen. As if someone else's perception of me could
compensate for my inability to perceive myself. I was in fact my own
phantom limb. And I assumed the world's caress would arouse missing sensations—which would be delightful. Yet the first sensation of
a foot that's fallen asleep is a ghostly distension. There is an impulse
to pinch that limb, to force it to feel. There's even at times a fascination toward one's own helpless self—a nonchalant savagery released
by happening upon a victim who can't complain. With what glee
did I, as a child, probe the crusted yellow heel of my own inert foot,

lavishing disgust, daring to feel toward it what I would never feel toward another person? My fingernails gouged it, I scribbled with a pencil on its miraculous surface—that surface so like the orangish paraffin of old candle wax, the shiny rind of a cheese—astonished to discover when I at last stood the tremendous suffering of which that foot was capable. My eyes overflowed. Poor foot! Each step agonized. As did something raw inside me these days, something unsheathed.

The weeping was interesting. It obeyed a subterranean pattern of its own. It surfaced at odd times: while I was driving to Shaw's Superstore for ground turkey and soy sauce, and had just successfully executed a brisk left onto Route 116 across three lanes of traffic; while walking to the laundromat late one afternoon with my shopping cart, noticing a Russian blue cat with burning gold eyes staring out a basement window.

In the laundromat, I pried the clothes apart. They'd rusted to each other in the black Glad bags, a sharp-edged puzzle of fabric. But in the water the clothes relaxed and were restored to their lives as supple shirts and socks. Like seeing planks of salt cod turn into swimming fish. I shut the lid and leaned against the listing white machine. "Mama!" shouted a boy clapping two tiny orange boxes of Tide.

"Shut up and sit!" she said.

"But—"

"Don't make me say it twice!"

The boy trailed over to the gray seats bolted together in a row. Janet Jackson sang. I sailed through the ceiling, through the cloud cover, breathing detergent. Maybe it would all be okay.

Later, walking the cart of clean socks and shirts home over the blue slate of Salem, I still felt inexplicably happy. Maybe I'll be able to work tomorrow, I thought. Yet how many evenings I'd felt this way! I gazed into the Colonial-era homes edging the Common— the chandeliers vast as hoop skirts, the forest-green dining rooms. It seemed as if the inhabitants of these homes had inadvertently given me a gift, a view available just at this instant when day ceased to cloak the world in innocuous visibility and before the maids drew the curtains.

Blue ginger jars tall as soldiers flanked a doorway. A mirror floated above a mantel. The rooms were hardly furnished, as if their people had left behind just the odd grandfather clock and Persian rug necessary for afternoons when they traveled up from their Beacon Hill apartments on a nostalgic whim. Abandoned rooms of aristocratic childhoods, like tin-and-enamel dollhouses only half-loved. Two blocks remained. The slate lifted platters of streetlight that shrank as my feet drew close.

I thought of certain people I knew who used to their advantage the opportunities they created. A journalist in a leather bomber jacket who swaggered into any room. An ex-student with blue-black hair chopped in bangs who instantly sent a rejected story back into the world until all were taken; she was married with two children, nonmonogamous, undeceptive. Envy seeped through me for those who could want something and know it and not be crippled by that knowledge. In the gutter, bouquets of light wove amid the indigo. What a waste of life to be unhappy now, when there was so much beauty! A thousand keys seemed to be strewn all over, keys like those for a diary were hanging in clumps from the bushes, gusting in the air like pollen, rattling like the husks of bees, dozens of charm keys jingling—all useless. Answers were everywhere. *You have to accept yourself. Ease up. Trust your impulses.* Perfect answers weren't rare. They were in fact ubiquitous. But I couldn't use them. They loomed like the streetlamp haloes in the gutter, impossible to pick up.

But it made no sense to be so stuck. Nobody had told me "Stop!" Not teachers, not my parents. Yet somebody must have. Someone was saying "Stop!" right now. Who? A woman or a man? The wind heaved in the treetops. A fist of rain stung my cheek. The small side window of my own house swung up like a lantern containing a swatch of blue futon, a green vinyl chair. But my legs carried me right past.

I walked until my calves were sore and my cart had developed a wobble. My face felt swollen, gritty, my jaw inflamed. Foil leaves pasted themselves to the pavement. Something was at my back, and I wanted to see it. I wanted it to jump out. I gave it chance after chance. Get in front of me. Go. Come on, whatever you are! Right now! The cart handle was ice under my fingers. Then a long screech pared down to the very core of my ears —

"Are you crazy?"

A truck had hurled to a stop three inches away. The driver's mouth flapped like a sock. Red, corrugated. "What are you staring at?"

"Sorry," I murmured. Snippets of light raced across the pavement like the freed legs of scissors.

"Watch where you're going!" bellowed the voice, deep as an air horn. But obviously I couldn't be run over! I was busy. I was thinking. I yanked my cart up over the curb, jangling its measly frame like some idiot child. "Come on," I muttered. My legs bounced, rubbery. My husband's car was in its spot.

"What happened to you?" he asked.

I wiped my face with my hand. How bright the room was — a Xerox machine with the light flooding up. "Took a walk."

"In this weather?"

I shrugged.

"Well, I hope you got the exercise you wanted, sweetie, if that's what you were after." He smiled, a sympathetic smile beneath his russet mustache. I came over to him and gave him a hug, inhaling. "You smell good."

"I smell bad," he said.

I sat in a vinyl chair. My fleshy chin seemed scoured, burning and numb from the cold, something punished. My hand rose to it. "I don't know what's the matter with me."

"You'll be okay."

"You think so?"

"Sure."

I gazed at him as he peeled a grapefruit and chewed it, watching the news on TV.

"You really think so?"

"I said so. What do you want from me?"

My shoulders shrugged. In the background was that siren, like something muffled by a series of shut doors. That, I felt like saying. Don't you hear that? Doesn't that bother you? But it lurked so softly behind all the ordinary sounds I didn't think I could ever pinpoint it for him.

My neck, I discovered a few weeks later, had become so stiff I had to carry my head sideways. It was like some oddly wrapped bundle on which I couldn't quite get a grip. Next door, a lady with silky white hair cut level to her chin swept her driveway of acorns. She had a blue plastic broom that looked like a toy. She bent to pick up something—a rubber band?—which she deposited in her coat pocket. If only my own mother could help me, I suddenly thought, and recalled Dorothy locked in the witch's keep. "I'm here, Auntie Em!" But Em, unable even to imagine the possibility of Oz, can't see her. "Oh, don't go!" cries Dorothy—again, I was in tears.

I strode to the video store for the movie. Then sat at eleven in the morning with the blinds drawn, watching the gray then Technicolor screen. I was amazed to see the female quest depicted there: the effaced, chastising housebound woman to whom one must return, the green-faced, potent woman one must never become. And that third woman, the good fairy, whose pristine, bridal femininity had dismayed me as a child, frightened and even repulsed me—it so far exceeded what I might ever achieve: her unsmudged gauze, the smug spectral soar of her laugh.

"Glinda!" said my husband that evening. "I had a crush on her, as a boy."

"Really?" I said with a shudder.

Girls had been attuned to *The Man from U.N.C.L.E.*'s Napoleon Solo, and I myself dreamt of rising out of a tiered cake at his stag party, clad only in a string bikini. My first sexual fantasy, age eight—it had disturbed me even then, the degradation of it. For I'd imagined possessing breasts like melting ice cream, hips that swelled to viola curves, a shape so heavy it lolls: the body desired by men on sixties TV. In my fantasy, I was far from Glinda. I possessed a lewd joke of a body with me inside, as if I were wearing the cake.

And there was a connection between this and my current problem, I suspected: the lingering suspicion that something grotesque encrusted me.

I sat in my husband's big blue terry-cloth robe all through October. Fever soared through me the first week, and for the next three I was possessed of symptoms subtle as their own last echo. From the porch I watched rusting roses swell to the size of powder puffs below a sky the blue of acetate. "I am not 100 percent," I murmured—as if that would summon the missing element. What if I remained this way? The way enzymes, after a high fever, permanently warp?

"In the Soviet Union people are sick so often they take it for granted," reported the doctor at the clinic. "It's just a part of ordinary life and they simply go with it."

"I can't," I croaked, longing never to remove the paper sheet, never to stop inhaling the clinic's icy scent of alcohol, which made me feel sicker and thus more curable.

One night a *Geraldo* show was on after midnight. It was an exposé about how some gypsy fortune-tellers trick people into believing they are cursed, using chicken blood and feathers. A man in a sun hat, glasses, and beard, had paid a total of nine thousand dollars to have curses removed. The man spoke in a slurry, hasty way, swallowing his words. It was obvious why the fortune-teller chose him: he seemed desperately shy, congenitally appalled by himself. Shame stained him like a birthmark. I swallowed and realized my sore throat was gone. Energy coursed through me. I swung open the fridge door and wolfed cold lasagna, cold chicken, potatoes, apple pie. I hippity-hopped around my house and kissed my husband until he pushed me from the bed, moaning, "I'm sleeping." The next morning, bright and early, I was at my desk.

But it was no better.

The boy's adventure story is about leaving home for the big world. The girl's adventure story is about relinquishing the big world for home. Dorothy rushes back toward Em the whole time she has Oz. In contrast, Superman and Oedipus, Moses and even Luke Skywalker are all banished from homes they can never return to. I crossed my arms, thinking, thinking, sitting on a kitchen chair on the back porch. Men are supposed to go out into the world to cure it; that's heroic. Of course, lots of women leave too, nowadays. Still, I couldn't understand daughters who settled a country away from their parents. How did they allow themselves? Didn't they feel guilty?

I pulled the blue robe tighter. It was late on a November morning, over two months after my peculiar dysfunction began. Suddenly I was possessed of the conviction that I needed to understand anorexia. Anorexia seemed key to what was going on. The orange-rust-crusted safety pin, long as a spike, jabbed my fingers as I unpinned it. I pulled off the robe and graying nightgown beneath, showered, and dressed. Then I drove to the vast library in Danvers with its Palladian windows and several porticos. Here stretched a shelf of books on anorexia. I grabbed all of them and had to tip my head high up to rest my chin on the top book as I toted them down the stairs.

And at my kitchen table—oh, I couldn't turn the pages fast enough. I identified without knowing why. I was thirty-two, not fifteen. My problem wasn't food (although it had been, once). Still, my heart raced as I recognized the good daughter's intimacy with the mother, her craving to please, her terror of others' contempt. I flipped to the back flap of the best book and gazed at the author through chipped yellow cellophane. Hilde Bruch. Her gray hair was combed straight back. She wore glasses and had an intelligent, kind expression on her face. She'd fled Hitler's Germany for London while a young doctor, her bio said, and had lived her American life in top positions at hospitals. Every now and then while reading her book I stopped to look at her picture.

She reported that one girl asked "rather desperately" why do I feel so fat? Yet her weight was below seventy pounds at the time. Bruch said to her: "You think 'fat' means the same as 'not being good enough.' And that's what you fear."

I loved the simple, old-fashioned names like Annette and Ida that she gave the girls. And I liked that she cared enough to really see

into them, girls—a category of creature I'd grown up holding in
such meager esteem it seemed a wonder that anyone highly intelligent would study them with interest and sympathy.

"Superficially the relationship to the parents appears to be conge-
nial," I read. "Actually it is too close. . . ."

But was such a state of affairs possible? Could one be *too close?*
The book said that the closeness came at the expense of "excessive
conformity on the part of the child" and of her developing an au-
thentic self. I simply could not think what the sacrificed parts of the
daughter might be.

Then it occurred to me that the most obvious of the sacrificed
parts were literally the anorexic's breasts. She does not become her
own woman; she resists becoming a woman altogether. Her mother
is the woman. She remains something else.

But what to make of this? Remaining close to one's mother is
worth some sacrifices, I thought. I recalled a dinner with my mother
at Tavern on the Green. The crystal palace had twirled around us
like a carousel with its waltz of tuxedoed waiters, chandeliers glittering, and elegantly clad men and women sweeping past. "Is that
Henry Kissinger?" asked my mother. And it was. He stood outside,
sweating in a rumpled tuxedo, actually talking behind his hand. It
was a wedding. We waited to see the bride but she never appeared.
At last we, and half the restaurant, returned to our seats. "I'm so
happy to be with you!" my mother exclaimed.

I grasped her hand across the table and smiled.

"I just feel so alive when I'm with you!" she said. "You're such
magnificent company."

What a fraud I was. Other daughters were really extraordinary, really beautiful. How much I wanted for my mother! How I wished I
could make her truly, truly happy!

I stood up and circled the table and kissed her cool cheek. "I love
you, Mom," I said. My words sounded lumpish to me, the words of
an ugly-duckling daughter. I returned to my side of the table, aware
of my clumsy hips, wishing I could be ethereal, diaphanous. "Well,"
said my mother—for the waiter had slapped down an American Express leatherette folder. She lifted her glasses, set on a metal chain,

and perused the check. I was aware of her handbag, a black leather satchel with gold studs, sitting on the floor beside her. I'm so expensive, I felt. How I wished I were rich! And with a flutter of my hands could make all the costs disappear—and make the flashing greenhouse of a restaurant disappear, too.

Had I ever really wanted it? The supper had an odd pressure to it from start to finish somehow, embodying my mother's desire for great festivals, celebrations, her longing to be for once where the fun was happening and to have it. She'd grown up poor, the daughter of an immigrant widow. And she was happy, here. But there was an almost excessive, forced air to her happiness. Why, it seemed as if the power of her own imagination kept the crystal palace turning, the perfumed women treading past—and when the waiter casually insulted us, as he did when slapping the check down, as he had when he said, "That's it? Nothing else?" when we both declined dessert, I glanced away, unable to bear seeing the magic waver, her dreams ridiculed.

Now, tucking the blue robe up to my chin, I thought, But it's one of life's great satisfactions, to make one's mother happy. I've been lucky to remain close. Yet even when the flu departed I walked around with a paperback on anorexia shoved in my pocket. I carried it in my pocketbook when I went to Boston to visit friends and tucked it in my brown leather jacket on neighborhood walks. The stories in the book gave me a feeling of greater likelihood. They made my own story seem more possible. Even the parts about my sister, Anita—although how she fit into the anorexic pattern wasn't yet clear.

She'd been, after all, fat, sturdy, with a churning piston of body that could conquer any city pavement. She whispered stories to me while we rode the subway, her mouth close to my ear. She explained about the pallid people who survived layers and layers below Grand Central Station, a sunless village, and the underground station at Eighteenth Street where no train ever stops. Once I looked out and saw for myself the explosions of light in the darkness, the secret sleepers, a boy in a cap with earflaps staring, a man watching a blue TV—the flickering pillars tossing movie frames.

"Guess what station's next," she screamed too loudly in my ear. I never could. She knew the anatomy of the subway before I realized it had one, when I still assumed the subway could stop anywhere, like a car. She even knew which mosaic hung in each station: the three-headed lady, the beaver balancing on its tail, the blindfolded woman seated on a throne. She'd organized the world when to me it was all still random, shimmering, and a beech tree might grow elm leaves, and a willow might flourish in a square of city street.

Once, lying on the backseat of my father's LeSabre as a girl, I noticed that one eye saw my slack hand floating, and the other saw it sunk; one eye saw my pink Cracker Jack ring, and the other saw it vanish. One eye saw my mother, and the other Anita, but even with both eyes open something was missing. I couldn't infer myself. What we see as blue is every color being absorbed but blue. I was absorbed entirely in others, and couldn't see myself. My story was a page edge flashing past, a radio band you've driven through before the signal comes in clear.

One morning the lady with a neat tulip figure on *Romper Room* stared through her hoop out into TV-land. "I see Jimmy," she said. "I see Susie. I see Nancy." I held my breath so long I thought I'd faint, nearly raising my hand to the black-and-white TV. "Bonnie. See Bonnie," I whispered. Suddenly the credits were rushing by. She was still saying names. She was waving. A commercial was on for Sugar Frosted Flakes. Wasn't she coming back? Was it over? Another commercial came on. Something prickled my nose. From the kitchen came the rap of a shut cupboard, the clank of sorted silverware. My mother was annoyed I was home. I swallowed. I was sick. My throat was burning sore. Or had I made it up? Had I invented this whole illness, forced the thermometer to heat by the strength of my desire? I was a cheater. I wanted home. And my mother knew it, which is why she resented my clinging hand, the grimy fingers that gripped her skirt. "Let go," she said, and I always did.

And found Anita, if she was home. Or waited for her, singing the songs she taught.

"Sit next to me," said Anita. "Watch me paste stamps in my book. Watch me do sponge art. Watch me weave a sit-upon." I sat so close our chairs touched. I was grateful for her busy fingers, her Girl Scout songs, her flesh that looked like it could endure a thousand pinches. I believed in Anita and gloried in her strength. I yearned to amount to something, too. Yet avoided myself. "Let go!" I told myself, and left myself in a hundred places. "I'm not who I was," I murmured, recalling something embarrassing I'd said an hour earlier. I slid from myself like the iron filings that assemble into now the bald man's hair, now his hat, now his beard, racing after the magnetic wand.

My mother was the magnetic wand, and my sister, too—and nothing yet held me in place. I'd always assumed that writing success, if I ever achieved it, would supply me my own wand. When even it didn't, when it too scattered me, for the first time I panicked.

I had not, as a child, been intelligent. My tests came back with red 60s and 70s, and sometimes worse. Then, at sixteen, I manufactured a mind.

Anita was away in Israel, my brothers at college. "Try writing down everything you remember," said my history teacher. "Then compare it with the chapter." I discovered I learned by copying, and copied everything—history, physics, lives of mathematicians, pages of Jane Austen. "'My dear Mr. Bennet,' said his lady to him one day, 'have you heard that Netherfield Park is let at last?'" Whatever I copied stuck. Senior year nights with the Lightolier lamp burning, yellow paper sifting to the floor, sheet after sheet of other people's sentences. And it was all still there the next day for the test!

One afternoon I overheard my mother describe to her friend Sylvia my oldest brother's life at Lehigh. She used a tone of disapproving admiration: "He lives a monastic existence. He's in the library until midnight!" I vowed to join that monastery. And when I got to college a few years later, I did. How I loved the stiffness of the library's spindly Windsor chairs, the way they made me shift and shift again like a wood corset. Mine was the last seat relinquished in the annex where a clock the size of a hatbox presided high on the wall, its two filigreed hands sliding closer and closer until they finally met to clasp straight up. The librarian jangled her keys.

At five past midnight the riveted library doors swung shut behind
me. The moon was a snipped hole in the sky, leaking bluish white.
Everything I could possibly do was done. Something clean as ammonia rinsed my veins. The earth was blue, lit by a fluorescent
moon. As I passed the dorms of partiers and sleepers, and the occasional man and woman holding hands, I shook my head. How com-
placent! Didn't they crave the sparklers that lit only after hours of
concentration? I couldn't understand it, couldn't understand it,
their renouncing the marvelous hardness of the desk, a matchbook's
stripe to strike against. It seemed to me that only by torturous rigor
could something original be glimpsed. And how I wanted something original! It was the only way not to disappear into the general
aspic of life, the general lemon Jell-O tallow.

My one achievement, I believed at the time, was the slimness I'd
achieved in high school. Senior year I'd got so thin that my period
went. I yanked the thin brown belt of my favorite dress to the tightest
hole and then past it. My father gouged two new holes in the belt
with a nut pick. Monday nights my mother and I sat on brown folding chairs at Weight Watchers at the Riverdale Y. I listened hard to
the stories: the lady whose teeth were wired shut and who put the
weekly cow's liver in the blender and drank it—that's how devoted
she was. The woman who traveled from beyond Gun Hill Road to
the one store in the Bronx that sold Frosted Treats and bought fourteen milk equivalents to last two weeks.

My mother slathered yellow mustard on iceberg lettuce. I
chomped carrots the size of billy clubs and whose yellowish fibrous
cores fell out like the middle of a hard-boiled egg. I studied the lists
of "legal" foods in the narrow pink pamphlet and the model menus
at the back with their single slice of French toast, their "Danish
Treat" of broiled cottage cheese. How nice to have just how to live
all written out in a pamphlet! And I liked that the pamphlet was the
same pink as the Hallmark datebooks given away in card shops—
books the size of a compact, and ruled into days tiny as Chiclets,
each day just big enough for you to write the letter *P* to signify your
period. What other use could there be? Days like saccharine tablets.
Days like the faces of blank dice. I cherished the free pink booklets

into which only the neatest life could fit. Weight Watchers seemed the path toward such a life. Here are the rules, use them. Until even the letter *P* became unnecessary. My period dried up. I read *Flowers for Algernon* and identified with the man poised in the doorway, glancing back in terror at the old stupid formless self in which he'd lived like a candle guttering in its own pool of wax.

Walking over a path at college one afternoon, a magazine in my hands, I stopped and stared at a sentence in an *Ellery Queen* my sister had sent. "He was asked to justify his existence."

What?

The character in the story sought admission to a club. This question comprised the entire entrance exam. But justify one's existence? Wasn't that like being asked to justify the moon or high tide? I shook my head and copied the mysterious phrase inside myself, to be recalled at the first instance when I in fact stopped trying to justify my own existence: when I succumbed to my paralysis, the rebellion I waged against my own desires.

For several months I lived in the blue robe, scribbling notes. Glinda and the Wicked Witch, anorexia, monastery libraries, yes, yes, but what did it all mean? Semaphores without the guide to understand them. And still I couldn't do my work.

Then one December morning, sitting down to my desk, I noticed that the sun had bleached the blank page yellow. It had sat empty on my desk long enough to stiffen and turn this marigold shade. I jumped up, strode the room, saw myself yellowing, hardening, turning to calluses the color of wax. I shook my head, sat down on the floor, dragged the phone over, and searched the pages of a dusty jade vinyl address book for the number of a certain therapist. I'd been in treatment with this woman once for a year when I lived in New Jersey.

The therapy had made no difference in my life. It hadn't mattered to me if I arrived late to her sessions or early. When I moved away we shook hands and I didn't feel an instant's regret. I'd gone to her to help me make a decision and she hadn't helped me make it.

It was a sign of my desperation that I resorted to her now. But perhaps some phone sessions would help.

Her Princeton number was answered by a recording. Her new number had an entirely different area code.

"You have reached Dr. Sing's office," her calm, melodious voice announced in some far-off place. "I cannot come to the phone but will return your message."

A slight southern accent, sexy and quite confident. I left my number, and walked around the block.

The phone was ringing when I unlocked the door, and I went flying toward it. "Oh, Dr. Sing! Thank you so much for calling back."

"Of course," she said.

"It's so nice to hear your voice!"

"Yours, too."

How calm she sounded! And unsurprised, as if we'd just spoken yesterday.

"But where are you?" I asked.

"Brunswick, Maine."

"Why did you move?"

Silence. So I plunged on and described my situation. Might she give me some phone sessions?

"Long-distance treatment?" She sounded skeptical. "Bonnie, physically seeing me and being with me are therapeutic. I need to be real to you, not just a voice over the phone."

"You are real to me," I said.

"Therapy isn't just words."

"I know that. I don't want just words." I wrapped the tan cord between my fingers, holding it tight.

"We need to physically be together for the treatment to work," she said. "I'm sorry, but I can't do it any other way." And then: "Enter treatment with me and you will write your book."

My husband and I owned a rusted silver Civic. This car was as small as a clown car; you could reach back and lock the opposite rear door while you drove. I dropped my husband off at his office in Gloucester amid the smell of fish and the ringing of masts. "Good luck!" he said. "I hope she can help you, honey." He kissed me and vanished behind the glass doors of his office building. The trip to Maine took two and a half hours.

Snow spread across the Bowdoin green like a fitted sheet. In Salem all had been dry and stone-gray. Here the steeple of the church thrust white into the blue sky as if to illustrate the definition of a straight edge. Women wore floral thermal underwear beneath their skirts and long stocking caps like elves. Every third person carried a hockey stick.

"It's good to see you again," I said eagerly as I rushed into Dr. Sing's office.

"It's good to see you, too," she answered, smiling. She shook my hand firmly—a tall woman with black hair brushed back in a ponytail held by a silver filigree clip. She had crinkly dark-blue eyes and wore a white blouse pleated like a tuxedo shirt. The only inelegant thing about her was her flat, heavy yellow hands with which I felt a strange affinity.

"I hope you can help me!"

"I'm sure I can."

"I hope you're not planning to move again."

She smiled and remained silent. Her office was at the mental health clinic run by Bowdoin. A green construction-paper chart stuck with gold stars was taped to the wall, and across from my bench stuffed tigers and bears lolled their heads on a shelf. They looked oddly sawn at the throat—as if their old sawdust contents had been emptied and new fresher sawdust put in, and then the whole hastily sewn shut. The land out the window behind her was winter-battered, the pink of old leather. A single row of books hung over her desk. This office was not really hers, I gathered. She used it in rotation with others. She was completing her dissertation. If she stood, it seemed her head would brush the ceiling. Everything about her was confident.

"I don't know what's the matter with me," I said.

"We'll find out."

"It would be nice to think you already knew." I smiled.

"I have some suspicions."

"I just want to dump it all out in front of you and let you make sense of the tangle."

She smiled, a beautiful smile.

"My mother once untangled something for me," I said impulsively, remembering the old rules. "A chain."

"Yes?"

But my heart quickened, and I shook my head. "I want to talk about what's wrong. I don't have a lot of time. I'm in a hurry."

"You're in a hurry," she murmured, nodding her head slowly. "You don't want to waste any time."

"Yes!"

She raised her eyebrows.

I laughed. "Oh, I would like to tell you about the chain," I said. "But I have only this hour and then have to go back. I want to know why I am this way, what's going on."

She sat silent, patient. Then said, "What makes you think the chain is unconnected with why you are that way?"

I smiled. "Oh, I'd like to believe it was connected, Dr. Sing. That everything's connected."

"What makes you think it isn't?"

For an instant, a spun-sugar construction—a dollhouse? a map? —seemed to shimmer in the air. What if nothing was wasted? What if it all linked up?

"It had gotten all bunched up, this chain," I said. "It was tarnished silver, an old present from Paul, my husband."

She nodded.

"I suppose I hadn't taken very good care of it. Well, my mother and I had gone shopping at Gimbel's, at the Cross County Shopping Center. We were in one of the changing booths, which are painted pink. These awful boxy garish changing rooms! I wanted to throw the chain away. It was tarnished and ugly and clumped up with knots, and it was cheap—but my mother, she said she would try to untangle it. While I tried on clothes, she worked at it with her fingers. She was so patient. And then she handed it back to me, ready to slip around my neck."

Dr. Sing nodded.

I blinked at the blurry hardscrabble earth behind her. It seemed to be Dr. Sing's own battered history, what she had traveled through to arrive here. "It was so nice of her," I said.

I could see the movement of Dr. Sing's head as she nodded, although I was looking past her to the earth.

"I'm just so angry at myself," I said abruptly. "I can't understand why I can't work. I don't know what's the matter with me."

"It's frustrating," she agreed.

We were both silent a moment, then she said, "You have some sort of impulse to throw things away. But you want me to prevent you. You want me to save these things, to show you they deserve to be saved."

I recalled a computer program I'd heard about called Psychotherapist. It parroted back what you'd just told it, but as a question.

"Sometimes I think there is a book of shit and there is a book of gold," I said suddenly. "I want so much to write the book of gold! But I'm afraid the other book, the dirty, disgusting book will emerge. I had this feeling that if I could bring my editor the bad book—just however bad it would be—then I could get it out of the way, and the book of gold could come."

"Bring me the book of shit," she said.

I laughed. "Impossible!" She was so clean. Everything in Maine seemed pure and wintry and pristine. She reminded me of Glinda in *The Wizard of Oz*. "I don't want to soil you."

"Don't you?" she said.

CHAPTER TWO

Aliens

During our second session I discovered that I couldn't tell her anything important.

If I told her a dream, I no longer cared about it. If I told her an idea I might put in my book, I suddenly no longer wanted to put it. I felt cold toward it. It was hers.

"Many writers refuse to describe what they're working on," I explained.

"Why is that?"

"It removes the mystery. Best to keep the idea inchoate."

"Ah."

"Until the right time."

Dr. Sing nodded. She was wearing a white peasant blouse with orange and brick-red embroidery down the sleeves, and a long blue skirt.

I crossed my arms. "You know, that chain I described to you last week—I have no feeling toward it. I don't care about it anymore. It's yours."

"You've given it to me?"

"You've taken it."

"Was there anyone in your past who appropriated your things?"

I could practically hear her turning pages in a textbook. "No."

"But inside you, someone is now appropriating your things."

I shrugged. "You know, that word 'inchoate' is just stuck in my mind. It's actually a word I hate. It reminds me of the word aliens. The undercooked diploid center of the word. The way that the *i* and the *e* are together. I wonder if that's significant?"

"The way the *i* is with the *e*," she said, musing.

"Glued. Tangled. Like a cell undergoing mitosis—the DNA's doubled but the two cells haven't separated yet. It's disturbing."

She nodded.

"My childhood fear was aliens," I said. "I was afraid aliens would kidnap my mother. I felt outer-space beings were watching my parents and my whole family. They had a very cold, analytical attitude toward us. They didn't care if we were harmed. They didn't know their vast power over us."

"Ah."

"You remind me of an alien," I said.

She smiled as if greatly pleased. "In what way?"

"You can do great damage without intending it."

"You're saying I must be very careful in how I treat you. That the slightest pressure can be painful."

I shifted in my chair, suddenly cleft by boredom. "Sometimes when you say something, I feel estranged from it. It seems too simple. I feel all sorts of complexities get lost. I'm shouting across a great distance to you. Although, in another way, I actually believe that you understand me completely before I've said a word."

"Is that what you wish? That I can understand you before you speak?"

"Yes." But then my heart beat hard and I added, "Actually, that's a scary thought—thinking you could get inside me, having no barrier against you. What if you're destructive? What if you decided to damage what's inside me, or to take it? It reminds me of how I used to stand outside my apartment door when I was a girl and think, What if my mother's been kidnapped by aliens? And what if they've left a monster who looks and behaves just like my mother? How would I ever know?"

She nodded, pushing a hank of hair behind her ear. "And you wonder if a monster might be substituted for me?"

"You might have a monster inside you, a cold, mechanistic, and cruel aspect of yourself."

"So there are two me's."

"There's the real you, which is warm and full of feeling. And there is this mechanical, dead, voracious, other being. Not you."

Again she nodded.

"I'm afraid I will lose the warm, empathetic you to the not you," I said.

"I'm unreliable."

"Yes—not that you can help it."

"No, it's not my fault."

I nodded.

She said, "I understand you perfectly."

And so it began, the clotted romance, the two lenses fused and sticking, the pilgrimage north. She became the yellow foot I gouged, and the suffering foot I cherished. I rose out of a cake for her, turning, exposing myself, clad in myself, the very stuff of me, staring her in the eyes, and she did not turn away. She never said, "Let go." If anything, she said, "Come to me" more than I liked. Within two weeks, I was writing the book I meant to.

The flip side to the therapist's power was her power. She made me feel she owned my words. She returned them when she pleased. Some days she couldn't be bothered. Those days, I couldn't write. Other days she relented, and after I left a message on her machine she phoned me back in the late afternoon, and cheated by giving me praise for my work, saying she liked what I'd described of it. Then, what glory! What a blaze leapt up, white-blue, struck from a subway's rails!

I thought about her so much, I half-believed I invented her. But she was real. She had a real voice with a Virginia accent, and a real body which was lean and unusually erect, as if she'd been a high school girl who grew too fast and had to consciously learn poise (she looked like she could stroll across a room balancing a book on her head), and she had real hair, blue-black. After several weeks it became obvious that she favored long blue skirts and white shirts with tubular, tight cuffs. Her missionary's costume, I thought. Perhaps she'd devised it so she wouldn't have to think about clothes. But what armies of blue skirts her closet must contain!—wool for February, cotton for August with pleats like cupcake frills. "I wonder why you're thinking about my closet," she said. "How could I not think about it?" I answered. "You almost always wear a blue skirt. Are you wearing one today?"—for we were having a phone appointment. We had one for an hour every other week, between times when I drove north for what were now two-hour sessions.

"What do you think?"

I smiled. "Yes."

"I wonder what else you see in my closet?"

"Just the skirts and white shirts. Boots. You're very well organized. Better organized than I am."

"Although I seem to own less?"

"Well, you're more selective. And there are depths to your closet. It goes back and back like a corridor. I can't see the end of it."

"That might change," she said dryly.

She tapped her Bic against her teeth while thinking. Occasionally, mechanically, she wound her pretty gold watch. I was so glad to have found her. I thought about her, dreamt about her, split her into two people in my dreams, both of whom she claimed were me but which I knew, beyond being me, were her. Sometimes it seemed strange that the woman who a few years before had been as easy to leave as an old magazine should now acquire such absolute necessity. What changed? I told myself that I'd put little into my treatment before, so got little out. Now she restored my clarity. She let me know that the shards of leaves that chased my heels on the streets meant something, clattering their cocoon bodies, scrabbling like spirit-mice, like her own rattling knife-blade skirts pursuing me.

And slowly I understood why I'd gotten stuck, why in the middle of my life my feet sank into cement. I could not become the successful woman I dreamt I'd be and remain the girl I was. I could not leave myself everywhere and also accrue. I could not shuck myself continually and gather my strength. I could not appall myself and be satisfied.

Since I'd never psychically left my mother's home, I now constructed a home up north that I could learn to leave. It was this woman's office, but when I closed my eyes it was the old neighborhood, home of the party line and mermaid wallpaper, and my sister's strong floury hands rolling dough on the table over and over to get it thin. And at the same time, my new home was strangely clinical, the air carrying a suggestion of alcohol evaporating, all boxy institutional edges and Sears art.

In seven years, I never lifted a tissue from Harriet Sing's box. I never broke an object. I never stole, at least on purpose. I begrudged every shift of furniture. I arranged the chairs the way I pleased. Like everything with transference swabbed over it, there was the suspicion she would lift off a paper that covered the entire office after I left and discard the soiled sheet. Then the office would look precisely the same for the next client.

Once or twice I dashed back into the room after we parted: Had she turned into a tin toy? Was she chatting with her boyfriend on the phone? Was she ordinary? Exhausted? Did she still exist? Those moments were the sweetest—the startled glance of her blue eyes, or her body stepping across the floor, existing in another part of the room, as if the cornered king on the chess board has just flown like a knight, and I'd tricked her into revealing she liked me before she could think.

CHAPTER THREE

Shangri-La

A horse loomed in the corridor of a ramshackle house, a house with Contac-papered furniture and bulging mint green walls. The horse's body was covered with welts that looked like erasers or pink mouths.

"Did you dream that when you touched the horse welts they grew in size?" Dr. Sing asked.

I swiveled on the couch. "Yes! How did you know?"

She scratched a note. "And there was a policeman."

"Have you *heard* this dream before? Has anyone else ever told you this dream?"

"No."

"But you know it."

"I know you, Bonnie."

"Oh." The sensation shivered through me that she'd invented everything my glance fell on—the walls, the ceiling, the spigot of the sprinkler system with its single impaled star, as well as the world outside, its racing pavements and scrolling skies. She'd pored over esoteric books at Princeton, I knew, having often seen leather-bound volumes piled on her desk, their gold-embossed letters mostly flaked off or dully glimmering. What mysteries had opened themselves to her? "Well, what does the dream mean?"

"Right now my telling you is not important," she said. "What's important are the associations you have to it."

I nodded.

"But let me conjecture about something," she added abruptly, leaning forward as if she couldn't help herself. She began to undo the bottom button clasping shut the columnar cuff over her wrist, then seemed to notice and let her hand drop. "Your mother was very depressed when you were young, wasn't she?"

"You know that, Harriet."

"And when you finally left home to go to school, you worried about her."

"True."

"And—after the age of six you didn't touch your own body. I mean"—she shrugged—"you stopped masturbating."

My mouth had a dry, odd feeling. This I'd never told her.

"And your desires seemed so big to you. Grotesque. Walls with lips jutting from them."

"Harriet! That's an image I've often thought—"

"And you didn't want to walk near the walls. You didn't want to touch them. You were afraid of being swallowed up."

A prickle swept down my spine. She held up one of her big yellow hands and gazed at me. "You thought something bad might happen to her while you were away. She seemed so fragile—like fraying plaster."

"Exactly!"

"But you see, Bonnie, she was much stronger than you ever knew."

"Was she, Harriet?"

"Isn't she going strong now?"

"Yes."

"You needed to see her as fragile. That way you didn't need to take responsibility for your own negative projections onto her." Her eyes were the blue of dusk but with something burning behind them, as if there were a barn fire far in the distance. "We all have them," she remarked.

"Even you, Harriet? But that worries me. Do you have negative projections onto me?"

"What do you think, Bonnie?"

"I think you do. It's what scares me." For it seemed suddenly that whatever she thought of me would be the truth of myself.

"And what do you imagine my negative projections might be?"

"I ask so much of you," I replied. "I think it makes you irritable. I think you're growing more irritable by the moment, actually." I smiled as if I were kidding. "Not that you can help it."

She nodded as if to say: You need never use that phrase again.

Thank you, my smile answered her. For a moment my mouth itself was too lazy to speak. I was convinced that she could read my mind.

"Yes?" she said.

"Oh, I was so happy for a moment." Were we speaking out loud? I had the strange sensation we weren't. But then where did the words exist? In the Picasso poster, the chickens on the shelves seemed as organized as files in a file cabinet.

"Were you?" she said.

"What?"

"Happy?"

An erotic sensation swept over me, as if my skin was rising toward her hand like fabric sticky with static electricity. I yawned. "Oh yes." I gazed at the framboise chickens, plump as feather pillows. Harriet's hand was playing with the button again. She half slid it out of its hole, then pressed it back in again and let her hand drop. Had she really guessed my dream, or was it just the impression I'd had of this session? I wanted to ask her; I suddenly felt quite unsure if in fact she'd told me about the policeman or if I'd told her. I must have told her. I'd certainly told her about the walls swollen with desires; it was just this drowsy delirium that let me recall it as her telling me. "This is nice." My voice came from someplace far away.

"But you were saying that you worried I was becoming irritable with you. Why would I become irritable?"

"Because I take so much, Harriet. It irritates you—like chafing your skin." I sighed. "You wish I would take less. I'm seeming greedier and greedier to you."

"Did your mother get irritable with you?"

"Hmmm?" The air cascaded with dust motes. "I don't know. No."

"Are you sure?"

"Yes."

Harriet nodded, and her nod seemed to say I agree that you believe what you just told me. However, I disagree with what you said. It was a very complicated but pleasing smile, and made me feel that of course there were things about my own experience that she knew better than I, just as a gynecologist knows a woman's internal organs with greater expertise than she knows them herself. I said: "But my dream of the welts and the policeman—what do you think they mean?"

"What do you think?"

"Sex and censure," I replied.

She nodded. "It's hard for you to take what you want."

"I want to learn to do that, Harriet."

"And I want that for you."

"Oh, do you? Because it seems that—it seems that if you really want that for me, then it will be possible! Do you really, or do you just think you do?"

She gazed at me. Her eyes were an Ionian blue, the supersaturated azure of a postcard sky, the sky over Shangri-La. "I do," she said, and I believed her.

I hadn't yet mentioned to her I was writing my book. I was afraid to notice this success myself. And I was afraid she'd unwittingly take my writing away, despite herself, the way she'd amputated my feelings toward the other things I'd told her about. Yet there I sat at my gnawed thrift-shop Ethan Allan desk every day, filling newsprint pages. My pen rasped across the coarse blank paper for hours on end while I gazed down through half-shut eyes.

And now everything I wrote, because implicitly linked to her, brimmed with significance. My own handwriting on the page appeared intricate as lines of alephs and beths crooking toward some brand-new meaning and vibrating like the Mexican jumping beans that shimmied down the grooves of my childhood racetrack, dozens of capsules pulsing with life—worms? snails?—the pills throbbing in my warm hands. My own handwriting seemed like that. Because nothing the mind leapt to was imperfect. Nothing was an accident.

"I'm sure your work is good," Harriet had declared one day when I'd begged for a response.

"But why is that?" At the time my face was covered with tears.

"Because everything you do has value, Bonnie."

An oracular sentence. I could take it in two opposite ways. It could be empty of significance—after all, everything that everyone does has some kind of value. Or I could take it in the spirit she seemed to intend, which was that I was special and that everything I did was imbued with meaning.

I chose of course the second way. And from time to time recalled her words while I was writing. "Everything you do has value." My pen raced more swiftly over the page. Dr. Sing conveyed to me the sensation that deep within me thought was happening. She was curious about what I found trivial: the yellow scuffed heels of my husband's wing-tip shoes, a glimpse of Paul asleep, unshaven, looking defenseless and handsome in the early morning, and my reaction to Paul's anxiety when he came home from volunteer work on Sunday nights at the homeless shelter on Crombie Street.

"There are people living there no different from me," he said. "A little bit of bad luck and we could lose everything, too."

I'd fallen asleep buried under quilts in front of the TV at 9:30 watching Joseph Campbell explain the different incarnations of Krishna, even though I'd kept murmuring to myself, "Stay awake. This is so interesting!"

"Those people might seem similar to you, but they really aren't," I said, turning on my side.

"You haven't met them."

"I know, but even if you lost everything, you have so much drive, Paul, that you would just find some kind of a job and apply yourself and build it all back. You would."

He nodded, considering. "Are you going to stay out here?" he said. "You're taking up the whole couch."

"Okay. I'll go into the bedroom."

I did, trailing quilts, and leaving the door ajar so I could hear Paul and the TV. *Booknotes* was on. Brian Lamb asked, "Did you write this longhand?"

"He always asks that," I shouted. I came back in, dragging my quilts.

"I thought you were going to sleep. It's my time to be up by myself alone."

"Okay," I said, a little hurt, and trailed back off to bed.

I told Dr. Sing all this. She nodded, leaning her head, chewing the top of her pen. She was an Anita saying yes to everywhere my subway car stopped, and if my willow unfurled aspen leaves, she didn't object. She did not ask me to turn myself down, or up, or to compliment her, or even—for a long time—to submit to my insurance company the linen-yellow bills from her that I was collecting.

What I'd assumed the contract would bring I received, instead, in her office. She imbued me with a sense of inner richness. Everything that occurred to me—my irritation with the sprinkler head poking down from the ceiling, my mother avoiding me when I was ten and singing "We shall overcome," the birds with sharp beaks my sister folded out of origami paper, a burr of sarcasm I found in the therapist's voice—all became fused and transformed, as if blown through a pipe to form a polyethylene balloon. I carried this balloon home, but it leaked air. Soon it was like many of my other objects, ugly as gum scraped off a shoe, and I marveled at my old ecstasy experienced at Dr. Sing's. Everything had possessed a mouth, and spoke: the thin carved legs of Dr. Sing's desk, the scratch of her pen behind me.

Together we re-created what once I achieved only by myself after hours of Colette, endless afternoons of Virginia Woolf and Flaubert: the world was shuttling looms, everything flying into place, crosshatched, assembling, even the honk of a bus just right. But at home, I missed the sensation of thrilling coherence. She fooled me. Or we'd been fools together, two village idiots blathering over the pavement, falling into raptures at pigeon spatterings, a galaxy of blue stars and comets! I could have wept with longing for the ecstasy of her office. For an instant—oh, an instant!—everything I'd craved had seemed true, and every bang in the pipes, every clang and gasp of the plumbing was part of the one big thought, not separate from it. I couldn't wait to speak to her again, for her to restore belief.

There must be a thief of happiness. When something goes missing, there must be a thief. How to understand the frequent loss of joy? Between the party and one's own bed, a thief of happiness. Between the rollicking bar and the bathroom mirror, another thief. Between yesterday night and this morning, a thief of happiness. Between good-bye and the phone striking the receiver, a thief.

My thief was not, in fact, some enemy of the writing contract. It was the contract itself, which, although I'd craved it, I experienced as aggressive. Judgmental. The father who steps into the room and commands: think. The moth, devouring. Confusion had afforded me a placid girlhood. Confusion had been the state of grace in which my dazzled girlhood passed, absolved of the passions that rattled my friends. Confusion was the smiling state into which my mind dissolved when my sister whom I adored pinched me hard, explaining this was called a kanip. "Am I giving you conniptions?" she inquired, my cheeks in the vise of her four iron fingers. She laughed, gloriously, and left my cheeks pounding as she dashed— but ah, she was thrilling!—out into the street.

"Why, you were abused!" declared Dr. Sing.

I smiled. Such a diminution of the English language!

Yet something *had* transpired between Anita and me. Confusion had allowed me to keep stroking her arm and kissing her hand.

CHAPTER FOUR

In the Gold Star Room

That first winter I drove to her through snowstorms, listening to AM radio. Anybody talking: Dr. Joy Brown exclaiming in a spasm of frustration "But what is your question to me?" to people fogged in with complaints, advice shows where the term "mechanic's lien" inevitably came up, programs where banjo clocks and collections of Flintstones cups were auctioned over the air and a homeopathic veterinarian gave advice on pets. The news and the incessant ads for Garleek-brand garlic on these stations were delivered with staccato urgency by what sounded like soldiers couched in foxholes. Static swallowed one announcer, and I spun the dial. "From the weather center in Montpelier, Vermont, this is mete-urologist . . ." I smiled: the man who always tripped over his job title. Then I recited along with the ad for Hooked on Phonics.

One Tuesday I rented a yellow Aries from Rent-A-Wreck. Our Civic was in the shop. Snow fell heavily after Newburyport out of a sky the color of a Band-Aid, and when I tapped the brakes near Portland, the front wheels slid. The whole front of the car initiated a slow swing to the left, into oncoming traffic. I marveled at the sublime calm that came over me. The headlights of the truck behind me shone straight at me through my front windshield. And still the Aries turned! On and on it went until the car came to rest face-forward, lodged in the powdery deep snow on the side of the road.

Blood banged in my ears. My chest felt tight. I'd been holding my breath so long it had come to feel normal, but now it actually scared me to draw breath again—is that when everything would crash? I shut off the engine. The car ticked, and then all went deaf. Silence had dropped over everything as abruptly as a cloth over a birdcage. White gobs of snow accumulated on the windshield. I closed my eyes, opened them. And inhaled. Nothing happened. Cars continued past, yellow low beams glowing, unearthly, an imperturbable parade.

Then I shook my head and carefully merged back onto the road, which narrowed and narrowed in the flying snow until the pavement was a long gray scarf. Then the scarf vanished. My back ached from hunching. I pressed into the muffled silence, blinking hard, the tires gripping feather down, the green digital clock ticking the minutes I must now subtract from my session like subtracting subtleties from myself. A boxy orange snowplow consolidated out of the welter and blocked my path at a steady thirty miles per hour. Dare I pass it? Plunge into the whirlwind it aroused? I bit my lip and pressed my foot lower, veering into the nonexistent left lane. White blindness, grease under the wheels. I let the car slip back behind the plow. The green clock purged another minute. I grit my teeth and dove into the whiteness again.

Her office, when I raced in, was toasty. Olive rubber boots stood on a sheet of newspaper; the bronze Athena gleamed on its bookshelf. And her notebook lay open on her lap. "Oh, thank God!" I cried. How many precious minutes remained? Could she possibly work her magic that fast? A full twenty-five minutes—gone!

"Harriet!" I said. "I was so afraid you might give up on me and leave. Don't ever do that," I said, allowing myself to sound childish. "Stay for every minute of my session. It's still my session, even if I'm not here."

"Of course."

At once, everything calmed. I owned one hundred and ten minutes of her every other week, and fifty minutes on the weeks in between. It was mine, she wouldn't give it to anyone else, she wouldn't reclaim it.

"We could have had a phone session," I said, considering. "But I didn't want to go another week without seeing you." I stopped. "Oh, I feel like I'm yelling. Like there's an enormous blustery gulf I need to shout across."

She tilted her head, considering.

"I feel like my words are clumsy, imprecise," I said. "Like if I don't shout you won't hear me."

"It is hard to hold on to me between sessions."

"You go away."

"We need to understand why that happens," she replied.

I thought of the whirling white, the minutes eroding, my eyes cutting between the road and the clock, and the experience of her as remote but essential, remote but in possession of all the keys to me. "It feels like you take something back. You reabsorb it. By the time I'm home it's gone."

"Perhaps you don't believe you deserve what I give you."

"It's not so great!" I exclaimed, surprised. My, how she flattered herself! How really incredible she must think she was!

"Yet you travel through a storm to get it."

I'd always smiled to myself when people referred to therapy as "work." Work! What a self-praising way to describe mere conversation. Yet when my friend Kate remarked, "But I could never indulge myself like that! Fifty whole minutes to just talk about yourself!"—conjuring an image of pink-and-gold glazed petit fours savored around a tea table while I detailed the detritus of my life like a woman showing her bunions, I replied, "It's no indulgence."

In fact, the treatment was inducing what felt like madness. Why, even this friend, who herself resembled a spectacular petit four, all gold-glinting hair and pink-frosted lips, her bare calves tanned and perfectly shaped as she paced the sand beside me at Singing Beach (it was already high summer when she said this; I'd been with Dr. Sing half a year), even she, Kate, whose company I'd always found delectable to the point of exaltation, now spawned bizarre resentments. The way she bowed her blond head as she listened seemed to indicate a sort of mock humility. Or her observation about my friend Juliet: "Hmm. If she said that what's important in writing is language, why then she really is a poet"—what arrogance! Who needed her to declare who was a real poet and who wasn't?

Ugly thoughts. I shook my head. It felt as if someone was planting them, inflicting them. In the deck of my life, odd cards were being inserted: bogeymen and gluttons, tiaraed friends doing a gloating dance, a mother as brittle as toothpicks, figures of grotesque appearance as if someone else's cards were being shuffled into mine. I was not playing with a full deck; I was playing with a bloated deck, a tampered deck. Harriet was doctoring it. I couldn't tell how but wished she'd stop. She replied that she was doing nothing.

Well, obviously, the villains were mine, were me. I'd just shied from them all this time. They'd been like the instant in a swinging glass door when your face distends, monstrous, and you glance away. Distortion. Surely not to be stared at, not gloried in. But now I couldn't help staring, frightened. How greedy, how devouring almost everyone seemed! As if, if I so much as picked up the phone, whoever had called would keep talking and talking until my day was consumed. And the more voracious people seemed, the more I craved Harriet.

Her assumption was that even my spasms of ugly thought made sense, what the mind flashed to pertained. The scaly green phosphorescence that lined my palms after peeling an orange as a girl; my sister tearing my mother's *Vogues* one after another, each perfumed month heaved apart in one trembling goaded rip, and Anita's arm bulging like a steelworker's. Somehow Harriet made the whole inquiry seem not just worthwhile but actually beautiful, so that for long moments, talking to her, it was in fact precisely like eating petit-fours around a tea table, delectable cakes with the icing dripping.

Who remembers learning to speak? Suddenly you are here and you are talking. You don't remember when you said "you" for "me" or "mmm" for "mother." Here I was, in my thirties, saying "you" for "me," and "love" for "hate," and "enemy" for "friend." I remember it all quite clearly.

On an afternoon in late February I told Harriet how I'd discovered artistic standards. Anita had come to visit my Brownie troop. She stood before us in her dark green Senior dress, her hair brushed back sleekly in a ponytail. She was teaching us to do sponge art. "Don't try to get it perfect," she declared.

We girls nodded.

In the center of each table sat a heap of yellow sponges and paint slopped in pie pans. A smell of damp wool and string beans hung in the air; the lunchroom was down the hall. If you closed your eyes, a plate of boiled yellow string beans with curling tails hovered in the air before you. If you opened them, there was Anita in her crisp green uniform and bangs cut short across her brow.

"Perfection is impossible," she declared. "Let me tell you a story. Once there was a man with a mustache that needed to be trimmed. He cut one side."

She snipped her fingers beside her lips. "Then the other. But then he noticed the first was now just a wee bit too long. So he cut. But then guess what he noticed about the other side?"

"Too long!" the girls roared.

"Yes!"

Anita raced her fingers back and forth, back and forth, the man cutting his mustache. The girls began to giggle.

"Too long!"

They shrieked. She was a success!

"But suddenly"—and here her voice acquired a soft tone of wonder—"he stopped and stared. Why look! There was no mustache at all anymore! Just a bald patch of skin. So remember"—and here her voice resumed its normal pitch—"the Man With No Mustache. And please don't try to get it perfect."

My first conscious lesson about art.

Anita brandished her fingers up in a dizzy, scissoring diagonal and the girls burst into applause. How fine she was in her dark green uniform!

Now everyone bent over her sheet of butcher paper. I gazed at Anita smoothing her skirt with her hands and chatting with my scout leader, Mrs. Minanski. Wherever had she found him, the man with no mustache? Anita and I went all the same places. This was the first I'd ever heard of him! And her diction: "a wee bit too long." Why, she didn't speak like that! What was she doing up there?

Anita circled the room, stopping at each child's place. "So much wonderful yellow," she said admiringly to Annie.

"Very nice," she intoned to Caroline and Margaret, speaking cumulatively.

She stepped up beside me, and paused. She tipped her head, one eye squinting. "Too much blue," she declared.

My face blazed. I hauled my paper close.

Yet hadn't she warned me? "I don't want anyone saying I play favorites," my sister had said that morning. "I'm going to be strict but fair. Understand?"

I'd nodded yes.

Now she stood two girls down. "Lovely," she murmured, "although you might try some yellow."

I gazed at my paper—a mess—and the man with no mustache seemed to speak in my head. "Don't make a mistake," he murmured. "Listen: get it right. It's entirely possible. Ignore what she said."

I smiled. Anita's man wanted perfection. Why should I want any less? Before this, I'd never really thought about doing a good job or a better job. Now I wanted to do a perfect job. Why settle for anything less? I thought of the man's pleasure as he merrily snipped this side of his mustache and that, his sense of immersion, his blithe engagement, and gazed through the diamond windows at the bony tree limbs lashing, my hands folded on the desk.

Anita continued to circle in her dark green uniform. And suddenly I could see there was a way she was both pitiful and bossy. How easy she would be to mock! She was fat. She wore a frilly hankie. She liked to roll up her frilly hankie in a long tight triangle while she was reading at her desk and actually nestle the point of it up her nose, a sensual habit. When she said the word *white*, she took care to pronounce the *h*. When she said her own name, Anita, she made sure the tip of her tongue touched the roof of her mouth. "The Spanish know how to make this sound," she said. "Not Aniduh!"

I stuffed my paper in the bathroom trash. At dusk, my sister collected the rinsed sponges and jars of paint in a plaid cloth shopping bag my mother had sewn with a strong brown lining. Then she and I walked home hand in hand. Hers was a stunted, dainty hand with dimples at the knuckles, and it felt strange, like holding a child's hand. Yet I held it tightly as we walked down University Avenue. My mind was full of the image of Anita's triumph, and I was suddenly afraid that she'd ride off on the subway to some glorious station where I couldn't follow. Or that she'd acquire more and more men with no mustache. I held her hand as we walked and over and over told her the truth: she was wonderful, everyone had loved her, and I loved her most of all.

"You seem the opposite of Anita," I told Harriet.

"How's that?"

"You take my side almost too much. You seem to say perfection is everywhere. That it's almost unavoidable, if you work hard enough. Do you believe that?"

"What do you think?"

I could tell she was smiling behind me. "I think you are a man with a big mustache!" I said, unable to resist the Freudian symbol.

"But I take your side almost too much."

I nodded slowly. "Yes. I'm not sure I'm reliable. I try to be, but I'm afraid I distort things. Once when I was growing up I told my father the price of something, a washing machine, I think. He looked dubious, and I insisted. Later I realized that I'd been wildly wrong—the entire order of magnitude was off, and I hoped he didn't believe me."

"You're worried I will believe you?"

"Yes."

"I'm the father," she mused.

"Why do you say that?"

"My big mustache."

I grinned. "Oh, I was just kidding."

"Naturally."

I crossed my legs at the ankle. "My father actually admired Anita most. She was the oldest child and better able to tell stories that could interest him. You are like a father whose attention I can hold."

"So, you are holding on to something of mine."

I smiled again. "Oh, yes. But it's like the long silk scarf a magician pulls out of his pocket. It keeps coming and coming, harlequin dia-

monds as I drive all the way home to Massachusetts. But at the end
it's just a trick handkerchief. Something bought at a magic shop."

"But you want to believe in the magic."

"Yes."

She didn't speak for a moment, during which the Picasso room in
her poster seemed to increase in color and brightness, as if infused.

"You want to hear me say the equivalent of 'Too much blue,' because that you would believe. But you also want me to say, 'It's perfect.' That's your predicament."

I nodded, deeply happy, but also unable to remember just what it
was she'd said. "Could you say that again?"

She did, surprisingly ungrudgingly, but the sound of her voice
was distracting. I said, "You have such a beautiful voice sometimes."

She listened in silence.

I said, "I feel like I would like to take a nap. Isn't that funny?"

"Would you like to take a nap?"

"In a way, yes. But the session's almost over. If we had more time,
if we had hours and hours, I'd take a nap."

She was silent. I didn't speak. I was looking at the Picasso room,
which was blurry. What a silly fool I was! Yet every second she didn't
speak seemed weirder and more delectable. It felt as if this was the
first time in my life someone had followed my lead, although this
couldn't be so. Still she did not speak. I thought my eyes would over-
flow. Absurd! I said with a laugh: "You must be getting uncomfortable!"—it came out as a croak because my throat felt so thick.

"I was quite comfortable," she said.

Even in December it was summer in that attic room. The air was
thin as the flaring, curling edge of a burning paper. Late in a session
an atmosphere of languor pervaded, as if she and I were joined in
the air at a thousand points, as if I'd somehow furred at my periph-
ery, atomized, mingled with her—this was the sensation toward the
end of our time together when she provided an interpretation, the
petit-four moment. I assumed this bliss was the point of treatment
and that when it was over I would in fact live in this sweet state.

Lying on Harriet's firm white couch, I gazed at the framed Picasso below my toes or surveyed the shelves of stuffed animals. A Native American girl galloped above me in a frame. I disliked her; Harriet refused to take her down. A heap of gold-and-wine kilim pillows at my feet hid the clock, which tracked minutes with red fingers and secretly communed all session long with Harriet, who could see it from her perch. I lay down, and my entire life flew up as if I'd flopped on the dusty sofa of my past, and it seemed the life outside this room was my sickness, and that I would be cured to the extent I could make that jumpy, shaky, flying life approximate this calm.

Harriet's remarks frequently suggested some new geometry of myself and my mother, or myself and Paul, or of the triple-decker house of my own identity, which in my new dreams swarmed with mice—tangles of baby mice and big-bellied pregnant mother mice rushing across the floors, impossible to exterminate. Harriet nodded. She leaned back in her chair. She offered no opinion of the mice, but accepted them with curiosity, as if they were distant relatives who had turned up at the wedding after all. When she did interpret, it had the disorienting effect of making some big things small and some small things big. An infuriating, shaming argument with a friend signaled merely a need to feel safe. A chance gesture of my mother's revealed a whole network of assumptions—the entire glass maze—in which I'd lived.

As Harriet spoke, for an instant I felt freed, detached. There was not always an apparent connection between this glorious lofting sensation and the particular words she'd said. The words cooled, hardened, like my car ticking on the asphalt after the long drive up. I walked toward the door mulling over her interpretation, feeling it already reducing in my hands like a clutched spider's web.

I turned—and she was still smiling, and I couldn't wait to see her again.

Calling her from home I sat in the unlit kitchen on the dirty yellow linoleum. I wanted to be in the worst place and find that she could join me. I wanted to be as sick as possible and find that she could heal me. The tan phone cord scalloped to my ear.

Her line was busy. I hung up, tapped the numbers again. I stared at the stove. Busy, busy. Gray tracks left by a sponge were suddenly apparent in the stove's upper left corner. What could she be thinking? Who was she talking to?

The sponge strokes fashioned a swollen glum face. This face had the porous texture of overrisen dough, portraying the dilapidated face of an abandoned king.

I dialed. "Hello, Bonnie."

"Harriet! Your line was busy."

"Yes. I'm sorry."

I took a breath. "But this is my time."

"Someone called at ten and I thought it was you. I couldn't get off immediately. I'll make it up to you at the end."

Ah. Yet time was stuck.

She said: "How did you feel when my phone was busy?"

How preposterous to be so moved that she's asked!

"Fine." The king's face unwound like an Ace bandage; it was just some sponge strokes, after all.

"You felt fine?"

"Oh yes. Anyway, that isn't what I want to spend my session talking about. If we talk about it, I'll feel I'm losing my session, that you set the agenda."

"If you're angry, I've set the agenda?"

"It's not what I want to talk about!"

It occurred to me suddenly that if I'd told someone Harriet had asked, "How did you feel,"—they'd smile. How rote: How did you feel? How did you feel? Like the cry of a mynah bird!

And yet when she'd asked, it was like being pierced by a tin compass point. A new globe could be described with a flick of the hand. It brought to mind how in sixth grade my class had been equipped with compasses, objects sharper than anything we'd been allowed to hold before. I, who couldn't draw, unfurled globe after globe. How marvelous to be given the right tool! My heart fanned open with each swerve of the gleaming leg. And at the end of the year I couldn't bear to throw the thing away even though rust had crept across its belt and you could only pull it open with a yank. Its precision was gone.

Still, I shoved it in my mitten drawer, which rapidly accumulated as well a pot of strawberry lip gloss, a black velvet choker with a cloisonné butterfly, wampum beads, a bottle of Arpege the size of a suitcase key, and at last, wrapped in toilet paper, a diaphragm my mother found among my things when I was in college. The toilet paper around this diaphragm rapidly withered to crepe paper, turning more and more brittle, until it seemed that time itself had purified it. I smiled sadly whenever I came across this ancient diaphragm, as if it epitomized my mother's hope that all pleasure would be mine. And among it all was that cheap tin compass with its legs that swung worlds on point, telling me that the perfect tool existed and one day I would find it.

This "How did you feel?" of Harriet's evoked the exact same feeling of the perfect tool. Although, if reported to an outsider wouldn't her words clank with banality? A lot of what Harriet said was like that. Hokey and banal and easy to ridicule, baldly unironic — these were usually the very words that could be most transformative. It called to mind how, on the subway, people often read Bibles: green ones the size of poker decks, big black leather-bound thumping ones with scarlet at the name Jesus, even comic-book bibles showing stumpy men in beards and lightning-bolt words from on high. Ecclesiastical words in the midst of the rattling number 4 train: seen one way, the words are rote and familiar, carrying a matte finish. Seen another, they are all shine.

"Something disturbing happened."

I stared at the white chickens, my fingers clenched at my waist. "It's because of this treatment. Remember I said I was going to New York?"

"Yes." She gazed down at me with serene blue eyes. Her gray sweater was pushed up off her wrists above a darker gray wool skirt.

"To see my editor and visit my parents?"

"Yes."

"Well, the ride down was just wonderful. Paul drove me to the Salem station and sat waiting with me in the car because it was freezing cold. It was still dark — 6:20 in the morning. It was so nice to have him see me off! On the railroad I drank Amtrak coffee and ate a bagel with Jarlsberg cheese I'd brought, and I read *Mrs. Dalloway*, and just had a really great time. But as we neared the city something very unpleasant started to happen. This big anxiety sprouted up. I was looking out at the factories and big billboards at the outskirts of the city. Soon we would be arriving."

I shook my head. "The closer we got to the city, the worse it became. It was like someone creepy staring at you. I was getting more and more upset. What is it, what is it, I wondered. And instantly, the anxiety—what's that word?—coalesced. It coalesced and had a name, and the name was Stella. My friend Stella! I was afraid she'd forget I was away and that she'd get angry at me for not returning her phone calls. . . . She almost always calls on the weekend."

I glanced back at Harriet, who nodded.

"Well, the train arrived at Penn Station and I phoned my father. The train was about twenty-five minutes late, and I felt very upset. Apologetic. So much of the day with my father seemed to be lost already. Ruined! It seemed a tremendous amount, although it was just twenty-five minutes."

Harriet nodded.

I fell silent, remembering how, as the phone rang in my parents' apartment, I shuffled my feet on the grimy, sticky floor in Penn Station. The Velcro sound of my sneakers lifting. "Oh, *Bon!*" my father had exclaimed.

"Harriet, he sounded just so happy to hear me. As if I was a big surprise to him and he was thrilled."

Her blue eyes met my gaze, and she smiled.

"He gave me detailed instructions about which subways to take and exactly where to stand on the platform. He said to please call when I reached 231st Street so he could come with the car to pick me up. He even asked if I had quarters for the phone call. He loves me so much, I thought.

"But this only made me feel worse, since I couldn't be really spontaneous and intimate with him due to Stella. Stella was getting in the way! I couldn't wait to call her. And as soon as I reached my parents' apartment, that's exactly what I did. I excused myself and went into their bedroom, where there's a door that shuts, and phoned. As it rang in her house I prayed that she'd be home. She picked up. Oh, thank God, I thought. I told her: 'I just want you to know I'm away this weekend.'

" 'You are?' she said.

" 'Yeah, so please don't be annoyed that I'm not returning your phone calls.' I was afraid that I'd come home on Sunday to a message machine blinking not just once or twice, but, like, eleven times. That happened once. Eleven different messages, all from Stella! Updates on her life. Different thoughts. A kind of diary." I smiled. "Actually, when it happened it was kind of charming. Although Paul thought it was excessive. But that was last year. Now the very idea of her calling that many times made me frantic. I just couldn't bear it. I couldn't bear to think she might be getting more and more annoyed with me."

Behind me, Harriet seemed to nod.

"Well, Stella was angry. She said, 'Do you really think I'm that dependent? Frankly, I find this whole call obnoxious!'

"But I didn't feel any relief. So I said, 'But you've left irritated messages on my machine before. There's a certain tone of voice—'

" 'All *right!*' she said, interrupting. 'I can't believe how insulting you're being. It's ridiculous, you calling from New York to say this!'

"Well, at last I could relax. She'd finally gotten my point."

"Which was?" asked Harriet.

I glanced back at her. "That I'd be away, Harriet."

"Ah."

"Now I could feel at peace. I told Stella I was sorry—and I was. I really was. I felt bad if she was hurt. I explained that I've been really jumpy these days."

My gaze fell on one of the white birds in the Picasso with its wings stuck out rigidly. Another little bird looked as if its flapping wings had been lacquered in place.

"When I stepped out of the bedroom, Harriet, my father looked worried. He asked, 'Is everything all right?'

" 'Fine!' I said.

" 'Is there something you need to do right now?'

"'Oh, no,' I answered. 'I just needed to make that call.'"

Yet how quiet the apartment had seemed when I stepped out, I recalled now. Set on the table was a snack: a red wax tub of Breakstone's sweet whipped butter, two flattish onion rolls from the bakery, and instant coffee in a ceramic jar beside a fresh pint of half-and-half. My parents always bought half-and-half in honor of my visit. My father was sponging off the blue vinyl place mats.

"Harriet," I said now, with alarm, "I didn't used to be so anxious. You've made me anxious. I used to be happy sometimes and I could get depressed—but this unsettled feeling, this ill feeling, this feeling of enemies: it's new. And it's because of you."

"There's a way I'm like Stella. I make you anxious."

"No," I said, although at that instant my eyes fell on the smug, neat letters on her Picasso poster which curled like claws.

She flipped a page in her notebook. "You wanted to get permission to forget about her for a while and have a good time."

"Yes."

"You didn't want her to miss you and make you feel guilty."

Suddenly I thought of something. "It's how I used to worry about my mother when I was away at camp. I worried she'd feel lonely."

"Did you worry a lot, growing up?"

I smiled. Worry was the texture of my childhood. As if the light-bulbs on Harrison Avenue were frosted gray. The helpless sensation that there were fragile people—my parents—whom I must protect.

"From what?" asked Harriet.

"Oh, just the rapaciousness of the city. The coldness and cruelty of other people. I thought my parents could be taken advantage of very easily by strangers."

"And what happened to your anger with your mother for sending you away?"

"What anger? I wasn't angry at my mother." I yawned.

Her page rattled. "This rapacious city. These cold and cruel 'other' people."

I nodded.

"Could they be an aspect of you, projected out?"

I nearly sat up. "Look, I want to understand what happened with Stella! I want to understand it before this session ends. Before I have to go out in the world again."

"This world which is rapacious."

"Yes," I said softly.

"And full of aliens."

"Please, Harriet."

"Look. There was a triangle: you, your father, and Stella."

"Yes," I said, "but my concern over Stella seemed like an aspect of me. Sort of like a layer of subcutaneous fat, a sort of inert bolster between my father and me. My concern about her made me feel over-emotional, irrational, inexplicable. That there was something about me I couldn't tell him."

"So, in order to enjoy being with your father," she said, "you had to first go behind a door and have it out with someone." She glanced down. "You said there was something about yourself that you couldn't tell him."

I smiled. "Oh, that's often how I feel with my father. Especially at the beginning of a visit. That whole huge swathes of me are inexplicable. As if they've been stamped all over with paisleys or erratic shapes. Like the shapes that fat forms on top of a soup."

"Fat again," she murmured.

"And he's so rational," I continued. "His mind works logically. Whole parts of me seem bizarre, when I'm with him."

"So you have a fight with Stella."

"I just wanted her to stop!"

Neither of us pointed out that of course Stella wasn't actually doing anything.

Harriet said: "And if you can appease her, make sure she expects nothing of you, then you can have your father to yourself."

"Yes."

"You needed her permission to feel happy."

"Yes."

"You were about to go off on your adventure—do you see how

this is like embarking on your writing project?—and you were getting very excited, your train was coming into the station, when suddenly you worried. Somebody might get angry at being left behind."

"It's like what happened the very first time I ever slept away from home."

I looked back at her. She lifted her eyebrows.

"There was a sleepover at my camp in the bungalow colony. My mother wedged the sleeping bag into her city shopping cart along with my pillow and clothing, and rolled it along the trails to the campsite. That night all the children in my unit gathered around the fire and listened to ghost stories. I was about five or six. But the darker it got, the more frightened I became. When it was time to go to sleep, I started crying. To my surprise, the head counselor took my hand and walked me home. He was a big strong man and held my sleeping bag under one arm. I was amazed, but he said it was nothing at all to carry a sleeping bag like that.

"When my mother opened the door, she was so startled to see me! I felt ashamed to have been brought home and to have surprised her. And I vowed that the next year I'd stick it out. And I did. But when I came home in the morning my mother said, 'I waited up for you all night. I was sure you were going to come home.'" She sounded so sad. I felt bad I'd disappointed her."

Harriet tucked a loose hank of dark hair behind her ear. "You got a mixed message."

"What do you mean?"

"Well, you assumed you would be rewarded for being brave and going out in the world."

I nodded. "But it seemed to make my mother feel abandoned. Worrying about how Stella would feel while I was away does remind me of that."

"Only this time you felt angry, not sad."

I nodded. "A strange reaction."

She raised her eyebrows as if to say, "Not so strange."

But my mind had skipped ahead. I was thinking how wonderful my parents had been to me, that night in the Bronx. My father had driven my mother and me to the Cross County Shopping Center. He'd sat outside the fitting room at Wanamaker's on a black leatherette bench while I tried on clothes and then stepped outside to show him. On the railroad trip back from New York on Sunday, the blue paper Wanamaker's shopping bags full of clothing and tissue paper rested at my feet, loaded, it seemed, with my parents' love.

Harriet nodded as I explained all this. She seemed happy for me.

"But Paul—I wish he enjoyed these presents! When I showed him the black silk pants, the white tuxedo blouse which I'd thought was kind of sexy—they seemed diminished. He doesn't get excited for me." Suddenly I said, "Do you think I should leave him?"

I turned to look at her; she lifted her head to meet me with her calm, considerate gaze.

"I'm afraid you do. I'm afraid you do and won't say so."

She said: "I don't think Paul is the real problem."

"Then who is?"

We both laughed.

After a moment Harriet said, "Perhaps you are afraid of my envy. Maybe I'll be like Paul and Stella and take away your pleasure."

"You do have a lot of power."

She nodded.

"But I *enjoy* coming up here. Sometimes, in fact," I said. "I actually feel grimy afterward. As if we've done something overemotional. Secret. Something I can't explain. But it makes me feel good and it's mine."

"Until you relinquish it," she said. "You see, you are very frightened of your own excitement."

I said nothing.

"The intensity of your anger at Stella indicates how very much you value the pleasure you give up."

Again I had the experience of delicious confusion while she spoke, as if her words were so true they passed straight through me without my hearing them.

"Would you say that again?" I asked.

She did, and I realized this was something else I liked about her.

CHAPTER FIVE

The On-Off Switch

A voice started speaking in my head.

"I don't like this," it said once when, late one groggy night, Paul very abruptly set his hand on my butt. "I don't like this," when he dropped my hand as we were walking along a street in Gloucester.

"I don't like this," I told the voice. "Go!"

But the voice did not.

Moods that had been mute spawned words. Waiting for my brother to acknowledge me after Passover services in Brookline, words swarmed in my head. My brother in his dark gray suit embraced his two daughters, said hello to his wife, began to chat with them, nodding, listening, responding, two fingertips set against his cheek—and all the while Paul and I stood on the pavement waiting at his elbow. We hadn't seen him in several weeks.

A frightening feeling possessed me: fire. My insides red and roaring. "I'm angry! I'm angry!" I thought. "And if I don't tell him, I won't stop being angry. I'll go home and be angry for weeks. I won't be able to do anything except be angry."

"George," erupted my voice, squawky, a bad microphone, "you didn't say hello. I'm standing right here." I grimaced, feeling distinctly insane.

"Oh. Hello, Bonnie," he said, straightening his glasses and smiling. "It's good to see you."

Words also arrived during an evening with Stella. "It's coming!" she shouted. "My piano's coming!"

She danced over the parlor floor. She yelled up the stairs to housemates behind shut bedroom doors. A friend had offered his old chestnut Steinway. She didn't know how to play, but it would look beautiful in her living room.

55 ∎

Stella and I had been talking quietly at the little kitchen table when the phone rang. "Yes, yes," she said, and hung up. Then suddenly she was shouting: "My piano is coming! My piano is coming!" But her joy seemed forced, coercive, greedy, desperate. I trailed her into the living room, where she yelled "My piano is coming!" to her roommates on the floor above.

I sat down on the shadowy steps, surprised by depression as swift as a guillotine. I was a girl in a gray dress sitting in the checkerboard lobby of an apartment building I didn't want my family to move to because it was too dark.

"We'll just put in stronger lightbulbs!" my father had said.

I bit my lips. Lightbulbs had nothing to do with it.

Now as Stella shouted and ran around the rooms, her gala emotion seemed theatrical, exclusionary, exhibitionistic, frantic. A gray sticky net had been thrown over me. Through it I watched the racing Stella.

But never in my life had I noticed such a moment! The plunge into ancient, nameless despair. An awareness of before and after. "Stop it, Stella," said the voice inside me. "Stop it."

And yet later in the evening Stella and I were as intimate as ever, sitting on a sprung pink sofa on her house's second-floor porch. This porch was so tiny that the sofa seemed hung in the trees. Oh, Stella was grand, really, and had been my best friend for the past three years, driving a ten-year-old lipstick-red Alpha Romeo Spider Velocci which she'd bought off a guy on the freeway, banging out her poems on a baby blue plastic portable to which she'd glued the words "Art is a house that wants to be haunted. —Marianne Moore," swimming laps so powerfully in a plain blue Speedo that men always tried to swim faster than she and rarely did (she'd trained on her college team), and wearing everywhere a wonderful black cloth raincoat she'd found at a thrift shop; it draped to her shins and gave her a faintly espionage-ish, Audrey Hepburn look. The first time I ever went to Stella's house she was living in a farmhouse in Iowa, and she said of a past love: "Oh, Nora's really magic! And with such a capacity for play! Like for instance, we might be sitting up in bed and have these empty plates in front of us, and Nora would just start pretending we were eating something—spaghetti, say—off the plates. We'd have a whole pretend meal. There's nobody else I could imagine doing that. You just laugh when you're with Nora."

Stella herself was much the same. I felt lucky to be her friend. "I have an idea for a comic-book character," Stella said now. "It would be called Well Actually Man. You know the way some guys hear you say something and they have to say, 'Well, actually, the velocity of the earth . . . well, actually, Bill Gates's *real* ability . . . well, ak-choo-a-lee . . .'"

We burst out laughing.

"Could you please not laugh so loud?" called a voice through the open window. Stella and I stared at each other and flung our hands over our mouths.

So wasn't I crazy to feel as I had earlier? All the way home I was shaking my head.

It was on a Thursday afternoon in September a few weeks after the episode of Stella's piano that I discovered the big on-off switch.

Stella and I were talking on the phone. She was at her data-entry job, and as we spoke I could hear her fingers clicking away. She was telling me about a woman from her therapy group who had a discouraging husband. This husband showed absolutely no interest in his wife getting a better job since then she would earn more than he. He felt this way even though he was a college professor, and you'd think a professor would be more progressive than that. Well, the wife interviewed for the job anyway, and when she came home from the interview her husband just sat reading at the dining room table. He didn't ask a single question. He didn't even look up. "Wait a sec," said Stella. I could hear the flip of a page. She said a few words to someone else and laughed her loud marvelous laugh. Then she said into the phone: "Okay, where was I?"

"He didn't even look up."

"Right. So finally she just had to say something, and she told him how much his behavior hurt her feelings. Well, Bon, you won't believe it. He just sat there and muttered insults. Poor Stephanie was so upset. Telling us about it, she kept crying."

"What an insecure man!" I gathered up two bent pins on the tablecloth from a new shirt of Paul's. They looked like slightly hunched people.

"I know."

After Stella and I hung up, I felt excited. I'd had a tedious morning, but now simply crackled with ideas. Sentence after sentence sprang into being for my essay. An insight occurred to me. Happiness! I reached for the phone.

"The real question is," I said, "why has this woman chosen someone who says nasty things?"

"Oh, everyone in the group thought of that, Bonnie!" Stella said. Ah.

Back at the computer, I had not one idea. I was dull. Eyes blinking. A lump.

The thought blazed into me: I have a big on-off switch! Stella had pushed my switch to off.

Well, of course, it must have been there my whole life, this switch. I'd simply never noticed. I had never actually distinctly noticed other people's effect on me. Or mine on them, for that matter. I'd lived inside my moods as if they were as inevitable as the weather. And without thinking how this could be true, I childishly believed that everyone occupied the same mood at once with only minor variations, the way people all occupy an hour of the afternoon.

But from that September afternoon on, when I heard a remark that damaged something in me, I noticed. A tightening occurred, a twist of piano wire. This tightening was highly uncomfortable because it was beyond my control and because it could last for days and even weeks after the disturbing remark.

After about half a year of living this way, I realized that I must say something immediately, no matter what, in order to minimize the effects of the remark. Even if my response felt insane. Even if it made no sense whatsoever to be alarmed by the remark.

An acquaintance wrapped her hands around her teacup in the

Cafe Algiers and told me, "Oh, the descriptive parts of books, my husband never reads those."

"Then he would dislike my work," I replied instantly. "I write lots of things with descriptive parts."

A white-haired man who volunteered behind the desk in the Salem library said, "Oh, you're finally returning the magazines you checked out!"

I stared. Why, I'd always assumed librarians were supposed to be like gracious pharmacists, serenely nonjudgmental. "It's a good thing I returned these magazines at all!" I declared. "I almost just threw them out." Which wasn't at all true.

But by the end of another year I'd arrived at a time when I could notice a damaging statement without needing to register disagreement. I was no longer on fire. I could dismiss the remark. It did not command me.

Before my discovery of the on-off switch I often felt bad without wondering why. Moods off-gassed from the vinyl of a couch. They seeped out from beneath radiators; sometimes the expressions of a cracked ceiling made them. You'd step into your apartment and there a mood would be, waiting. I'd never thought about it until now. In Iowa years earlier a few friends had come up the stairs to my studio apartment for a drink. It was someone's birthday. One of my friends walked in, sniffed, and announced, "There's a garbagey smell in here!"

I'd laughed, blushing. Then fetched the trash under the sink and ran downstairs to pitch it into the garbage can.

"You are attracted to aggressive people," Harriet remarked.

"How do you know? You haven't met them."

"But I hear what you say about them."

"Exactly. What if I'm putting the wrong spin on their words? What if I'm distorting the context?"

For was this friend really aggressive? With her heaps of legal pads curling with stories about expatriates, her leather bomber jacket and clacking boots, her collection of tin wind-up circus toys, her affairs with older men—she was inspiring. One felt drunk, buoyed up, in her company. Still, I recalled her voice bellowing up my stairs, "Better get your bike out of here!"

"Think lovelier thoughts," I coaxed myself often now, riding in the Civic, or letting the cool air gust up to my face from the freezer in Purity Supreme. Please think lovelier thoughts.

"I was lonely on Sunday night driving home with Paul. I just felt so melancholy." I shook my head, gazing at the green floor of the Picasso room. "We were on the Tobin Bridge and had to merge left to get on Route 1 up to Salem. . . . Just a Sunday evening feeling, I guess."

"Perhaps you were lonely for me."

I turned and stared. "For you? I wasn't thinking about you at all!"

My, how the woman flattered herself!

"It was so hard to get here through the blizzard. The whole time I was afraid the car would spin out."

Dr. Sing shifted in her chair. She was wearing a tentlike, fish-gray dress and for an instant when I walked in I'd wondered if she was pregnant. But her face was too thin for that. Still, this dress marked a big change from her usual outfit. She looked cozy and warm in it and yet strangely impenetrable, as if she were wearing plastic carpeting or the prickly core of an artichoke.

"My back hurts from hunching over the wheel," I said. "I was afraid my car was going to spin out the way it did that time I was in that boxy rented Aries."

"I wonder what it would be like if it was easy for you to get your therapy. I suspect you would create other obstacles to having me."

"The obstacles to you are real!" I cried, staring at the snow pelting the window.

"Yes, but if there were no storm, I suspect it might still be difficult for you to come here and have a full amount of me. Reality is distracting you."

I laughed bitterly. "Well, you know, reality is a big distraction.

Maybe for you, in this warm office, paid so highly, what I call reality provides less of a distraction."

"Do you think so?" She shifted within her poncholike dress.

"Yes."

"Well, what is your fantasy of my life?"

I sighed. "Oh, I imagine you own a big house with a cozy, brick-sided kitchen. I can just see you standing there blowing on a steaming mug of tea. You're wearing wool socks and a long sweatshirt, and you're about to curl up on the sofa with a psychology journal. It makes me happy to think of you that way," I continued. "I want you to be happy and satisfied. That way you don't resent giving to me. My treatment is a relief from what might become boring in your too-cushy life." I smiled.

"Ah. You are doing me a favor by coming here."

I looked back at her and smiled again. "Yes. You are in danger of becoming sore. Like a breast that is too full. I provide relief."

"Thank you," she said. We laughed.

Then she said, "So you wish me well."

Instantly, my mind filled with disturbing violent images I didn't wish to share. Razors attacking a breast. Teeth biting it. I shrugged.

"Some might think it would make you resentful," she continued, "that I am such a Lady Bountiful. So loaded with marvelous things."

"I'm happy you're well provided for."

"I appreciate that. But do you see how hard it is for you to receive from me? You have to tell yourself that in fact you are not receiving. That in fact my surplus of good things is in danger of harming me. You are relieving me of that peril." It occurred to me that she even seemed dressed like a breast today, albeit a grayish single iceberg of a breast, a walking igloo.

"Yes," I said softly.

"You tell yourself that because you work so hard to get me, you deserve me. But what if you weren't tired when you arrived?"

My face grew hot. I glanced down at my thin, prone, hungry body, my arms that felt weak from grasping the steering wheel. "My exhaustion doesn't count to you much, does it?" I said. "You just want me to be here. You don't care what it takes. That's just nothing to you."

"On the contrary. I care about it very much," she said softly. "That's why we're discussing it."

"I'll speak to you next week," I said at the end of the session.

"Yes."

I left her door ajar behind me and had almost reached the waiting room when I found myself racing back.

"Harriet! Harriet!" I called in a panic in her doorway. "Or before." The magic charm that meant I wasn't separated from her.

She smiled. "Yes, of course. Always."

"She might eat hamburgers, you know," remarked Paul. We were in a souvlaki joint off Boylston Street on a Saturday afternoon. Paul wore a white shirt with burgundy stripes, and chinos. "Can you imagine her eating a hamburger?"

"No."

"She might. On a picnic. The grease getting on her chin a little."

"No."

"But she might." He took another lusty chomp of his gyro and smiled. Some yogurt sauce dripped onto his paper plate. "Is she a vegetarian?"

"I wouldn't know."

"Maybe she sits in front of the TV at night and shovels spoonfuls of ice cream into her mouth. Have you ever considered that?"

"No." I crossed my arms. "She doesn't look like she does."

"That's because she's bulimic."

"You're just being perverse."

"Oh, *I'm* perverse."

"What does that mean?"

"You can't even imagine this woman eating!"

It was true. Harriet would not eat even tofu. Her perfect mouth did not admit food.

* * *

"I can't imagine you eating a hamburger," I reported.

"That's because you idealize me." She sat in a starched denim skirt with a white angora sweater, her hair pushed behind one ear.

"No one has ever given me so much."

She nodded. "It's like giving you vitamins."

Such a plebeian image! And it didn't even seem accurate. Surely what we did together was far more nuanced than that.

"An idealized person is in a very dangerous position," she observed, gazing away from her yellow notebook.

"Why?"

"Their height is unnatural. Their position is fragile."

"But you helped me when no one else could. You are extraordinary," I said.

And the more I praised her, the happier I felt.

"He makes me feel dead inside," said the voice in my head, referring to my husband. "He doesn't inspire me. He never compliments how I say something. His highest compliment is to argue. He envies me. He begrudges me."

Paul was driving. He began to hum. "On a clear day, rise and look around you. . . ."

I sighed.

He slammed the steering wheel. "You just can't stand for me to be happy!" he screamed. "You scrutinize me all the time. You want to eat my head. You look for me to say one wrong thing, and then you despise me."

I half-shut my eyes, gazing out the window at the gritty landscape streaming past. Why argue? When I try to explain my experience, I told myself, all he hears is criticism. I imagined opening the car door and just stepping out as we flew along. Paul accelerated.

"If we have an accident, I'll divorce him," said the voice in my head.

I pictured myself bandaged, in a hospital, declaring "I never want to see you again."

* * *

"Are you having an affair?"

I'd just shut the door behind me from my trip to Dr. Sing.

"No."

He gazed at me from the couch, his eyes steady and hard. It was nine P.M. He was still in his rumpled business suit.

"I wouldn't have an affair," I said. "It just tears a relationship apart. I know that. I'd get a divorce before that."

"Why are you talking about divorce?"

"You brought up affairs!"

He continued to watch me.

"I'm getting something valuable from Harriet," I said.

Something you're incapable of giving, I suddenly thought. Something neither your father nor mother were able to give you. You deserved it, but they just couldn't give it. It's sad. Still, how can you give me something you've never received?

I turned around and opened the door to the house. "I'm going for a walk," I said. Before the door shut behind me, I could hear him click on the TV.

"I am afraid you'll pull back."

Silence.

"I'm afraid you'll think I'm too much."

"Why?" said Harriet.

"I want so much. I'm afraid that secretly, despite yourself, you resent it."

I recalled an afternoon when I was nine and had stumbled upon something almost unbelievably wonderful. In the empty kitchen, standing on a chair—an ordinary brown grocery bag. But when I reached inside I discovered packets of brown and white molded cowboys and Indians, boxes of intricate horses, colored metal jacks with an orangey-red ball, mercury in a maze, clear tubes of pick-up sticks, and Golden Books with foil bindings.

"Get your hands out!" screamed my mother.

She stood in the doorway. "They're not for you!" she said hastily. "You'll ruin them. They're for your guests."

"Guests?"

"For the birthday party. They're consolation prizes."

I gaped, astonished my mother had invested so much time and money in my party. Yet my hands in the bag itself seemed to have physically hurt her.

"You are like a mother who doesn't resent me exploring what's inside," I told Harriet slowly. "You don't push me away. My real mother felt that I was 'too much.' My needs were too much. I felt sticky and hot and intense and smelly. My touch ruined things. You let me explore."

"Yes."

"You know, that bag of prizes reminds me of the writing contract."

"How?"

"Well, I thought it would make me so happy. That it was in a way full of rich, wonderful things. But contact with me seemed to spoil it."

She leaned back in her chair. "Kleinian, isn't it?"

I nodded.

By chance I'd bought a paperback of Melanie Klein's essays years earlier. A compelling, mythic quality suffused her work. She proposed that to the infant the mother is the world of well-being. When the mother is unavailable too long, the infant feels hungry, helpless, unsoothed, upset. Mysterious internal pangs stab him. He is rattled by his own shrieks, which seem to come from outside him. He feels altogether attacked. In response, the infant fantasizes about hurting the envied breast, gouging it, injecting his own worst elements into it. But then the infant becomes anxious, fearing retaliation from this "spoiled" breast.

All this seemed to me disturbing, melodramatic, grotesque, developmentally impossible, and yet conceptually of use. "You mean that the contract was what she calls 'the good object'?"

"The good object, yes. Which, in your case, makes it inherently unstable."

I nodded. "I assumed the contract would absolve me from certain painful doubts."

Like a mother who infuses the child with bliss, I thought. Yet the instant I possessed my ideal object, I became terrified it would be stolen. "Remember how furious I was with Kate?" I asked. "I felt like she was taking my joy away. I didn't know how to make her stop."

"Yes."

"It was so frustrating and mysterious."

"But now it makes sense?"

"A little."

Kate had invited me to visit her in St. Louis, and that's where I was when news of the contract arrived. We found a congratulatory message from the editor on Kate's machine. I raced downstairs to return the call, leaving the door slightly open behind me because to shut it completely seemed rude. Still, while I was speaking with the editor I was aware of Kate sitting in the kitchen at the top of the stairs, three inches from the slightly open door. I didn't want to express my delight in too strong a fashion. I could tell already from Kate's gleaming, overexcited face and curt gestures that she felt envious. "I'm very happy," came my voice—dull and flat. "I'm looking forward to working with you, too."

Yet even as I climbed the stairs I maintained the feeling of being chastened. Kate poured coffee from her Mr. Coffee machine. She began to cut slices of pumpkin bread she'd baked. "How'd it go?" she asked, throwing me a bright glance. And for the first time in our decade-long friendship, I experienced Kate as greedy. Smug. The way she laid one hand flat on the loaf as she drew her knife down in perfectly even strokes, the way she flipped the slice neatly onto a blue glass plate, even the paleness of her hands with their translucent almond-shaped nails—all seemed to express an exaggerated humbleness and a naked superiority. Every gesture of hers seemed to announce: "This is how it ought to be done!"

So monstrous did she seem, in fact, that at dusk I sat crosslegged on my bed in the basement scribbling nasty, novel thoughts of her in initials—a covert, eroded language of hate I invented on the spot. W.A.B.S.I. What A Bitch She Is. S.S.S.E. She's So So Envious.

Since Kate seemed hurt by my news, I tried to minimize my joy. I'd feel it later. But after we said good-bye in the airport I still couldn't feel it. And on the plane ride home it wasn't there. And even a month after I was back in my house in Salem it was still gone. Kate was stealing my joy! I didn't know how to make her stop. This was madness, I knew, but it made no difference. Instead of my object defending me, I discovered that I must defend it.

"But do you see how it's the same scenario as Stella and your father all over again?" asked Dr. Sing. "Another triangle. Always a triangle. And the person outside the triangle is taking your joy away."

"Yes, I suppose."

"Who do you think that person is?"

"I don't know, Harriet. I suppose you think it's my mother."

When I glanced back, Harriet's beige skirt looked voluminous, composed of gigantic folds and crevasses.

A whiff of horseflesh rose from her black boot. "And who do you think it is?" she asked.

"Kate, sitting at the top of her stairs."

"Idealization is a corollary to persecutory anxiety—a defence against it," I read in Melanie Klein. "The former idealized person is then often felt as a persecutor . . . and on to him is projected the subject's envious and critical attitude."

I nodded and turned the page, sitting on my futon couch.

So, I'd won the ideal object but without obtaining its enthralling, milky content. Harriet became my new coveted contract; she was the source of goodness. Yet I couldn't help feeling, even today, that Harriet was in fact truly withholding, exhausting, cold, insensitive, greedy for my money, insufficiently approving, and above all, that she reduced me to a state of aching dependence. I was a doll whose wind-up key was tucked in her pocket. But why was my key in her pocket? How had she become such a thief?

"You look fat," I whispered. My hands were clasped so tightly together they hurt. But I felt that if I didn't say exactly what came to mind, I would be beyond her help. "Just today, not usually."

"Maybe that's because you think I demand so much praise."

I nodded. It was a relief to be with her again. I'd arrived early and trod about the Bowdoin green, on which chunks of ice were still melting. The ground splooshed softly underfoot and the sky was a wincing blue. Now, as I lay on the couch, my toes in their gray socks were cold and wet. I glanced back at her.

"Your face has a blemish." I swallowed, and shook my head. "It looks like someone's scratched you. Why did you chat with me at the end of last session when I was writing your check? I hate when you chat! It's unworthy of you to chat! Were you nervous? Tired? What is that smell of instant onion soup?"

"Is there a smell of instant onion soup?"

"Yes. It's revolting."

"I shouldn't eat?"

"I don't want to smell your eating. You shouldn't eat anyway right before my session. You should be lean and intense and excited."

"The way you are."

"Yes."

"You dislike how much I consume. You dislike how much praise I require. Why do I require so much praise?"

"So that you don't leave me. So that you will continue to like me. You are insatiable."

"Yet you don't want me to eat and feel satisfied. I wonder who's really insatiable. You empty yourself of what I give you, and so you are constantly hungry. Perhaps it's you who feels insatiable."

"Oh, it's true! Harriet!" I exclaimed with relief. "Often I do feel empty and gray, or anxious, until I see you again."

She nodded.

"Harriet," I said softly, "I'm so sorry I said these horrible, hurtful things to you just now. Please say you forgive me."

She was silent.

"Please!"

"Bonnie," she said calmly, "you know all your feelings are welcome in here."

"I don't feel that."

"Because you don't welcome them yourself."

"How can I, when some are so ugly?"

"Which?"

"My attacks on you. I think I drain you. I think I exhaust you. I see you as a lean, fragile, damaged person."

"Like your mother?"

"Yes!" I said, my mind full of wonder. "My mother when she ran to the sink once to get water because reading to me exhausted her. It dried out her throat, she said. My pleasure hurt her. But oh, it had been so wonderful right before she jumped up. She'd been reading to me from *The Cat in the Hat.*"

"And what would it have been like if she was happy that you received pleasure?"

"I don't know."

"You see, Bonnie, you are so afraid of being punished for your pleasure that you cut yourself off from it. But why is pleasure so shameful?"

I shrugged. "Why ask me? It's our culture, Harriet. The Puritan culture."

"And what if it weren't our culture?"

I imagined a swollen earth-goddess, hot wet sounds like walruses slapping.

"Maybe my soup revolts you because you don't want to know I have a body."

"Your body is of no interest to me," I said.

"Isn't it?"

"No."

"Yet you remark that it is fat and blemished and that you dislike the smell of what I feed it."

"I'm sorry I said that. I told you I was sorry."

"Yes. I wonder how you feel when you stop praising me."

"Apologetic, apparently," I said with a smile.

"Because your praise is a defense against your insults?"

"I suppose. I'm thinking of Anita's chin. It was fleshy and seemed lacking in nerve endings, and yet it had tiny white X's where Anita had had stitches. She'd fallen off her bike. I always felt bad for that chin of hers. The stitches hurt me to see them. She was so vulnerable."

"You felt guilty she was hurt."

"Yes."

"You loved her."

"Very, very much."

"I know," she said.

Here was a dream of a poet who lost her ear underwater. It was recorded on a scrap of loose-leaf paper glued into a notebook. And here was the Button King, on Johnny Carson's couch in pants and shirts that seemed made of buttons, so closely were the buttons sewn. He held up a photo of a car, which also appeared composed of buttons, and explained that he stayed up late and glued. And here was the story of a girl whose parents lived in a mustard room. I'd turned the pages of this notebook before but it had always seemed to me that even my handwriting in it was stupid. Now I found myself leaning close, interested in what the girl who wrote it had to say.

What a change!

I told Harriet in my next session. She smiled. The Mexican needlepoint women striding away from each other on Harriet's wall hanging seemed to have exchanged a whispered secret as they passed. The poppy-red lamp swelled plumper. I felt proud of myself and proud of Harriet. I glanced up at my enemy riding over me on her pony. Even she seemed happy at my news.

CHAPTER SIX

Red Masks

Demons flew out wearing the faces of friends. I had a date to see Janice in a week. As the day approached, her face inflamed in my mind to a red mask: she appeared voracious, demanding, and impervious to my needs. I strode from wall to wall. I stared at the phone. I yearned to yell at her: "Stop! I can't bear another instant!"—although I scarcely knew of what. It was as if I were molded from rubber, a hot-water-bottle woman stretching and stretching to escape the pinch of my oblivious friend.

No, I could not breathe with Janice's name set on my calendar two days hence! But how weird. This was Janice, best friend and maid of honor at my wedding. We'd met when I was seventeen and came upon her in an empty classroom freshman year at college, Wallabees propped on the professor's desk, Derrida open in her hands and a dozen silver-paper ashtrays glinting all around while she munched a Drake's red-cherry pocket pie. I'd opened a wood door searching for a quiet place and discovered her presiding over a spectral class. "Mind if I stay and read?"

"Suit yourself." She flipped a page. "Weren't you in 'Language as Cosmos'?"

"A day."

She smiled without looking up.

The professor of the seminar had smoked clove cigarettes, famously studied at the Sorbonne, and informed me I lacked sufficient preparation. Janice was allowed to remain. A drop-shouldered B. Altman's coat cut identical to mine draped the back of Janice's chair, although hers was russet and mine pine green. We took this as a sign of kinship. We strode to supper later, and snow shook out of the night, sparkling under the streetlights and melting into the red-gold thicket of Janice's hair. We talked about our mothers, Simone de Beauvoir, *The Island of the Blue Dolphins* and the tree-stump home in *My Side of the Mountain*, and the mystery of why people look so entirely like themselves even though we knew our own faces to be as arbitrary as dealt cards.

"Camus said that by the time they're forty, people have the face they deserve."

"He died in a motorcycle accident, right?" I said.

She nodded thoughtfully.

We talked too about the oddly passionless women on our halls who seemed to chew through their courses like cows masticating, steady and unswerving. How strange these pragmatic women seemed, toting their lacrosse sticks, highlighting their texts with canary felt-tips! Why, it was as if they'd coated even their minds in a rich conditioner so there was never a snarl. She and I craved the tangles and mazes, whatever pointed inward and then inward some more—a sentence we found in a book and could hold before our eyes like 3-D glasses, a few lines of poetry about a sensation so subtle we'd never heard it set in words. We stared into the dark from which snow emerged as if from slit pockets, welcoming the dizzying effect. "You too? Is it the same for you?" we cried across the crystal lawns and up the hill to where the lit circular dining room full of other students glared like a flying saucer.

From that day we ate supper together every afternoon at five. We chose the same Waldorf salad and cottage cheese and snow peas, finishing off with coffee and milk released from a spigot you controlled by gently pulling a lever shaped like a bloated golf club. Then we walked together to the library. At the stroke of six I sank into my Windsor chair, the sun waning across the lawn in rivers of light. The spokes of my chair gave the sensation of riding a chariot. Janice preferred the modular orange couches on the top floor that could be assembled into a perfectly square, body-sized cube. She inserted herself into this cube or, if she needed to write a paper, advanced far into the depths of the library stacks that clanged under one's heels like the iron levels of a penitentiary.

Often Janice or I appeared where the other was studying. "Break?" we'd whisper, and pad down to the vending-machine room in our socks, which were mismatched in the style of the day, a yellow one with a black one, a green with a pink. The shallow marble steps pooled beneath one another and held a chill even at the height of Indian summer when the windows were stuck open, as if reason itself had coalesced coolly underfoot.

Janice plugged her quarters into the machine. It launched individual pie pockets, heavy pastries glazed with sugar. She was ashamed of her love for them—cherry, apple, and a ghoulish pineapple so artificial it achieved a sort of kitsch fascination, like pink Sno-balls or Count Chocula; it was a sign of her comfort with me that she let me see her eating them. I gnawed chocolate chip cookies that had dried to pencil shavings, or the occasional waxy, mealy Red Delicious apple, or the squarish orange whose peel yanked off in one piece, like a sweater, revealing a fruit the size of an egg. We both swilled the scalding vending-machine coffee, which coated one's mouth with powder and for which it was possible to acquire a taste, which we had, a mild perversion as if we fantasized we were drinking the pulverized library itself, a potion of straight intelligence. We scarcely spoke during these breaks, but ate and muttered. It was reassuring simply to have each other's company, and this reassurance continued all evening, each knowing the other was somewhere nearby.

So how could she have become anathema? By what reversal of blazing energy? Craziness, but I couldn't stop it. Inadvertently she would insult me in some indelible way, I felt. She would reduce me to slag. I would become my old sniveling self (for suddenly I felt this was how I'd often been in her company), inarticulate, placating, my spirit in defeat.

And the same worry infected my friendship with Kate, my other maid of honor. Or matron of honor, rather, a horrifying title discovered by my mother in a bridal handbook, but which spared me deciding who I liked best: I could have both.

Kate had been a friend of an even more elemental sort. Meeting her was falling in love. She leaned toward me across a hundred lacework-iron café tables in Madrid, a semester abroad, showing me her mother's feminine script, her secret husband's staring photograph like a face advertising a military camp, her own poetry whose movements down the page amazed: How did she get from here to there? How achieve these chimes and transfigurations? "*La rubia y la morena*," sang a man who spied us bent together in the corner of a bakery against the steamed glass: the blonde and the brunette. We laughed. "*Otra café con leche*," we called. My back ached with hunching toward her as she hunched toward me.

When we returned from Spain, she offered her study to be my bedroom. We lived in a tall blue house with a glass-walled kitchen and a living room painted the color inside a nectarine. Her husband sat in a corner of the living room and practiced classical guitar, the instrument tipped high and his head drooping as if studying his own heartbeat. He played thin, endless, inconsolable Bach as if muttering under his breath; it sounded as if he were playing an accompaniment and in an instant he would take the solo.

I'd complained about my housemates. So Kate and her husband invited me to be theirs and to live among the Audubon birds whose very drabness mystified—the dusty red of the tanager; the bluish black of the crow—why frame such plainness? Although I knew, if I could simply train my eyes to see like Kate's, a hundred invisible constellations would become manifest. And she did instruct: she remarked on the stark winter tree branches whose elegance I'd never noticed, the scattering of birdseed on snow. Time after time she plucked beauty from nothing. And the closer I stood to her, the more I saw it.

Then, in the early spring, Kate pulled the bedspring from beneath her husband's mattress and wedged it into the corner room. She slept there now, although when I lay down on the bedspring once, it felt like a hundred fists. Kate wore white crepe-soled nurse's shoes and took a day job at the Friendly's, moonlighting at a posh restaurant called Town Farms. She kept wads and wads of dollars coiled in an old Chock Full O'Nuts can. On Wednesdays, in part to give Jim and me a chance to know each other better, she said, she stayed overnight at her parents' in New Canaan. Those nights especially I holed up in the library until midnight, then wandered home slowly down the empty road. Still, he was always waiting. "I'm tired," I said. "So splash cold water on your face," he replied, in irritation. "She's my best friend," I said, turning away from his annoyed expression. Through the closed door of my bedroom I heard him playing flamenco—a swift fan of the hand before he clamped the strings.

Kate and I donated blood one hot afternoon at the Red Cross and bought a bottle of Kahlua on the walk home and baked Maids of Honor—cornmeal cupcakes with cherry jam inside—and put on a record of Spanish rock—*"Rómpeme, mátame, pero no me ignoras, no mi vida!"*—and we collapsed on the sofa, laughing and half-drunk. I'd never ever been as happy. What did I care if her husband stayed or went, as long as I had her? For thirteen years she aroused intense joy—until now. When abruptly I couldn't bear her company.

I purchased a box of immensely elegant note cards at Bob Slate, in Cambridge. Butter cream, with envelopes the size of toast points, lined with gold paper. In my prettiest handwriting I conveyed to Janice the modest fact that just now I needed to be out of touch. This has nothing to do with us, I explained. In fact, I would miss her. In fact, I already did! Still, I couldn't see her, couldn't phone. Had she ever gone through a time like this? I loved her, I added. I hope she understood.

But a provocative phrase nicked my ear. "This has nothing to do with us." Well, obviously it did. I removed another card, sighing over the loss of the now-unmatched envelope.

"It's just that I feel an enormous pressure inside." But didn't that sound as if I were blaming her?

Out came a third card. With each revision I cut explanations and apologies until the card seemed to smile in its own rectitude. The more I simply stated what I wanted, the more airily unobjectionable it seemed. The message grew smoother and smoother, as if I were blending a balm thick as pancake batter to soothe my friend's infected throat, as if there were something quite irrationally the matter with her and if I could simply formulate the right palliative she'd be at peace and I could slip temporarily from the friendship without her notice—and the horrible clasping pressure would be relieved.

Why, contemplating this imminent peace I became almost merry sitting at my desk with its bud vase holding three bluish-purple irises. What a lovely color! I poured another coffee. Cha-chaed across the floor. I sharpened all my pencils, one after another, with a decisive satisfying crank of their shafts. Then I cleared a space for them in my top desk drawer, shoving back all the messy old checkbooks and papers. At last I sat down and completed the note. How eminently reasonable I was, after all. And when I reread the part about how I loved Janice, how I missed her—my heart ached! An impulse swept me to call her and exclaim, "Oh, I love you!" Instead, I signed my name.

A smile rose to my lips. The handwriting latticed in an almost indecipherable filigree. I licked the gold flap, and strolled across Salem Common, my heart lofting higher at each step. Ah, I couldn't wait to get back to my work! I couldn't wait for the lightness that would be mine in three steps, when I would be free!

But just as the card swept into the postbox's innards, my heart rang. It went off like a fire alarm. My very bones vibrated. For Janice might be angry when she read my card! She might be furious, she might—oh, what a fool I was! What a mess I'd made! Now I wouldn't be able to get any work done at all, all week. How could I feel safe enough to write? She might call at any moment, furious! I must devote myself entirely to awaiting my friend's response. My teeth clenched. I stared at the grass, which was a spiky yellow. No, I'd just have to call Janice and apologize. Ask her to ignore my insanity. I strode back over the stubbly grass and grabbed the phone, nearly yanking it out of the wall.

And so I begged myself back, each week from a different friend.

"You acted impulsively," said Harriet, "and see what happened?"

"What? I thought and thought about the message. It took two hours."

Harriet shifted. She neatly folded back the sleeves of her white shirt, which was as stiff as paper. "Okay, not impulsively. Half-consciously. You set up a whole unnecessary drama. You should keep your feelings about Janice where they belong: in here."

"But you have nothing to do with it! If anything, you're the *anti-dote* to her. I look forward to seeing you. You make writing possible. You make imagination possible."

"Didn't you once feel that way about Janice? That you could tell her anything?"

Fog suffused my head. "Maybe. Yes. How did you know?" I turned to her and she smiled down at me with her Ionian blue eyes. Relief seeped through me—the first all week.

"Let's look at that," she murmured.

"At what?"

"Let's treat it as an association. What you just did."

I stared into the Picasso room, frowning.

"You turned and looked at me . . ." she prompted.

How small the painted chickens really were, consolidating, shrinking into themselves. Hard as concrete. "So?"

"Well, do you remember why you suddenly looked at me? You see, everything that happens here is part of the same conversation."

"Is it? Isn't there something new that ever gets in?"

"That's the issue exactly!" cried Harriet. "You always want to be-lieve it's something new. You want to believe what's going on now is unrelated to what's gone on in your friendship before. You want to believe it's an aberration, that it's something I'm doing to you."

"It certainly feels that way."

"Yes," she said softly, but this time I didn't turn.

"I feel very far away from you." Tears wanted to clog my throat. "A loss has happened."

"Why is that?"

I shook my head. "Because I don't want to turn and look at you."

She seemed to nod behind me.

"You are very far away, and soon I will be gone from this room en-tirely. It feels as if you won't allow the kind of closeness I want." An-ger jolted in me from somewhere. "Soon I will be out again in the world and tense about Janice. It's as if I'm trying so hard to get you to understand, and you haven't."

"And what will happen when I understand?" she murmured.

The Picasso room blurred. "Hope," I felt like saying, but didn't. "Then you will know, Harriet," I pronounced grandly, "that the way I feel for you is really and truly utterly different from how I've felt about Janice or Kate, or anyone else." I turned and allowed myself to look at her. She was smiling.

I turned back and she sat silent.

"I wonder what sort of an association that was," I said.

Still she remained quiet.

"Looking at you makes me feel close. Suddenly I wanted to feel close."

"Perhaps to overcome your anger at me."

"Why would I be angry?"

She didn't answer.

"You know the answer to my quandaries, I feel, but you just won't give it. Like this situation with Janice. You seem to understand why it's happening—all this tension, this animosity. But I can't tell, is my friend bossy or is it me?"

"Well," she said, closing her notebook, "you're not psychotic, Bonnie. There is a reality factor to the incidents you describe. Janice sounds like a very assertive person."

Ah. A reality factor. Once, years earlier, Janice refused to drive me someplace I needed to go. A small incident, minuscule even.

Yet it burned like an infected splinter because it reminded me of tinier incidents I couldn't name, like coral abrasions too small to see. I'd been visiting Janice in Cambridge from my home in Iowa. My brother had a small pink suitcase I needed to fetch. It would be twenty minutes with Janice by car if she drove me (a New Yorker, I'd never learned to drive) or an hour and a half each way alone on the T.

"I spend my whole week driving," Janice said. "It's over an hour to the clinic. I just can't bear to get in the car on the weekend." Perhaps she'd wake up at six the next morning, she offered, and ride the Red Line with me.

But the next morning at six she did not wake up, and I departed to fetch the suitcase. The whole laborious way, while I waited for the Red Line to Park Street and then rode the Green all the way out to Riverside, past tracts of wire fence and suburban parking lots, I recited, "I won't forget this. She'll pay!" Although I really didn't know what I meant.

It was simply that I'd have driven her, I knew, no matter what. And I couldn't conceive how she could send me off on this sojourn of dragging a little stuffed heavy pink suitcase block after block— even if she'd had nothing to do with stuffing the suitcase or my need to regain it.

Of course it was Janice's very self-possession I resented. Her ability to say no, to tolerate my resentment which, she may or may not have assumed, I'd dispatch with, since its unwieldy weight constituted a small burdensome stuffed suitcase of its own.

I arrived back at her door on Hubbard Street at last. An apartment mate let me in—a blond fellow with sleep crusting his eyes and big raw boney feet. I set my suitcase in the closet, and shut the ceramic-knobbed accordion door upon it, each knob decorated with its dainty blue sprig.

Janice smiled and began to pour me what seemed like a quart of orange juice in a vast blue glass. I stared as the sun beat hot on the tangle of plants in her alcove beneath a crystal on a string that, in rare moments, tossed rainbows across the wall but mostly, as now, hung gray as a dusty grandmotherly glass stopper.

Soon, however, I was smiling. There was nothing to do about my anger. If I brought it forth, she'd snatch it and turn it against me. She could use my anger—I knew from experience—more brutally against me than I could use it against her. "Stop crying!" she'd once declared, years earlier. She'd been crying first and—she accurately perceived—my tears were meant in part to stop hers.

I'd left her earlier in order to eat supper with my boyfriend. When I knocked at Janice's door around ten, she swept it wide and shut off her record player, which had been playing Joni Mitchell: I wish I had a river . . .

"Sit down," she said. She explained in detail how angry she was. She began to weep. I felt unhappy—I tapped into a reservoir of sadness—and tears came into my eyes.

"Don't you dare!" she cried. "I'm the one who's been hurt here!" Instantly my eyes dried and I sat across from her, "giving her attention" as she wept, and blushing with shame—although in a quite separate room within myself I recalled the pleasure of my supper with my boyfriend, the American cheese and kaiser rolls and his kisses, all of which now transformed to glue in my stomach. Janice could name her emotions in a way that made mine clot and fur and become unidentifiable. Inside her stood a botanical garden with labels riveted to the trees; inside me was a blurred jungle with one thing growing into the next.

The evening of the day I fetched the suitcase, Janice threw a party. She sat in a marigold-wool snug sweater with pearl buttons the size of monocles and bent toward a man with whom she was plunged in intense conversation. He was a tall pale man with the body of a contortionist. He sat on her couch cross-legged, his feet upside down and their heels flat as irons, the arched chain of his spine draped like a fishing rod, nodding almost in synchrony with Janice while the two of them kept their gaze locked upon the couch cushions between them. Janice left the rest of the room to fend for itself.

She didn't notice Thea shifting from leg to leg, or Daniel studying the titles of her social worker texts. The blond housemate still had sleep crusting his eyes; it was an orange almost phosphorescent color; and he alone, aside from Janice and the pale tall man, seemed perfectly at ease, hunched over a Pyrex dish of brownies, eating one after another, scraping the dish with a knife. Thea went to the bathroom and emerged smelling of Shalimar. Daniel slid a book from Janice's shelf. Other guests poured in, the blond roommate opening the door. Janice nodded to the pale man. Her laugh soared out. She was having a fine party. For the second time that weekend I was amazed at the license she allowed herself.

The bookish passion that had once melded our youths together had long deserted us. Janice now had Polaroids of herself in a lumpish burnt-orange dress with her arm around an awkward, smiling boy of around ten. His name, Timothy, was written in her rounded stuttering ballpoint underneath and the photo was taped to her wall. There was also a picture of a girl named Sally who wrote, "I love you, Janice," on a green piece of construction paper, and a child named Raymond who glanced up from long-lashed eyes to barely meet the camera's gaze, while Janice stood beside him in a boxy, white, too-big shirt smiling into the lens.

These were Janice's clients, to whom she gave therapy. At the time I knew almost nothing of therapy, but still it seemed odd, acquisitive, to mount these expressions of love, as if she wanted something unfair from them. Janice had also taped up on her bedroom door a picture of herself from when she was five or six, with enormous unfocused brown eyes and half-parted lips, as if she were swimming underwater in her plaid dress when the camera had rushed up. Her face ran from margin to margin. "It reminds me of wonder," said Janice, "the way I once felt it," which statement itself sent me into a state of wonderment, that it had been so long ago for her, as if this blurry child were a seraph that, if she was very good, she might someday become.

She read gossipy novels now, and fresh-minted handbooks on therapeutic issues. Her new friends were placid, plumpish women, many of them social workers. The word *intellectual* sent across their faces a look of dismay, smacking as it apparently did to them (I later understood) of elitism and pathological introversion, and of an almost willful obsession with obscurities, the cilia and pseudopodia of phantasmal thought—whereas to me the term had an almost totemic joy. I'd been blindly lost inside myself until I discovered the skein of intricate prose; I assumed they were the same way. As if our very minds had been invented by those sentences that spun into richer and richer meaning as your eye traveled their length, and which gave the sensation of far corners, a flashlight beam illuminating distant furnished rooms heretofore unsuspected, as if the mind, chaste until now, had been made love to. Life was complex, revealing leagues upon leagues, and there was no need to be alone in it skimming across its surface like a waterbug when in fact you could surrender to its hundred-page depths and enter its sunken ballrooms where feelings you hadn't even noticed you'd had were handed to you etched in black and white, giving you the sensation of being both infinitely complicated and infinitely graspable. When I said "intellectual" to Janice's friends it was to evoke this shared knowledge, a shared experience, and one valued most especially by Janice.

But her friends' noses wrinkled; they gazed at the floor. They believed in pragmatics: social work rather than psychoanalysis. They were friendly women who nodded easily and laughed warmly, and yet among them I felt bizarre, rococo, unable to recognize myself in their blithe assurances, their spiritualistic bonhomie, their sincere compassion and ironed, pastel wardrobe. These were the new people Janice gathered around herself.

It was as if the lacrosse players had won. They soothed something in her. They provided a sort of mammalian happiness. She seemed to bathe in the wheat gluten and Pearl Drops health they radiated. It was as if her entire life now were a conversation in the vending-machine room, the murmurings and sighs of convivial company without the vast exertion of all those books. And yet, at this moment of her party, bent toward the tall pale man who lolled toward her like a heavy-headed puffed dandelion, she struck me as vastly mysterious—questing for her lost wondrous girlhood in the eyes of her child patients and in this man's sticky gaze, while ignoring the guests who tumbled through the door at her own party.

If it were my party, I knew, I'd have run around trying to liven people up and to extend myself like mortar between the social bricks. I'd have wanted to get people excited and talking, and forgetting themselves so that I could forget myself—all of us whirling, rising, talking, leaning, spinning from disparate sand into clear molten flowing glass.

"I jigged," I told Harriet. "I used to have this mock tap dance thing I did." Charlestoning in the kitchen. Seizing my grandfather's cane and looping my throat and crying "Take her away! Take her away!" as I lugged myself offstage. I pattered my feet and smiled like a loon, injecting happiness—I hoped—into the shadowy house. In a red restaurant chair at DeFemio's in Yonkers at the age of eight I'd sung along with *Cabaret*: "What good is sitting all alone in your room?" My father said, "Listen to her. It just lifts my spirits!" and I discovered my calling: to be cheerful.

I loved being cheerful. Saturday mornings I appeared in an apron, holding a pad, at my parents' bedside. "May I take your order?" My father ordered eggs, my mother plain toast, and I dashed into the kitchen to whip it up. "I like this restaurant," my father said, sinking his fork into the eggs. "Delicious toast!" said my mother, and I grinned from ear to ear. "How well put," declared my father upon reading a birthday card I'd composed in which I enumerated all the traits of Anita's that I appreciated—her singing voice, her hiking vigor, her keen-eyed spotting of distant birds in trees without even wearing glasses. "You say just the right thing," my father said. It seemed to me most people scarcely thought about the right thing to say. They spoke at cross-purposes. They did not read the tension in the brows, the sigh, the pinched lips, the half-finished sentence. They said what they wanted to say, which resulted in myriad hurt feelings and bewilderments. My cheerfulness was a talent like playing the piano or being good at paddleball. I smiled, and it almost always felt genuine.

Anita was not cheerful. She glowered; she raged; she wept; she sang. She had many emotions. Anita stood in the hall and pointed a finger at my mother and said, "That was WRONG!" I held my breath and kissed my mother's pale cheek, fascinated by Anita's fury: the red cheeks, the sweaty face, the incomprehensible accusations. How did she allow herself? Of what did she consist? It all seemed to do with her being fat, as if my mother had imposed this unfair body on Anita, so of course Anita was entitled to be crude and eruptive. How would you feel if your body were suffocating you?

"It's Anita whose rasping throat seems to need a palliative," I said. "The childhood Anita."

Harriet nodded, winding her watch.

"All my friends are reminding me of Anita. You know, Janice and Kate are both oldest sisters. Somehow I never noticed."

"Maybe you did notice. Maybe that's why you chose them as friends."

I shook my head. "No. I want to agree with you, but it simplifies the truth of my friendships."

"What does it leave out?" She glanced up from her wrist, letting her big yellow hand drop.

"The love. And their particularity. Their unique ways of being brilliant."

"But now they seem like Anita."

I nodded. Janice now seemed domineering, even cranky, as if a subcutaneous irritability crawled through her, while Kate possessed the calm grace of an icon, the beauty of the older sister in pleats and darts, her hand clasping a green rapidograph with a stiletto-sharp nib.

"Even Paul," Harriet observed, "can appear to be like Anita."

I nodded. He could seem pathetic and sad, in my misperception, needing me to take care of him and cheer him up, as if he were some job.

"And now I want to be the older sister," I said. The center of my own life and not its audience. The girl with an opinion.

"You feel mean when you don't take care of others," said Harriet.

"Oh, I don't know."

"But you feel Janice is."

"She is! Janice has an ability to absent herself. To sort of hum to herself and get quite internally absorbed. She once invited Paul and me to a folk concert and it turned out to be awful, one banal local performer after another. The audience kept shifting in their chairs. Lots of people left. But Janice just smiled and shrugged. She didn't once apologize. I would have said, 'I'm sorry,' a dozen times."

"How would you have felt, apologizing?"

"Oh, desperate. As if I'd messed up. Undeserving of my friends' having come to this event." I looked up at the light blue Picasso sky.

"Janice chooses not to feel that way."

I nodded. "But it makes me feel invisible, that she wouldn't even acknowledge she was disappointed not to have pleased us." I folded my arms. "Actually, Harriet, it just occurred to me that maybe she feels too lousy about herself to apologize. Years ago I had scabies— itchy microscopic bugs under the skin. I phoned Janice so that if she was scratching a lot she'd know why and could treat herself with Kwell. Well, she told me that I'd caught the scabies from her! Everyone in the halfway house where she worked had them. They'd been infected for months. It made her feel disgusting so she never mentioned it to me, although she knew that she should. When she dried her hands on my towel, she must have left them, she said."

"It's hard for her."

"She didn't really have the independent joy I attributed to her," I said slowly. "I wish you could see her: the way she digs her hands into her pockets and trudges. I once made split-pea soup for the collective house we lived in: a whole potful. Janice held up her bowl of soup and said, 'I didn't get any peas!' I looked in her bowl and said, 'But Janice, it's all peas! That's what the entire soup consists of!' I used to drive home from Janice's enumerating for myself the ways I got her to laugh, how I'd drawn her out of herself, how we'd had fun. It made me feel successful."

"But now you don't want to do that."

I gazed at the prongs of the barren Picasso tree. "No. In fact, it frightens me now. That I will get lost in her."

"In trying to placate."

I nodded, recalling the way Janice laid a plank of satin-rippled cool butter on cornbread, the way she ate a pot of warm Annie's-brand macaroni and cheese, stirring it so the noodles crackled. Here, too, she was absent, absorbed in her pleasure.

"And you want to get lost inside you," said Harriet.

"I have to be able to let go, to do my writing. If I think of someone who might want me, suddenly I can't do anything but think of them."

"You are so used to feeling that other people are holding you hostage. Your best friends, even."

"How did you know?" I said, surprised.

She was silent.

"I think I chose friends I was afraid to cross," I said. "I felt good at conforming. Then I knew my friend was happy. So I could be happy."

"Were you happy?"

"Oh yes, Harriet."

I knew she didn't believe in my old happiness. She wanted to call it something else. But it really was happiness.

CHAPTER SEVEN

A Hundred Bakeries

"It doesn't seem to me as if you had these negative emotions inside you all the time, suppressed," said Paul. He spooned up some of his cereal and chomped. "It feels as if something nutzoid has been added." He was eating Grape-Nuts at the ceramic-topped table on the back porch, dressed in his suit.

I nodded, my foot shaking. "But isn't it good that all this stuff is coming up?"

"But I'm not so sure it *is* coming up, sweetie. It's paranoid. It seems to be coming from something new injected into you." He crunched on another spoonful of cereal.

"Maybe that's because you just don't like it," I said, sensing that I was being unfair.

"Well, baby, it's true I don't like to see you this way, all cuckoo for Cocoa Puffs. But I've known you a long, long time," he said calmly. "And it feels like something has been added, not that you were keeping something suppressed that's now released."

I missed my old way, in fact. Since I'd begun treatment half a year earlier, I hadn't been happy for a single day or even a single hour. A shivery tension inhabited me. I was a tuning fork constantly being struck.

I told Harriet about a fabulous evening three weeks before I'd begun treatment—I'd met Stella in Boston and we walked around the North End. The bluish cobblestones gleamed like iron loaves and a hundred bakeries had their doors flung wide; the air smelled of anisette. It was dusk. Stella wore a funny beautiful little black wool coat with a fur collar and red lipstick and laughed her big round laugh, balancing herself on nubby-heeled shoes. We ate spaghetti with delicious garlic sauce in a joint crammed with tables, then walked to a café with copper cappuccino machines. We'd both promised to bring stories but Stella seemed to have forgotten.

Late in the evening, though, she unclasped her purse, which was the size of a coffee-cup lid. Out sprang a wad of paper like a chrysanthemum blossom. She smoothed the pages, squinted, drew out a set of tortoiseshell reading glasses from the same impossible purse, and read aloud sentences as wonderful as the rainbows in just-washed hair.

Then she asked me to read, but my pages seemed to hold nothing coherent, nothing that was anything. "Well, why don't you just read that." Her finger fell on a cluster of ink. I read that little spate, and she said, "It's wonderful. It really is, Bon." I blinked. I'd been convinced that all I was writing was nothing, nothing.

The next morning when I awoke an ice storm had glazed the trees, but the sun had broken out. The sky was china blue. I stepped through the icicle grass in the yard, sucking on a cracked-off blade. Each leaf of the shrubbery seemed sunk in a shimmering shot glass, dilated, the pear yellow leaves and the diseased-looking leaves, as well as the bright jade leaves—a thousand crystals of a scattered chandelier. I sat down in the frozen hammock and lay back on the web of ice, which crackled under me. Leaves flashed like mackerel against the sky. I practically shone with happiness.

"But your joy was based on having devalued yourself for a very long time," explained Harriet.

"Oh, I don't care! I don't care what it was based on. I miss it. I want it back."

She shifted. "But wouldn't you like to be able to feel happiness on a more regular basis?"

Of course, I thought.

She silently waited.

"I don't believe I can be happy while I'm in this treatment. It makes me too anxious."

She listened.

"I can't be in treatment and be happy."

"That's a very interesting assumption," she said.

And we disputed it for the next six years.

* * *

"It makes me anxious to think of seeing Kate this summer. I've been dodging her calls."

"Well, what does it mean to be *in* contact with her?" asked Harriet. "Why do you want to be *out* of contact?"

I raised my eyebrows. For an instant Harriet had resembled Kate: the pursy, particular way she'd uttered those phrases. I glanced back and had to suppress a shiver. The arch of her fingers on the notebook, the smug pleats of her blue Parisian skirt—these echoed Kate, too.

"It's the sensation that my friend will destroy me," I said. "That my friend will say something, perhaps even in passing, that makes a belief in my own viewpoint impossible. I can't protect myself."

I looked back at Harriet again. How high her head seemed to be today! Rising atop the long alabaster column of her neck.

"Why not?"

"Sometimes I don't even know it's happening," I said.

"Do you think you could learn to notice what is happening at the time?"

The room filled with sleepiness. A dusty ambiance like the inside of a shut car parked in the sun. As soon as this session is over, I decided, I'll drink coffee. Great scalding cups, with cream.

"What?" I asked.

She was silent a moment, then repeated her question.

"I suppose. But it feels like, if I defend myself, I might be overreacting. Making something out of nothing. I'd be the aggressor."

"You mistrust your own perceptions."

"They're so different from anything I felt before."

"Are they?"

I thought. "It's as if, before, there was interference on a radio band—at the very beginning of seeing a friend, for instance—and I'd hear a different conversation coming in from far away. But then as I tuned in more precisely, that other conversation went away. This treatment has turned up that other conversation. But whose hand is on the dial?"

She was silent.

"I can't protect myself from my friend," I said, "because often I immediately agree with her criticism, and my work afterward seems weak. It seems destroyed."

"Your friend has so much power," murmured Harriet.

"Doesn't she?"

Janice had the session before mine and was running over. She gazed into Harriet's eyes as she spoke, standing in the middle of a squalid public clinic with green linoleum floors. People with sallow complexions lounged about in chairs, half-drowsing.

But Janice just kept cutting further and further into my session! She was talking and talking, and all the while Harriet maintained an expression of polite interest. Oh, it was wrong! Outrageous. Blood pounded in my ears. At last, I couldn't stand it another instant. "You have to stop," I yelled. "You have to go!"

Janice ignored me.

I grabbed her and started shoving her toward the door, shouting furiously. She didn't acknowledge my shouting, but oh, I could have yelled at her for hours! What a release!—while at the same time it made absolutely no difference, she seemed not to hear me, and I myself seemed anesthetized to my own screaming. Still, with one last push I thrust Janice out. In the hallway, she straightened her clothes and left.

I turned. And there was Harriet, her smiling eyes focused on mine, noticing everything. But only two-thirds of my session was left, and despair dropped over me.

"I'm struck by the fact that you weren't angry at me in the dream," said Harriet.

"Janice was the greedy one."

"It's still so difficult for you to be angry at me."

"But I'm not!"

She sat back, her pen clacking against her front teeth. "I wonder what it would be like for you if you could have as much of me as you wanted."

Ah. Living on cake.

"You see, Bonnie, you are also Janice in the dream—or rather, you dream of being Janice, the girl who runs over. Who takes what she wants. Who insists upon her right to have it. You are angry at this girl because you think it's her fault you don't have what you want," she continued. "Yet you resist speaking up because you believe such behavior is greedy, is ugly."

"Yes," I said. And I realized that Janice was like Anita, and Harriet was the mother we both wanted. Yet the politeness on Harriet's face —what was it if not my own estranged childhood politeness? I recognized her dream expression from how it felt on my own face.

Before Harriet, there had been a different woman with whom I wished to get close—closer and closer, and we were never close enough.

After the divorce, Kate lived in a breathless attic *sans* electricity which rented for seventy dollars a month and where, lying on her cot after she'd blown her candles out, she gazed up between the rafters at splinters of night and stars. During the summer it smelled as if the pine rafters were smoldering, and in winter ice crystals seemed to hang in the air. The chill scoured your face. A long table was wedged under an eave. This table held books—Chaucer, *Sir Gawain*, and *The Joy of Cooking* with her grandmother's own Radcliffe penmanship (indistinguishable from Kate's) in back giving her boeuf bourguignon recipe, and her mother's almost identical handwriting conveying the salad dressing she'd invented, with its secret ingredient of sherry. My eyes always fell on the Tiffany-blue hardcover, about which Kate once said, "There are so many things I just love in it! 'Dough the consistency of an earlobe!' Isn't that wonderful? I'd like to use that somewhere"—meaning in her poetry.

I smiled at her. I never noticed such things!

And here were her Norton anthologies whose translucent onion-skin riffled in the breeze from the open window, and her *Beowulf*, her Spenser, and the candles half-burnt in their several candle-sticks.

She was studying to take the English Achievement Exams for graduate school. Around two A.M. she came home from her waitress job at La Boca, half-drunk on sombreros. She took her ankle-length

Lanz nightgown out of her closet downstairs and changed in the communal bathroom. Then she carried a lit taper up the attic steps and sat wrapped in the green down sleeping bag, reading Elizabethan poetry. With a sharpened pencil, she jotted phrases on a separate sheet. The wind rattled the window frames and occasionally carried, she said, the suggestion of an mbira. A Ghanaian musician had killed himself two years ago in that attic. Sometimes the notes of a thumb-piano played just as she was drifting to sleep, and once she heard it as she was coming up the stairs.

"Oh, that's so scary!" I said.

"Really?" She smiled. "I'd actually like to see a ghost. I try to have receptive thoughts when I hear that mbira. It's not ghosts who scare me, but living people."

I nodded, surprised at our opposite fears. Kate's own husband had owned a thumb-piano. She'd shown it to me once—small as a cigar box, a double row of fifteen raised steel rods which you flicked your fingers off, hard.

"Wouldn't it sound better if he pried the bottle caps off?" I nodded toward two decorative Yoo-Hoo caps that imparted an unfortunate buzz.

She smiled, bewildered. "That's part of the music!" she said. Ah: a dirty, reverberant rasp, like playing a Sucrets box, a rattle I'd have excised in favor of a bright calliope ring. How much I had to learn!

"But don't you see that the more you build up your friend, the more you diminish yourself?"

I shook my head. "Being close to such a fabulous person, I feel *better* about myself. That she would choose me. And yet . . . something is changing. Harriet, it used to be that any new book in the bookstore seemed wonderful. I couldn't see any flaws. Now some sentences seem lazy or boring. Some sentences seem weaker than others."

"You used to idealize whatever you read. Now you are getting a little bit of distance."

"A lot of distance."

She nodded. "I am trying to give you something that a malicious remark cannot destroy."

"What might that be?"

"You tell me."

"I think of something hairy and indigestible. Like the twine my father uses to wrap packages to me. Or the tough white strands that seem to hold this couch together. Fibrous, strong, artificial, indestructible. Like the gristle you cut off a lamb chop."

"It's not beautiful," said Harriet.

"Oh no. Not in me."

"But in somebody else?"

"In somebody else I would admire it."

"And you want that for yourself?"

"Yes."

Harriet nodded, as if this were precisely the thing with which she intended to endow me.

"I'm writing something longer," Kate had said one afternoon three years earlier.

I was standing in my parents' dinette in the Bronx, under the 1960s light fixture with its freehand stars like asterisks, holding the powder puff–pink phone in my hand. "A novel," I murmured.

"Maybe. We'll see."

A boomerang shot into my stomach. "Where's it set?"

"Nepal, mostly. I want to get in the smells and sights. It's a love story."

"Oh, I'm glad for you."

She laughed. "It's no big deal. It's probably awful. I'm trying not to think about it. The whole trick is to do it in a nonchalant way."

Yes, of course. That was suddenly the best way. I was so earnest and perfectionistic! Of course, the offhand approach is best.

"I remember Kate," Mark said. "Such a little Puritan! Her poetry is boring—I mean, it has to be! She was such a priggish little soul-deadening person!"

"Was she?" I shook my head, confused.

We sat barefoot in my friend's Provincetown apartment with its blue-gray–painted floorboards and its glimpse of beach. Mark sat at the piano. He'd been writing an opera.

"Frankly, I don't understand why you ever made so much of her, with her long blond hair and perfect WASP manners. Just the thought of her makes me want to kill myself!"

I smiled. Kate once told me years ago, when we lived together, that she hardly ever spoke in class because she was shy, but that others sometimes mistook her for arrogant. I'd been surprised. Who could misjudge her so?

Mark raced his fingers up the piano keyboard. He sat in red-and-white shorts and a white T-shirt.

"Really?" I said. "But do you really remember her?"

"Tallish, hair to her waist?"

"Yeah."

"Oh, come on, Bonnie." He slammed the keys into a powerful chord. "She was such a little prig. Say, 'Fuck you, bitch!' Let me hear you!"

I smiled. "Fuck you, bitch."

"Louder! 'FUCK YOU, BITCH.'"

"FUCK YOU, BITCH!"

He turned and grinned. "You're on the road to mental health."

"I thought of her as a devil doll," opined Leon, another friend from those days. "She appeared innocent but in fact had a very superior, condescending attitude."

I nodded, recalling a supper Kate had cooked and to which she'd invited Leon and me: leaf-thin moo shu pancakes with a vegetable filling, plum sauce in a tiny blue shallow dish, brown rice in a brimming bowl.

"Pass the flapjacks!" cried Leon. He'd grinned and rubbed his palms.

I flinched. He couldn't help teasing her—goading her, really. Leon was often willfully crude around Kate. Now I saw that he'd perceived her refinement as a judgment, as if she were continually reminding him of his working-class background, as if he must tweak her for her poise.

"Pass the flapjacks," and I wanted to smack him.

Kate smiled and lifted the plate and passed it to him.

"Your flapjacks," she said.

Now I said, "Really? You saw her as a devil doll?"

"The miracle is that you didn't."

Yet even now, although Leon's viewpoint provided a certain solace, it didn't seem reliable.

I just couldn't get a fix on my old girlfriend. It was like trying to train one's gaze on the beveled emerald edge of a mirror at the same time as looking down into its lustrous surface. "She's half an inch thick," says the beveled edge. "She's depthless," replies the surface.

"I'm so sorry, Kate," I tell her, a year into therapy. My voice sounds dead. "I can't bear to hear about your novel. It's just that I admire your work so much. I know this is an unfair request. I have no right to ask it. But would it be all right if we didn't talk about your book?"

"Of course!"

Still, the subject keeps cropping up. She's taking a break after finishing a chapter; a certain person reminds her of a character in her book. Taking a shower this morning she couldn't help visualizing her book as a movie. It would actually make an excellent movie, she says with a laugh.

I smile across the white-and-red vinyl tablecloth. I want to prove I'm stronger and saner than she might think. Some days I even introduce the topic myself. Yet eventually I always make my request again, more emphatically.

"Fine!" she says, brightly. "There are a million other things to talk about!"

But why exactly was the idea of being around Kate so very threatening? Why could I suddenly not bear to hear about her book, I wondered one spring night in bed.

She'd diminish me by being close, I sensed. I'd become like a gray, disconnected lightbulb in her radiant presence. How ugly I felt in her company!—as if I were the brown-clad, stained, galumphing child, ordinary to the point of disappearance, while every skein of words she invented rang with an almost mystical music. Yet I'd never been like this before! She'd been writing her novel for three years and I could always tolerate seeing her and hearing about it. It was just since therapy began that I needed to impose this absurd request. Don't talk about your novel!

I shifted on my side, one hand on Paul, who stirred in his sleep. My eyes gazed past the open French door toward the backyard, lit by moonlight. The streetlamp on Pickman rasped like fabric tearing, someone ripping a seam.

No, I'd never been like this before. But now I had something I wanted—this contract, the chance to feel really good about my work—and I refused to give it up. Yet hadn't I ever had something I desperately wanted and dreaded to lose?

In the past, losing cost nothing. Playing rummy with my brothers when I was six, it upset me when I picked up my cards and discovered an entire row of royalty. I stared at the kings and queens, and felt sad for my brothers, who had the weakness of actually needing to win. "I was lucky," I said when I showed my hand. They burst out laughing. "You were losing so much," said the older brother, grinning, "that when you went to the bathroom we set up the cards so you'd win!" I smiled, confused. But I hadn't at all minded losing!

Now, though, I had something I knew it would hurt me to lose. Possessed of my contract, I could not afford to be dull or stupid anymore. Up until now, being stupid cost me as little as losing at cards. It hadn't really mattered when my tests were returned with 60s or 70s on top. If a friend pumped advice all over me, if a woman in biology class proclaimed with a smirk, "That blue sweater! How many days in a row are you going to wear that blue sweater!" while the girls around her actually tittered (I glanced down at the comfortable blue sweater, surprised because I'd believed I was half-invisible and also that as long as you changed the shirt underneath, a sweater was something you could wear ad infinitum, like a coat), it didn't matter.

Secretly, in my deepest core I'd believed that inside me was something special. I had to believe this. And I believed, furthermore, that at some unspecified time, like Cinderella rising to her feet in glass slippers, I would display this specialness. This was the fantasy in which I lived. It made insults to me free. My day would arrive, I told myself—never thinking how this might come to pass. And now it had.

So the contract had become an impossible, craved demand. Now I understood what it felt like to be the instrument of another's will. Something was controlling me and it was not me. Invisible jutting objects pressed into me like the corner of a table pulled too close. My friend Mark's mother's voice on my answering machine forcefully inviting me to have lunch in Boston—what an outrage! Didn't she understand I had work? Stella sending me a story with just a yellow sticky note saying, "Bon—Pls. read this." How high-handed!

The only way I could understand the seizures of rage that began to shake me, that filled my nights with burning houses, was as madness. Just as someone throwing up a bad meal experiences it as a symptom of illness, not health.

I was leaving my girlhood of passionate gratitude. I was doing it gracelessly, violently. I was leaving behind the time of thanking my father profusely for buying me eyeglasses, of wandering the windy gray streets in old clothes, eating Devil Dogs and potato chips, wishing wildly for the thing that would prove my value.

"I hope if you are successful, it won't change you," Janice had said.

"I hope it will," I prayed.

"You are looking for ogres," she told me. I nodded, trying to ignore how her mouth had stretched like an ogre's even as she said those words.

"See you soon!" says Kate, in a pleasant voice.

"Yes." I smile, feeling blessedly sane. What a relief after the recent wild distortions!

We've finally planned a meeting for early July. It's late spring. After hanging up, I begin to wash dishes, my hands plunged deep into water. The phone rings. I let the machine get it. "It's me again, Bon. A question occurred to me. Do you think it's too old-fashioned to include a letter in a novel?"

A letter is immediately the most enthralling development a novel can contain. I see the letter on the page—the sprightly italic type racing from margin to margin, then the body of the novel framing it. One's eye is eager to reach the letter. What will it say? Something clever and fun, something Kate can knock off with a flick of her wrist.

Yet why did she feel the need to phone me back and pose that question? What was she asking? Is it too old-fashioned to include a letter? Our friendship ends on that question.

Three months later she leaves another message, following a series of letters that I toss in a drawer, still sealed. "It's Kate," she says. "I thought I'd give myself one last chance. I don't know what's gone wrong between us."

But how downtrodden and lackluster her voice sounds, coiling itself into the spools of the answering machine! Yet now, in the silence, I detect a nasty, goading quality in her words. What does she mean, "I thought I'd give myself one last chance"? She means to give *me* one last chance, doesn't she? I press the button. Kate's voice rings out again, shockingly friendly and warm. After a moment of silence though, the mocking quality returns. I shake my head and erase the tape.

"False memory syndrome" is the phrase the radio journalist uses. I park the car and sit rigid in the Purity Supreme lot, listening with all my might. Parents are suing their children's therapists. They claim that the therapists induce supposed memories of incest when in fact no such abuse ever occurred.

My heart pounds. They're so dangerous, these therapists! They have no idea whatsoever of their power! I myself am suffering not from false memory but from false reality: my perceptions are distorted, my nightmares run wild in the world.

"Make it stop," I tell Harriet when I see her again.

"But it comes from within you."

"You always say that, but I was never like this before."

Still she's silent.

"You think I was like this before."

"Secretly, yes."

"Frightened of my friends."

"Yes."

"Angry at them."

"Yes."

"You're wrong. I loved my friends. They delighted me."

"I'm sure that was true, too."

Janice and I make a date after four months of not seeing each other. A few days before our supper, Janice calls to say she really needs to shop that night for a dress for her doctoral presentation. Should we cancel our date or might I want to go shopping?

"I'd love to shop with you. The whole point is just to spend some time together."

We meet at the Chestnut Hill Mall, but first Janice wants to select a bouquet to sit on the table during her presentation. At the florist, she turns cardboard after cardboard of the big varnished flower book, gazing studiously. Then we walk into Bloomingdale's, and Janice pushes the matrons' garments across the rack. "Would you mind holding my dresses?"

"Of course not."

She scrutinizes each dress, frowning, turning her head. She hands me a long brownish dress with flowers and lace at the collar. She hands me a pink drop-waisted dress with puff sleeves. Minutes pass. She doesn't bother making conversation. She hands me another dress, absently. I make a remark; she grunts. Fury begins to afflict me. I feel rendered invisible, insulted—that Janice allows herself to become so absorbed in her search that for twenty minutes she's mute. I feel like dropping the dresses on the floor and stamping all over them. But I will go crazy if I speak! This isn't the right moment, anyway. After all, she needs to find her dress.

Later, in the ladies' room, I say, "It makes me feel invisible when you treat me like that. When you don't bother even to make conversation."

She blinks at me, drying her hands on a paper towel. "I knew something was bugging you."

"You did?"

"Sure. You're so easy to read!"

"Well then, why didn't you say something?"

"I had to find my dress."

"Janice," I say, "I need you to make even just a little chitchat with me at a moment like that, to acknowledge I'm there."

"You didn't used to need that."

Yes, how marvelous I used to feel when I sensed I was "being of service." It was as if my friend and I had achieved an Olympian, privileged sense of intimacy. What an honor, to be so accepted that one's presence could be taken for granted! "No, I didn't," I agree.

A month later she calls midmorning. "I'm submitting my thesis tomorrow. May I go over a few grammar questions?"

"All right."

She reads an entire page of her manuscript, building to the question. I nearly hold the phone away from my ear. Over an hour passes, during which I give my opinion on grammar. Finally, I can't contain myself. I tell the truth: "I'm feeling a headache from tension now. I have to get back to my own work."

She gasps. I hear her gasp. And then the phone goes dead. After a moment I hang up.

She cannot change for me, I tell myself. It is hard enough to change for oneself.

"Splitting," I read in a book Harriet recommended, "is linked with increasing idealization of the ideal object, in order to keep it far apart from the persecutory object and make it impervious to harm."

A description by Hanna Segal of the theory of Melanie Klein. I copy it into my notebook. My new life seems more and more split, with Harriet on one side, and almost everyone else on the other.

Once upon a time, before I met Harriet, I'd experienced myself as an ordinary, drab, gray-clad girl. I was content to sit lost among the other girls until my gift expressed itself and redeemed me. I believed then that someday some gift of mine—I didn't know what—would select me, would press me into visibility. It never occurred to me that one's gift was something to be insisted upon and defended. Ambition seemed ancillary to it. One worked hard, and the reward happened by itself, if it was supposed to. How much time I'd lost to passivity!

Yet once I gained Harriet, I yearned to possess the specialness with which she endowed me, as Kate had once endowed me, and Janice before her. But where my eyes saw Golden Books and candy cigarettes, my fingers grabbed leeches and razors. It was my own hands—sticky, dragon-scaled—that transformed the prizes. And the more Harriet gave to me, the more paradoxically frustrated I became. She sat in a pretty blue French skirt and dangling silver earrings, reaching for her notebook. I pushed off my scuffed torn shoes and lay in my stocking feet. My skeins of association were things she could fascinate herself with and master; my insides reflected her beauty. Whereas to me they brought increasing dismay, since the more I trusted her, the more primitive were the images that forced themselves to mind.

"The fears you had about your friends are really your fears about me," she said one day in high summer. "The fear that I will enslave and demand, that I am impervious to your needs."

She'd explained transference once. Now I understood her remark as both a statement of fact and an invitation. She was a particular person, but she also took pains to remain hazy, a shimmer. She made a business of providing a medium in which to encounter my ghosts, the ones about which I had no direct knowledge and which I experienced as imposed upon me.

Adam Phillips says about transference that in one's relationship with the analyst one unwittingly relives and thus discovers one's emotional history. The instant she suggested my fears were really about her, I could see it was quite true. Harriet's imperviousness to my needs seemed flagrantly embodied in the way she smugly swept her skirt beneath her, and the exorbitant payments she exacted. The treatment was using up my car, my money—even my life, I felt—all of which she sucked up and prospered by.

"So I am the greedy baby. You see how you turn things around?" she inquired, didactic once more. "This is something you do. Instead of giving to you, you actually experience me as taking."

"You do both," I said.

"Projective identification produces a variety of anxieties," writes Hanna Segal.

I was again copying into my green cloth notebook. I swept some crumbs into my palm and walked over to the trash, then returned to the book.

Chief among these is "the anxiety of having parts of oneself imprisoned and controlled by the object into which they have been projected. This last anxiety is particularly strong when good parts of the self have been projected, producing a feeling of having been robbed of these good parts and of being controlled by other objects." I nodded.

I was now no longer friends with Janice and Kate and Stella and Margaret and Pearl and Kathie and Martha.

"You're getting scary," said Paul that evening as I stood calmly chopping tomatoes.

"No, I'm getting healthier."

"You're dropping people left and right. I'm afraid I'm going to be next."

"Don't be afraid," I said. "All these people were really aggressive and insulting. They were always taking from me, though I couldn't see it." I tossed the tomatoes in a bowl and reached for the cucumbers.

"But these were your best friends!"

I smiled. "I thought they were," I said.

Yet even I noticed that whenever I excised a friend it brought only brief relief from the oppressor who'd taken up habitation inside me.

My behavior had assumed the talismanic traits of a perversion whose allure resides in the sense of gods propitiated, calamities forestalled, of sacrificial acts performed as a precaution against far worse. And still my respect for the inner gods grew from day to day, for there was no sidestepping their dictates. If I didn't call up Lucy and cancel, I could not work. I could go for a walk, I could sit on the lawn in front of the ringing yellow daffodils, but I could not relinquish myself to my work. Something in me was commanding. Something within me was unbudgeable. Something had arisen in me that appeared as my greatest enemy—a compulsiveness, a rudeness, a greed.

Thinking about it, rubbing the tops of mushrooms with a moist paper towel one evening, it occurred to me that Kate's novel had, in my mind, constituted a world more enthralling than any I might chart. In Spain once we'd made a plan to meet at eight in the morning at the Ochoa bus station. When we met at the bus gate she told me she'd woken before dawn. She didn't have a clock, so she grabbed her knapsack and a ripe banana that she'd set out the night before. The banana was her breakfast while walking through the dark to the corner. At last the bus arrived, and she asked the driver for the time. It wasn't yet 5:30, so she went back home and got back in bed.

I recalled at the time feeling envious of even that walk to the bus, which struck me as full of adventure. I envied even her mouth eating that ripe banana as she walked through the blue dark, the streets damp from the cleaning trucks. Kate was inside herself. And I longed—I saw now, gazing down at the cutting board—to be inside her since I didn't know how to be inside myself.

"I'm feeling so anxious about my friend Lucy," I reported one day during the second September of being in treatment.

"You need to come into treatment more," declared Harriet. "You need to come up every week. If you don't, you'll drop out of therapy."

"Why do you say that?" Her prediction rattled with a sorcerer's magic.

CHAPTER EIGHT

The Blue Valentine

I drive reading a book. I drive drinking bottle after bottle of water. I drive eating peanut butter and banana sandwiches, Smart Food, grapefruit, granola, chilled American cheese on hamburger buns snatched from refrigerator cases, vitamins, echinacea. I know the exit for every good bathroom on the highway, and the exits that loop you onto local roads that weave for miles into the landscape with no Texaco in sight. The Civic dies and we buy a wine-red Camry that is soon crusted white like a January mouth. She is a secret I tell myself, a cult I've entered.

My session falls on a Jewish holiday and I phone from my parents' bathroom, sitting cross-legged on the powder-clogged blue rug facing the blue wicker hamper. It makes me feel bizarre to call from there, but it's gratifying to have my other self, my self as Harriet knows me, make an appearance in the corner of my parents' house. My knees touch the blue wicker. The bathroom door is wedged shut on the stretched cord of the phone, and I feel momentarily like my parents' crazy daughter, like Anita, willful and unbounded, insisting upon her idiosyncratic wants.

Vacations, I phone from motel rooms, my eyes finding patterns in the quilted vinyl bedspread, nestled thunderbolts, infinite right angles. Even away, I'm not away from her. Every calendar for seven years has her name inscribed on every week. Once, exhausted while driving back from a writing workshop I led in New York, I take an exit off the Mass Pike and find a hotel lobby. I'm scheduled to lead a workshop in Framingham, Massachusetts, that night, and it just seems like too much to drive all the way up to Bowdoin for my session and back down by evening. I left New York late, planning to call her from the road. Standing in the phone booth of the hotel, I watch the sweep second hand of my watch. The arrowhead swings past the 3, the 6. When the arrow brushes 12, I lift the receiver and dial. I explain where I am. "I'm sorry, Harriet," comes my doleful voice.

What effort, to speak! "Please say it's okay."

Silence.

Electrical ganglia prickle down from my armpits. My fingers grasp the ugly, wound steel coil of the cord.

"*Where* are you?" she asks, although I've said.

Her tone seems to imply I'm calling from a madhouse. And indeed, with the lobby door flashing, elevators ringing, the blather of voices, it suddenly feels like a madhouse. I explain again.

She says, exerting an obvious effort to keep her voice uninflected, "Why did you plan your week so that it was so difficult to reach your session?"

She is not interested in any explanations having to do with real distances between real cities or with real days of the week. "Talk about your resistance to coming up," she instructs, and I lean my forehead against the steel torso of the phone. My gaze falls on the oxblood wing-tip shoes of a salesman in the next booth, the legs of a matron walking past in hose like Ace bandages. The smell of lunch food—knockwurst, stewed meats—rolls in from the dining room.

"But I *want* to see you," I insist.

"I'm not asking you to feel guilty."

"No?"

"The feeling comes from within you."

Ah. "But say it's okay I didn't come up."

"Bonnie, can you see what would happen if I did? The opportunity you would lose?"

The salesman in the next booth sets his hand on the phone receiver, waits a second and plugs more money in. "Maureen?" he asks.

"*Why* do you think you feel guilty?" she says.

When I step outside, the parking lot carries an after-effect of motion, the vestigial shimmer of things that have rushed into place, as if the highway had hung in the sky and has just swung onto the ground. Everything looks more right. I'm light-headed with relief that the phone session is over.

And she has a good point, I think. I always feel guilty. It's ridiculous! Why, I'm used to wearing my culpability like an abject coat, like some tormented character in a Dostoyevsky novel who wishes his wretched garb would absolve him from further punishment, which he heartily believes he deserves. But why this craving for forgiveness? I stand beside the Camry door and jingle the keys. The afternoon light is rinsed, tropical, its molecules floating about in a delirious amplitude.

Harriet wants me to question my persistent guilt. Those childhood calls to friends when I didn't want to go over: "I wish I could come. I miss you! I'm so, so sorry!" I'd set the phone down confused, hollow, stricken with a crazy pining for my friend. But wasn't I in fact *glad?* Hadn't I really *wanted* to stay home? So why wasn't I happy? I'd gaze at the phone and drift blindly from the room. "All better?" asked my mother. "You told her you can't?"

My head would nod. Various dials seemed to be turning in different directions within me. I sat and gazed at my mother's confident arm if she was ironing or the glinting needle of her sewing machine if she was stitching a dress. Classical music drifted in from the kitchen radio, WQXR, and a seasick sensation swelled over me, reversals within reversals, held from floating off the dull, meaningless earth merely by the steadiness of my mother's foot on the treadle, her sotto voce, "Moon river. . . ."

Standing in the parking lot, it occurs to me that I habitually ascended to almost mystical states of guilt. Yet at the same time I perceive, quite sanely, that Harriet actually wants me to feel guilty right now. "I think you underestimate the importance of these sessions to you," she'd said testily. I'd stopped breathing an instant, and wanted to collapse into compliments: "Yes, yes, I'm sure you're right. Please be patient!" Her irritation frightens me. She is my well-being.

Every morning now I clutch at dreams before they diffuse into a haze of inconsequentiality: people dive into the icy ocean, preferring sensation—any at all—to their state of persistent numbness; a man I crave is far away and I never have the right change to make the phone work, never the correct combination of quarters and nickels, although I'm desperate for him.

In the morning I spend hours compulsively transcribing these dreams. I'm trying to do for myself what Harriet does, but my thoughts aren't hers, my interpretations don't predict her own, and when I stop it's with precisely the same unease with which I started. The click hasn't happened. Insights arise about these dreams but they never bring the sense that I've pulled myself out of the dream and into the day's activities. I have the feeling that with the right insight, the dream will collapse shut like a tin cup I can use later. It will be smaller than me. And even when I despise spending two hours transcribing dreams, I must, since if I don't set these phosphorescent scenes on the page they'll be gone by noon and then it will be as if I ignored arrows that appeared at my feet. It's hard to believe there was a time I didn't have to do this.

The writing that arrives in the afternoon, however, is as strong as has ever come. I step down the back stairs to a corner of the basement where I've set up a card table. The boiler rumbles into life behind me and the scent of oil hangs in the air. I'm on the very last essay in the book.

The places where Janice and Kate and Stella were have filled with Harriet. If I say I felt lonely, she responds, "You felt lonely for me," and I know she's right. A journalist with whom I had coffee writes me a flirtatious letter and I compose a flirtatious response. "Don't send it to him," she advises. "It's meant for me."

Others represent a distraction. A mere flight from our work. Harriet encourages my absorption in her, although it needs little encouragement. The patient "must accept falling in love with her doctor as an inescapable fate," I underline in Freud. "When a patient falls in love with her therapist, no matter how amenable she has been up until then, she suddenly loses all understanding of the treatment and all interest in it, and will not speak or hear about anything but her love, which she demands to have returned. There is a complete change of scene; it is as though some piece of make-believe had been stopped by the sudden eruption of reality—as when, for instance, a cry of fire is raised during a theatrical performance."

I nod. Despite the apparent sexism of this description, with its abrupt transformation of the rational female into an obsessed nitwit, I feel I understand what Freud means. Now instead of talking about various people outside the room, Harriet and I talk about what is going on between us. Instead of dealing with descriptions of my interactions with others, we don't deal with descriptions at all. A raw big emotion occupies the room with us. We both feel its heat. "To urge the patient to suppress, renounce or sublimate her instincts the moment she has admitted her erotic transference would be, not an analytic way of dealing with them, but a senseless one," says Freud. "It would be just as though, after summoning up a spirit from the underworld by cunning spells, one were to send him down again without having asked him a single question."

And something *has* been summoned. It crowds my dreams, devours oxygen, bids me to look forward to seeing Harriet as if anticipating a wedge of bliss. I commit to memory the conclusion of the Freud essay: "The treatment must be carried out in abstinence. . . . If the patient's advances were returned . . . she would have succeeded in what all patients strive for in analysis—she would have succeeded in acting out, in repeating in real life, what she ought only to have remembered."

Harriet seems a veritable icon of abstinence. In her royal blue skirt bordered with red roses, her white blouse folded back at the cuffs, she gazes down with serene blue eyes that hold an expression of compassion, curiosity, and a sort of glinting mirth. "It's your Princeton training," I say. "That must be why you never seem even tempted to do anything that would compromise the transference. Oh, it gives me such confidence to know you received your training at Princeton!"

She smiles happily back at me.

I no longer miss my old friends. I recall mostly ugly things about them—Janice's stolid unbudging buttocks in her high-waisted Gloria Vanderbilt corduroys bought six at a time at Bloomingdale's once

she married Dov; Kate remarking about a poem of hers in the journal *Poetry* that she'd come to write it because she'd read a syllabic
poem of her husband's and thought, "I can do better." She'd raced
upstairs with her pencil, and did. These critical thoughts about my
friends are reassuring, although occasionally my love for them stirs
uncomfortably. A new story is being written through me, and I don't
know if I like this new story or even believe it. It is not as lovely as the
story I would have written if I'd had the choice. The story I would
have written would have carried the scent of boxwood in the south
of Spain, and it would have been full of ineffable experiences—bird
songs at dawn, darning needles hanging iridescent over a pond, a
perfect omelet cooked in a battered pan. This new story is full of
squabbles. People are darker and smaller in it, as if I'm using the
lens at the optometrist's that makes the letter A into a black, filled-
in chunk.

In early December Harriet says, "I'm moving my office."

"Why?" I ask.

"I'm going into private practice."

"You got your doctorate!" I cry. "Oh, Harriet, I'm so proud of you.
A Princeton doctorate. Congratulations."

"Thank you, Bonnie."

Her new office turns out to be at the top of a thin yellow house
with white shutters off-campus. I think of it as the pineapple house.
Gables as lean as witches' hats rise on three sides. Scarlet carpets
race up and down the rickety stairs. Silver radiators like skeletal burros are stationed below the wavery glass windows, and bowls of dried
rose petals are strewn on doilies upon flea market side-tables at a
thousand Victorian turnings. Other therapists and a spate of realtors
occupy offices in the rest of the house. Across the street is a freshly
paved parking lot.

Now our therapy is interrupted by great cracks and then long
hisses as the steam comes on, and sometimes I crave for Harriet to
open a window as the feverish air settles over us, leaving me sweaty
and almost panting. The idea never occurs to her. She remains miraculously impervious, her hands dry as sandpaper, her color wintry
and pale, although I'm rosy from the heat.

* * *

"You can call me if you're anxious," remarks Harriet at the end of a session in late March.

What qualifies as sufficient anxiety? Sometimes now I find a thought is cantering around in a circle in my mind, faster and faster until I must pick up the phone. Harriet never says, "This is why you called? How trivial!" And often, just knowing she is going to call back, I can relax. The thought stops cantering. It vanishes over a hill. When the phone rings I wish it hadn't. Now I'll have to fetch the thought back to tell her, as justification. Besides, I enjoyed having her to look forward to.

I missed Harriet, I realize, before I knew that it was a person I lacked. In the late afternoon I used to stroll the gritty streets of Salem and end up at the Derby Square Bookstore. There I scoured others' books, desperate to find the answers to my book's problems, hoping to discover the scene I ought to write next, but the only answers I could see were: no, you do it wrong, you don't do it like me.

When I looked myself up in Harriet, though, my entry existed. There I was, alive on her page, known, assessed, translated. Certain memories sprang up again and again with Harriet: the dentist's waiting room on Grand Avenue where I sat turning the pages of *Highlights for Children* beside my mother, and where the Venetian blinds were blades of dusty sun and the drill behind the wall was a narcotic drone as if time itself had slowed to the point of audibility, gluing my mother and me in a tarlike clot so tough it seemed we could never step out into happiness. And here was Mrs. Claw, my third-grade teacher with the dancing gray eyes and knob of gray hair, giving me a valentine change purse the size of her palm. Mrs. Claw had stood in her stocking feet on a chair beside our inkwell desks, sorting a high shelf. When she discovered this purse she handed it to me, although I was three seats away. "I laced it myself when I was in the hospital," she said. Silvery blue vinyl fixed with a snap. I was amazed; I thought I was so ordinary I was indistinguishable. And Mrs. Claw had been in the hospital! Why? I stowed the purse in my private mitten drawer at home as if it were Mrs. Claw's heart itself, and as long as it was hidden it could never be damaged by others' envy.

It's interesting how something you've known all along can suddenly display itself. You've never forgotten it, you have the feeling you've thought of it often, yet suddenly it looms like a person stepping out of peripheral vision.

I recalled especially the first thing my mother ever made for me: a sweater, crimson, knit from February all the way into August, the ball of wool leaping from my mother's beige satchel onto the grass of the bungalow colony, the needles rubbing and tapping while my mother bent over the pamphlet of code. At last the cable knit was done. Done! I tugged it on, even though it was summer. But the second time I wore it I stumbled into a patch of briars that lined the corner of the yard, and the sweater got spiked with burrs—scads of them taking up residence deep in the beautiful cables. To take them out was to shred it. The sweater had become a garment of scratches, and every time I wore it I wondered how it was possible to ruin anything so fast. And here also was the shadow that flew up in me when my mother's hand brushed my face, and the agonized silence of the last year with my first adult boyfriend, and the secret to why a person feels alive at times and at other times inert. "Good-bye!" I cried at the end of a session, turning back for one last look.

She smiled. "Good-bye."

"I'll talk to you next week—if not before!" Adding the desperate charm that allowed me to feel connected to her, not cut off.

"Yes," she answered, smiling. "Always."

My mother was never so entirely mine. She had drowned within herself. She sat at the kitchen table in flesh-colored anklets and wine pedal-pushers, turning the pages of a *McCall's*.

"I was so depressed I was practically out of my mind when you were two," she told me when I was long out of college. "I was sick in the hospital with something the matter, my fever was rising, the doctor was going to discharge me. We were afraid I would die. Walking to the apartment to take care of you, my mother fell and broke her hip. I felt she was in the hospital because of me."

Because of me, too.

They both returned from their hospitals, but in our apartment my mother brooded, sighed, seemed to be working out a dolorous problem within her—or else she'd given up on solving the problem and simply lived in it. Sometimes, though, she sang a frantic song, *chhh-chhh-chhh, chhh-chhh-chhh,* wheeling her hands like Betty Boop. "Yes, we have no ba-nah-nahs!" she sang. And: "Oh, the monkey wrapped his tail around the flagpole!" I'd gaze at her in admiration. Her lifted hands wheeled in her washerwoman gesture; her mouth stretched in a smile. "I have a lov-er-ly bunch of coconuts!" Yet her joy seemed brittle as tinsel. I didn't know where it came from or why.

"Go out of the room. You tire me," she said when, seeing her sad, I imitated her manic dance. "I can't look at you," she said.

When she saw me as a child, what she saw was wrong. I erased my chalked answers with my palm and calculated new ones—more wrong. On Open School Day, the teacher looked from my blackboard multiplication to me to my mother, who sat in the last row in a funny fake-fur brown hat and fancy dress. An innocent expression hung askew on my mother's face. I longed to protect her, as if she were the impossibly big number I'd scrawled, a miscalculation in her fancy dress and hat. She'd seen my math work on the board and shook her head no! I hastily worked out a different number, which, it turned out, made even worse sense. My mother bit her lip. "Parents, please do not help! The children need to learn to make their own mistakes," the teacher had intoned. Now she frowned at my mother sitting in her elaborate lace dress. My mother's hands twisted in her lap.

An awareness of my mother's vulnerability had flooded me even earlier, when she fetched me from nursery school. We'd stood on an island in the midst of University Avenue, cars roaring left and right. Something blond bounced up the road. "My hat!" she called, desolate. Her silly, faux sheep's wool, pillbox hat! It rolled among the careening, gritty traffic.

And it seemed, with my mother's desolate cry, "My hat!" that at that instant an immeasurable loss had occurred, that nothing could be as good again, that the hat was the single most wonderful object she possessed and a chaotic force had snatched it and flung it beneath the oblivious male traffic—such despair sprang out of her, as if this really was the last straw, life with four children had pressed her to the limit and then beyond, and all that had redeemed her plight was this hat.

A few months later my mother came home from adults' mosaics class with a clumsy brown-tile ashtray rimmed with talon red. Someone had taken hers, she said. She'd glued her tiles—yellow and white, lemon cupcake colors—neatly to the tin frame and left it to dry. But when she came to claim it, it was gone. All that remained was this forsaken object, sloppily arranged, each brown tile with a milky oval in the middle like the yellow eye of a level. Still, my mother saved this ashtray for over thirty years—she has it still—set on her bureau holding necklaces and pins, something not hers yet hers, proclaiming by the stubbornness of her possession of it the extent of her yearning—as if the ashtray were a clumsy bookmark holding the place of an enormous disappointed wish, her unabated desire for the other thing that this suggested.

Still, I never quite believed her fingers hadn't arranged these erratic tiles, that her eye hadn't purposely chosen this brown. Secretly I identified with that ungainly ashtray as I stood before her with my tangled hair and sticky palms. And when we walked calmly hand-in-hand together, an abortive, scratching maelstrom seemed to gust around us in the city streets, and my toothpick mother could scarcely withstand it. It grasped at her hair, her dress, her legs—she was a haggard shadow tugged a thousand ways by her family—so I was just as glad to see her stowed away in the long gray kitchen, safe as the knife-blue valentine locked in its drawer.

"Don't you think it's strange you never found a way to get angry at your mother and negotiate with her?" Harriet asked.

"Not at all!"

To be angry at my mother was impossible, it was to be Anita. To be angry at my mother would shatter her like balsa wood. She needed quiet and calm. The morning my mother enrolled me in nursery school, I recalled, I wasn't angry, but sad, since the cost of nursery school was so high. My mother had gotten dressed up in a bright pink skirt and jacket that she'd sewed herself and high-heeled shoes dyed to match, and she'd taken me by the hand and walked me to a red-brick private house with Georgian arches above twin doors. I'd thought nursery school was run by nurses and was surprised that the two women we met weren't dressed in white. A smell of sour, warm milk pervaded. We inspected a basement space where very little light leaked in. We were shown the red hollow cardboard bricks to build with, and the beige beagle that quacked as it wheeled its legs on a string, and the box of tambourines and triangles.

When the skinny woman with the tall, red hair told her the price, my mother bit her lip and stared at the linoleum. Then she carefully made out a cheek. "So much," she muttered later as we walked away across the cool, tree-shaded street. She shook her head. "They have some nerve." She gazed down at the pavement while I clasped her hand. How I wished I cost less! And yet the nursery school frightened me, the strange gray space, the oversized lightweight bricks, which I could see were required to be put away neatly on their shelves.

"Thank you so much!" I said, kissing my mother's hand. A feeling like illness crouched within me from sheer worry.

"All right," she said with a tired smile, detaching her hand.

Her high heels scraped on the sidewalk, an abrupt, womanly sound. When we returned home together, she pulled off her dress and hung it on a hanger, then stepped into stretch pants and a blouse and apron. "Go outside and play," she said. But I didn't want to go outside. I didn't want to let her out of my sight. I wanted to make it up to her, but every touch or kiss of mine only cost her more. So I sat as quietly as I could, watching her sort laundry. She needed protection. She needed walls of cotton wool. She was a doll who needed to be safe in a shoe box diorama while the wind shook the outside world.

"Bring it in here," said Harriet.

"What?"

"That wind. The wind that shakes the outside world. Bring it in here."

Surprised, I looked at her objects glittering, the silver Buddha and the bronze Athena. I thought of Harriet herself propped behind me like an Easter Island god.

"But I need this office to stay calm."

"Well, Bonnie, it's in danger of turning into that dentist's office," she replied. "You and your mother were glued together. Everything bad stayed outside."

I nodded.

"You couldn't imagine separating from your mother without an act of violence," she continued. "You tried to keep the disruptive, loud, chaotic emotions out of your relationship with your mother."

"I didn't feel them. They weren't me."

She nodded. "They were not-you. But they can come here. I think you'll be surprised by what happens. Your anger will be returned to you as something else."

I turned back and looked at her. A whiff of perfume drifted to me, a scent of roses. "As what?"

"What do you think?"

"If I got angry at you?" I asked. "You'd retaliate, even if you don't mean to. Frankly, if you didn't retaliate, my anger might feel ignored, unreal, dismissed." For suddenly I felt quite angry—at her smugness, her pristine femininity. Her Glinda qualities. And I was seized by the absurd sensation that she'd been ignoring this anger. It was as if I'd been raging—screaming in a paralyzed dream—and she didn't deign to respond.

"There is a third option," she said.

She is a steady hand making something she will not lose. She is satisfied by her work. Every week she opens the same yellow spiral-bound notebook. Every week she sits in the same chair behind the couch. I come in sick on envy, frantic about ambient noise, wild to make contact with that thing that happens four-fifths of the way through the session. Can't we get there faster? Why must she make me work so hard?

"I make you work so hard," she says, considering. "And what if you didn't work?"

Value would fall out of the world. "Hard work makes me feel less guilty."

"About what?"

The sweater I wove with briars, the mother I depleted until her health flew off, everything about me that cost too much: even the Oreos I carried to nursery school. There they were, columns of brown and white, like thermoses, and so neat I stroked the cellophane. Too expensive, my mother murmured. I was too loud for her, too wild, too tearful, too in love with her. Goodness leaked from her in the form of lemon-cream mosaics and perfect clothes knit by hand, and by desiring what it was she offered—her quiet calm— I spoiled it. I wanted it. I was desperate not to feel so rashy and twisted, my tights crooked, my mind springing like something electrified. She sat reading. She turned a page of her lady's magazine. I reached out my hand and smeared her with my want.

"Your desire is offensive," reflects Harriet.

I think of my husband occasionally pushing me away when I reached for him. His remark once when I sat on his knee and kissed him, "I appreciate all the beers you've had." His response when I heard his foot on the stair at dusk and raced to him across the Iowa apartment, "I'm tired from work. Let me sit."

"But why don't you imagine that satisfying you would be mutually pleasurable?" asks Harriet.

"It seems to be for you." I smile and she meets my glance. I turn back. How beautiful she is with her cobalt eyes! I add, sadly: "Although I hope I don't tire you too much."

"Do you see how quickly you go from feeling gratified to feeling guilty?"

"As if you had swollen skin and it was irritated by my touch," I murmur, saying the very first thing that comes to mind. Since I've started coming up every week my sessions have become richer with free association.

"Taking makes you feel greedy and so you put the greed inside of me: I am swollen."

My face burns. I gaze into the Picasso room, the hot rumpled chickens and the nonsensical limp broccoli, and beyond them the coolness. I would like to go into that room and shut the door and plunge into the coolness.

"I love how your scarlet lamp exists in both this office and the room in the poster," I say. "It's as if this room and that are a Venn diagram that overlap in the lamp, or as if the lamp in the real room is showing the way into the imaginative place."

She nods, listening.

"It's like all the objects I've told you about. The silver-blue valentine. The red sweater. They exist between us somehow. Or rather, they exist in me with greater reality because of you. They feel more mine. They used to feel inconsequential. Now they just feel more real. Isn't that funny? There was a time when telling you something took it away from me. Amputated it. It became yours. I couldn't feel it anymore."

"That reminds me of the blue valentine you hid," says Harriet. "You hid it because you were afraid of your own destructiveness."

"No, I was afraid of someone else's," I say immediately.

She remains silent. I glance at where she sits behind me, and she meets my gaze with her contemplative blue eyes.

"It's funny," I say, turning back, "because storing that valentine purse in the drawer with my white cotton Girl Scout gloves, and some old pieces of chocolate . . . storing it there really just made it invisible. I mostly forgot about it. In a way I did destroy it."

Again she says nothing.

Suddenly I recall how passionately interested analysts are in people's behavior toward objects. Our things are diaries of our fantasy lives, attacks and restitutions and enthrallments, all grafted onto the doll or purse or car. I think of the red sweater.

"Part of me wants to say it's all just silly, ascribing so much importance to these objects." I gaze at the painted balustrade. "Yet they're the story of my life."

The room is warm. Harriet does not shift in her chair. After a while my time is up.

My mother did not want this many children. What she wanted was indescribable. She married and gave up work, which she enjoyed (as an office manager; she'd earned more than my father) and was so nervous during the lunch hour when the jeweler measured her finger that he measured her trembles, too, and the diamond ring never fit right. My maternal grandmother had assumed she'd live with the newlyweds. But my mother couldn't endure her remarks. "You haven't dressed them warm enough!" said her mother, gesturing toward the children on a spring afternoon. "Feed them meat!" she declared, although we children hated meat and wouldn't open our mouths for it. After my parents married but before my mother was pregnant, my grandmother said to my father: "What are you, a cripple?" Meaning: Why wasn't her daughter pregnant yet? And so her mother lived four blocks away on Popham Avenue, behind the Daitch and Dana's Bakery.

Tuberculosis had taken my mother's father when she was less than two. So she grew up with just her seamstress mother and two brothers in an apartment near Crotona Park in the Bronx. Friday nights in summer with the windows pushed open and the air like oil, they strolled beneath the big dark indigo trees, my mother's fingers twitching at her side as she practiced steno. She studied it three years at Walton High School. The pirouettes that meant two words, the curlicues and loops that were whole phrases—she could transcribe faster than her teacher could talk. She sat in front of the Emerson radio and copied the news. She sat over black coffee at Woolworth's and surreptitiously copied the waitresses' conversation. Not a word escaped her; not a murmur or hiss. She kept a battalion of sharp pencils in a wood case and a mint-green shorthand pad on top of her books, and it seemed the secret of life was transcription, that she would spin a steno ladder out of the open apartment window, and climb down to freedom, to someplace far from Fulton Avenue.

Her widowed mother worked from seven in the morning until midnight, stitching, bent over the sewing machine. "I never see the light of day," she said. And it was true, my mother told me. Their apartment was in the back of the building. Some days her mother didn't set foot outside. "I'm a slave," she said to my mother, who took her hand and kissed it. She still assumed her mother would live with her after she married, and she looked forward to imagining her mother with her feet up, gazing at the television set, her mother with her own bedroom, from behind whose door would come the murmur of her conversation with an as-yet-unmet friend.

The apartment was dominated by the cutting table. This was a piece of Old World furniture so big it devoured the living room from the back wall to the doorway, where it lapped out into the foyer, a shining walnut tide. My mother was eternally sliding around it and banging her hips against its beveled lip. At any time of day demanding, wealthy ladies appeared with their bridal daughters or just for a fancy dress they needed by Friday, latest. My mother opened the door to find strange women in their slips, her own mother on her knees before them, mouth studded with pins.

"At Kress's I can get this dress off the rack for ten dollars!" ladies often declared, "That's what I'm going to pay you." Or they protested the length of the hem they'd approved last week (her mother never pointed out if they gained weight). They unclasped pocketbooks big as bakery boxes and produced pictures ripped from magazines: "Make me that!" My grandmother was famous for her designs, one of the wizards of Fulton Avenue.

The door shut behind them and my grandmother reached for her long, sharp shears. She snipped, and newsprint women formed across the table. She could invent a pattern to match any dress. *Vogue, Simplicity*—why waste good dollars on a packet of tissue? She snatched what paper was at hand, and sometimes my mother had to read the president's last speech across a paper woman's waist, and the march of armies along a sleeve, and tomorrow's weather below the brittle throat. Even after she graduated high school and was dating, she fell asleep to the hum of the sewing machine, which wove through her dreams so that sometimes, in a corridor at a dance, there was her mother sewing, at Roseland where she did the foxtrot, at a Catskills winter mixer where she set her napkin on the table and strolled to the bathroom to reapply lipstick, saying, "Back in a sec—" her mother in a hallway, half-hid behind a rack of coats, bent over the machine! Or her mother, wielding the pinking shears with its alligator grin.

When she came home from night school, my mother paused outside the door. She smelled the apple cake fragrant from the oven, the challah whose strands wove together into one sweet loaf. All day she'd lived on black coffee and iceberg. She refused to be undermined. After a girlhood of chubbiness, my mother had at last achieved a slender, American waist. She worked in a Manhattan office right across from the Empire Hotel and attended Baruch College at night, and she smoked cigarettes sometimes with one of the office girls to kill her appetite. So at her mother's threshold she stood a moment, steeling herself, before stepping into the aroma of cooking.

Her mother glanced up, her steel-rim glasses flashing, her gray hair tucked under a scarf. "You look starved."

Already! "I'm not."

"Still, you have to keep up your strength. A glass of tea, at least. For me. How was work?"

"Fine."

"That Lansky. His hands he kept to himself today?"

"Yeah, Ma." She sighed and set down her bag, and got talking, and her hand strayed to the apple cake already cooled and set out on a plate. Just one slice.

Her mother tried not to look. She said, "You left lipstick on the cup. You wear too much. It isn't nice. Another slice—take! Come on! And a kiss, please." She tilted her cool cheek.

My mother kissed her, and touched her thin shoulder.

How to ever leave? Impossible without resorting to her own sharp shears. She sat at the enormous table that always seemed to crowd her and trained herself not to eat even here, learned to snip herself away, to regard the alligator mouth gnawing at her stomach as good, as freedom. She dated boys and never took a sip of gin or ordered so much as a slice of cherry pie to go with her coffee, black.

She got so skinny, she told me, that her period dried up. Her mother, a woman who searched for the O-U kosher seal on everything and kept her head covered and waited six hours between meat and milk—made her daughter drink blood. A tumbler of traif. She collected the blood from kashering (the slanted wood board, the coarse salt glinting like sequins) in a pot: that's how desperate she was! "I told you. Too skinny, you'll ruin your health! Now, drink!"

My mother gagged. She held her nose but still smelled the hot feral scent and wetness—it coated her lips. Once a week, this blood, and at last her period returned.

Veering between crazy grapefruit diets and bakery feasts so it wouldn't happen twice, she maintained a decent weight and dated two men at once, a green-skinned Orthodox boy on Saturday who wouldn't turn up by surprise on Friday, which was when she dated the man who became my father. My grandmother nodded when she heard that my father had proposed. She'd already snipped out the newspaper dress.

It came to life as a Skinner satin confection. A picture of my mother wearing it stands on my parents' bureau. Down the back, a row of pearl buttons all the way to the cinched waist. Long, tight sleeves and a trailing skirt. As the wedding approached, my grandmother sewed through the night. And although in the mornings my mother stood groggy before her, steadying herself with a hand on the walnut table while my grandmother pinned, my grandmother seemed if possible even more awake, as if stars were coffee cups.

Two hours before the ceremony, it was done. The creamy skirt swirled around my mother's legs, engulfing them like so much frosting. The sleeves started as puffs but ended snug as a second skin at the wrist. Still, my mother's happiness was spoiled when she had to come home early from her Florida honeymoon. She'd contracted an ailment, a lassitude that a dozen doctors could not diagnose. Her tongue was pocked, she wept from fatigue, she vowed to her husband that he wasn't tricked, she'd never been like this before. At last a name was found for the ailment: mono. Her mother came over with meat broth. "Leave everything to me," she said.

"No, ma. We're getting a nurse."

"What nurse! You've got me."

"She's hired already."

Her mother gazed at her. "It's your life."

"I'm sorry."

Her mother shrugged. "I want you to be happy."

"I know, Ma."

"At least let me bring food."

"Okay."

Her mother brought chicken soup, which she left in an enormous pot on the stove. But my mother could not eat it. She gazed at the rich dollops of oil on top and turned her head away. Her horror of getting fat possessed her even while she was sick with fatigue. The German nurse took the soup for lunch, and my father had it for supper, along with the boiled chicken my grandmother left. One afternoon, though, walking past the pot, my mother grabbed a slotted spoon and fished from the soup one of the circles of carrot. What harm could there be in a carrot? She slipped it into her mouth, and instantly her eyes teared. She couldn't believe it! So sweet and rich! It was as if she was eating the Old World furniture and newspaper patterns and her mother's own exhausted glance as she looked up from the sewing machine at my mother in her nightgown, heading for bed. She couldn't finish even that piece. She removed the carrot from her mouth and wrapped it in a napkin and set it aside. If love had a flavor, it was that carrot. Let Larry and the nurse eat it. If she did, she would have to ask her mother to move in.

A sarcastic burr in Harriet's voice, a starchiness in response to a request. Her French skirt crackles like tissue paper. Her dangly white earring swings like a chandelier.

"I like your earrings, Harriet."

"Thank you, Bonnie," she says with a voice as cool as Noxema. Her detachment makes my palms feel sweaty and grimy; her poise makes me desperate. And yet I can scarcely speak about it. Still, I'm coming to see that there are aspects of myself that are stunted, hidden because they might be appalling to someone antiseptic. I felt dirty from an early age.

"What's that all over your dress?" the kindergarten teacher had asked.

I glanced. Blue smeared across the bodice of my dress—a shameful stain, a big sticky cloud. A moment before I'd been immersed in my wild colors and jumped at the sound of my name. Wasn't it strange how your name could hook you from out of a dreamy place? My name jolted me and I stood before Mrs. Sandler, staring down. See how messy you got when you forgot yourself? "Blue," I whispered.

"No." The kindergarten teacher peered at me. "*Trees!*"

Ah. Well, certainly there were trees. A forest covered the dress, cherry trees and burnt-orange maples and dark green pines, each the size of a quarter. My mother found the fabric in a store below the El on Broadway and had sewn this A-line dress.

"Go to the principal and show her." The teacher wrote out a note.

Mirage puddles shimmered on the waxy floors. Echoes murmured from the classrooms—the shrill of children and the deeper gong of teachers. At last the frosted glass door rose before me. But was it blue I was wearing or trees? A mess or trees? The principal, I knew, was a firm woman with Brillo-gray hair and a megaphone voice. The door swung; a man brushed past as I stepped in. The blue was all over me. My face was something to throw in an icy lake.

"Mrs. Sandler sent me." I handed her the paper and stared at the neat surface of her desk, the glass holding a single red rose.

"Thank you," she said. I curtsied and left. Behind me the door fell shut.

If a scissors lay on the floor I would snatch it, I would cut cut cut until neither dress nor girl remained.

Mine is the dirty wind snatching, the tiles pushed crooked, the tin bulging with botulism, everything sticky-fingered and grasping and sprawling long shadows. I am an alligator with a ceaseless appetite, a thousand clothespins biting, something my mother made that spoiled, bristling with thorns, studded with spite.

My mother kept trying and trying to choose me. She wanted three children and she got four. She wants to want this fourth—but my hems fall, my hair lumps with knots, and when she sees me she sees her own dissatisfaction, her own restless, scavenger heart. She turns away. Flips the magazine page, looking for something else.

Harriet saw my hems and palms. Whatever flashed to my mind,

she saw. The shark fin, the scissor tooth—the one withheld thought might be the very thing that would make her hate me and so I confessed it at once.

My mother's face looks like a witch's for an instant. She grabs my hand and pulls me across Broadway. I clench my teeth. All afternoon she's jumped into my sentences. It's Friday, a week after my last session with Harriet.

"The house is really—"

"Too big, too dark," she says.

"Yes, but the thing that's wrong with it is—"

"You haven't quite moved in."

"Let me speak a moment!" I say loudly.

A hatchet of silence falls. After a stunned moment my mother says softly, "I'm sorry." She's stopped in traffic. My face flushes hot. I shut my eyes, mortified. But then the world resumes. A coarse voice croaks out of me: "It's just that it doesn't feel *ours* yet. Maybe because the man we bought it from keeps coming back to get things."

How can I be so lacking in my mother's elegance! My adolescence has arrived all at once, monstrously, at the age of thirty-four.

Yet my mother listens, scanning my face as if she doesn't know how best to encourage me. She suppresses the urge to agree. Her eyes are large and blue gray and highly intelligent. We finish crossing the roaring, dusty street. She didn't mean to cut me off, I know. She's just excited to be together. She just wants to connect.

"Do you want to go here?" she asks at the window of the Opera Café.

I glance at the menu and nod.

We sit in the back, in a vinyl booth patched with silver duct tape. "Black coffee and a fruit cup," says my mother. She urges me to have whatever I want, a tuna sandwich, a piece of chocolate cake. She sees me as her big, healthy daughter without a weight problem. I stir my coffee with the flimsy spoon, and break off a piece of Chinese cookie. My mother scoops an icy ball of honeydew. "This is good," she says, gesturing with her spoon to the pink-skinned grapefruit whose flesh is ridged like crepe paper. I start to tell her of the recent turmoil with friends.

"It used to upset me how you let your friends push you around when you were little," my mother says.

"Really?"

"It used to make me angry," she says. "You were friends with so many bullies."

So there is an aspect of accuracy in my new perceptions!

"You couldn't tell them the truth."

"No," I agreed.

"They twisted you around their little finger," she said. "I wished you could stand up to them."

"I didn't have the confidence."

The waitress slaps the light green bill on the Formica, her thumb leaving a shiny stain.

"I'll be right back," says my mother. She grabs her big black pocketbook with its pattern of gold rivets and tugs her marvelous blouse past her hips when she stands. This blouse is black, with a texture like crumpled tissue paper. It's snug at the hips, like a toreador's sash. She's slim, I think; she doesn't need to wear cover-up clothes. She looks wonderful at seventy-two. I wish she knew it. Her life has been structured by dieting. Her gesture of covering up hurts somehow. I glance away, toward the street, and then watch her walk to the bathroom in her slacks and black Reeboks. She knows just where the bathroom is, having come here often before concerts.

I admire her prowess in New York. It's like her card sense, her knack for mah-jongg, a certain shrewdness that lets her find her way: she doesn't tip too much or too little, she's nobody's fool, she says "thank you" to bus drivers at the end of the trip, she remembers the name of her doctor's receptionist, her handwriting is elegant and poised and not overly large. She has a sharp, quick intellect. I shut my eyes, wishing for my old ease with her back.

I noticed that I dislike it when my mother brushes the hair off my face. I freeze. I dislike it when my mother extravagantly praises my work: a wild disparity opens between what I've accomplished and what I feel she really wants. I dislike it when she kisses me very, very gently on the cheek with a sound like the tiny click of a purse.

"You are ruining one of the best parts of my life," I tell Harriet.

"But I'm not doing anything," she insists.

"Still, I never had had these feelings before. You put them there, or at least allowed them to fester until they're grotesquely big."

"How would you feel if I told you that you'll get used to these feelings and they won't seem so bad?"

"Horrified." I shake my head. "I don't want to become someone else."

How frightening she is! "You don't love my mother, which is why you don't care what happens between her and me. It's not a loss to you." My throat aches.

"But I know you do," she says softly.

"Yet you are destroying one of the most precious things I have."

"How? How am I doing that?"

"I don't know, Harriet. That certainly doesn't mean you aren't." I refuse to look at her.

"Now I am the witch."

I smile. "Yes."

"And your mother is vulnerable and good."

"Yes."

"You see, Bonnie—" she begins, and I interrupt.

"I hate that phrase."

She's silent a moment.

"And I hate," I continue, "that I'll have to feel anxious because of the tension between you and me. Because when I'm afraid you're angry, it terrifies me. You have too much power. So, soon I'll have to apologize so I can get through the week."

"This is how you felt toward your mother."

"It must be very gratifying to have all the answers."

Again she falls silent.

But did I feel this toward my mother? That criticizing her was intolerable because she was my well-being?

Well, yes. Of course.

Still, there is something beautiful which Harriet is trying to smash. It is something I have treasured very much, something which has filled me with happiness. She wants me to drop it so I can grab hold of something bigger. But it is my mother herself which I feel I am holding on to, the hem of her ceramic skirt.

"Do you mind if I sit over here by the door?" Harriet asks right after I lie down. "I've been feeling a chill on my back."

"All right."

We reorient ourselves. Now I'm lying with my feet pointed toward the tall gray window, with the Picasso room behind me.

"I didn't want to switch directions," I report.

She remains silent.

"I did not want to have to think about the chill on your back."

Her ballpoint rubs the page.

"I don't think you should ask your clients to accommodate you at the expense of a certain continuity in their treatment. The client is supposed to see the same stimuli every week so it becomes a blank screen to project on, right? But everything I see right now is new."

Scratch, scratch, says her pen.

"I didn't feel comfortable telling you no," I say, my throat tight, my voice rasping. "I was afraid you'd feel resentful and it would distract me all session. But I think you made a mistake. Are we to be switching directions every week now? Why should we switch directions? So what if you felt a chill on your back! That chill is your business! You shouldn't have burdened me with it." My face is hot and I keep shaking my head.

I stare out the window at air the gray of ice. "I don't want to apologize," I say.

"So don't," she says. "Don't apologize, Bonnie."

"Yes, perhaps it's you who should apologize." I continue looking at that ice sky. "I saw your car on the way in, Harriet. It's so ordinary! A regular car. A boxy blue Ford. It's not commensurate with your status."

"Which is what?"

"Oh"—I smile—"exalted. I wish you drove a Rolls-Royce or an armored car, a German car."

"So I could withstand your attacks?"

I laugh. "Yes. Sometimes your car seems so ordinary it's pathetic. Just so vulnerable and fragile."

"Which is good in that then I can't attack you."

"I suppose so. I don't like being aware of your weak back. Your back which feels a chill."

She nods.

"I don't want to have to take care of you. Everything in your office seems so small to me right now, like the contents of a diorama, miniature, junky, stupid, lightweight, as if bored out by insects. As if built up from mere coats of varnish."

"You are very angry."

"Must you always state the obvious?"

She's silent. I don't hear her writing.

"I associate stating the obvious with all those stupid, meretricious therapists. The inept ones. The ones that are like little tin contraptions you wind up."

She's still listening.

"I'm sure many of them do very valuable work," I add.

She laughs.

"Why did you laugh?"

"You don't sound very sincere," she says.

"But perhaps I am! Perhaps I'm more sincere than you know."

"You could have told me you didn't want to switch directions. You know you could have said that to me."

"We're looking at what you said to me, for once. And it was wrong. Yet I want to apologize. I hate seeing everything here as junky. I hate this entire session."

She's silent. "It's a start," she says.

In the car home from Harriet's, it occurs to me that my mother's helplessness frightened me as a child; I believed that she was powerless against wild forces: me. Her depression entered me and expressed itself as the thorns studding my sweater, the butterfly that turned to a moth in my hands, my own inability to hold on to a good thing: her.

I was astonished as a child when she brought me to a Hanukkah party at the downtown Y, a children's party she suddenly carried me off to, where all the other children were in dresses and gray trousers, and I wore playclothes. When the singing happened at the end ("She mixed them! She fixed them! She poured them into a bowl!") I was torn between joy and melancholy. The dark winter night pressed against the windows, and my mother stood waiting outside in her last-minute light blue slacks and a lilac blouse, doing something for me, doing something so exclusively for me that it made me sorry for her—because my capacity for joy was so inhibited, my capacity for worry so inflamed, that I could not possibly warrant this trip to a party.

Boys squirmed on gray folding chairs. A happy woman wearing a ribbon corsage waved her arms as she sang, her mouth exaggerating its shapes. A goldenrod mimeoed sheet was passed to me with the words ("You may not guess it! But it was the latkes! That made the Syrians recoil—oil!"). Someone had gone to all the trouble of typing and mimeographing the pages for this one afternoon! For an instant I could not sing. That someone loved us so much! Oh, foolish person! But who was it?

I looked at the happy woman waving her arms. I didn't think it was she. I looked at the steel-haired, big-bosomed teacher up front. I didn't think it was she. No, it was someone's mother, probably. How could we be happy enough to deserve it? I smiled and smiled, hoping she would see me, wherever she was.

When the big party with the strange children was over, the doors in the back were flung open and we streamed out. Parents hugged their sturdy offspring and took their preoccupied hands. "Let *go!*" I distinctly heard one girl say. I'd never say such a disrespectful thing!

Many of the parents obviously knew each other and chatted in what seemed even then like a debonair, downtown way, fathers in tweed jackets, mothers riffling in little white purses for a cigarette. For a moment I didn't see my mother and then I did, behind a clump of others, searching for me, alone, breaking into an eager smile when our eyes met. "How was it?" she asked breathlessly. "Did you have a good time?"

"Oh yes. Great!"—hoping I sounded sincere.

In the car ride home the dark city streamed by. Upstairs I couldn't turn on enough lights. I wasn't the least bit hungry. I just wanted to sit among my family. I wanted my brothers to be loud. I wanted my sister to "monopolize the conversation." I wanted to sink back into them and disappear.

Now, it occurred to me, driving along Maine Street in Brunswick, that I was ceasing to disappear. Now I was appearing more and more fully. And I was seeing my mother in a new way: as a woman who could endure my temperament and remain near. As someone occasionally peevish, who could be overtired and annoyed. Who'd been very depressed for her own reasons when I was a child, but who loved me nonetheless. We'd been so close to each other we were as joined as the newsprint woman pinned to the fabric underneath, stitched by a hem of steel. And in another way, it occurred to me, my anger might have nothing to do with my real mother at all. It was my own unconscious fury lugged about from here to there like a cotton sack loaded with windows and oranges, a bulky, stabbing just-discovered absurd burden.

Oh, it was too bad I'd been born so late in my mother's life and that my needs had overwhelmed her! Still, there was so much pleasure yet to give each other. There were lovely things I wanted to bring her, and more and more I could appreciate the enduring beauty of what she'd given me, the tree dress with its maples of burnt sugar and its dark red cherry trees—a fabulous Crotona Park—the crimson cable-knit sweater, the sotto voce melodies.

What was good I characteristically held away from myself. I could see this now. The blue valentine, the contract's yes, even my mother, whom I cost too dearly. I snatched things away from myself, then wondered why deprivation clawed. And while the blue valentine lay stowed in the drawer its edges seemed to sharpen to the blade of an X-Acto knife. I stuck my fingers in to grab an old chocolate, and gasped. Mrs. Claw! She'd cared for me. And yet I'd stowed her gift away, hoarded it, allowed its edges to curl, its snap to acquire a rim of rust. I'd spoiled what she handed me—hoping merely to save it up, to protect it from infestation by briars, the darting eyes of other children who might be envious, my own spoiling hands. I wanted to preserve it for when I could truly deserve it.

And I realized for a flashing moment, flying down Route 95, that my mother really intended for me to have good things. The songs and holiday food, the downtown ambiance—she meant them for me. She couldn't help it that we came late to the party, that we found out about it so very late. She still meant for me to have it.

CHAPTER NINE

Walking Under the Earth

Little mattered now beside Harriet Sing. Everyone else was merely metaphoric. The world beyond her door was a dream that manufactured images to present her. She nodded and transcribed them into her yellow notebook. I'd been in therapy two and a half years.

Paul and I had moved to a big blue four-bedroom house in Boxford, Massachusetts. I slept on the couch in my coat. It was an orange fiberfill coat that could get quite stuffy. During the night I woke, drank water from the kitchen sink, and sank back down on the couch, gazing at the gray lawn that shone like concrete beneath the moon. A smell like onions drifted up from the coat. I repositioned the couch's bolster under my head; it was as firm as a roll of paper towel.

My husband would fall asleep by the TV and eventually make it to our bed upstairs. In the early morning his scuffed shoe-heels clacked down the steps in what sounded to my ears like a petulant gallop. I held my breath until the roar of his car faded into the phlegmatic rattle of the fridge. I drowsed three more hours, coaxing myself, "Don't think. Not yet." When at last the couch consolidated beneath my reluctant body and became too hard, I sat up.

Trees surrounded the house. I'd never lived among so many trees and I'd never wanted to. In winter they looked like bones and in summer their dark green leaves massed sticky and claustrophobic. I missed our old town of Salem, where I could walk to a store and where there were people my age. None of the people who lived in my new town seemed my age, especially the ones who were.

The entire downtown was two buildings: the post office/bank/café where you could buy a fresh glazed cinnamon roll and a sheet of stamps, and the Victorian house across the street that held the library. If you left your car parked on the side of a road anyplace that wasn't downtown, the police phoned you. The most beautiful time was right after a snow, when everyone was inside and the sky resembled the inside of a pillow. A marvelous taut silence held then, like the stillness after the crack of a stick.

Most days the couch became too hard to lie on at around ten A.M. I slipped my feet into my shoes. Wearing the T-shirt and jeans I'd slept in and the orange coat, I drove five miles to a general store that sold the *New York Times*. If the store wasn't open yet, I slipped quarters through the mail slot and carried the newspaper to the coffee-shop. I ordered a croissant that stained my napkin like French fries. Around me hearty blond women jangled the keys to their vans and arranged when they'd pick up their children from sports practice. Old men in ventilated baseball caps sat at the central table, joking, ruminating, mostly about politics. They showed a strong Republican turn of mind. Some of the men scarcely spoke. They slurped that first hot sip of coffee and ate their breakfast, then shrugged and sat back. It was interesting to see what counted as friendship among men.

The skinny counterwoman in her white cap recognized me. She smiled as she slid me the coffee in its thin white plastic cone set in a tan holder. I smiled back. I thought: If I kill myself, they'll say I was the girl who came in every morning and read the *New York Times*.

Because, actually, I often thought about killing myself those days. It provided a certain reassurance; it wasn't the least bit alarming. I allowed my mind to drift to thoughts of suicide at luxuriant moments, when driving around in the Camry while the reddish-brown woods flickered past, or when a familiar song came on the radio, "Sometimes the snow comes down in June": a noose in the living room, kicking the chair free.

I'd never considered suicide before in my life. I'd never understood those who did. What an unbelievable torture life must be to them! Not to want to wake up tomorrow? Not to want to taste chocolate cake again? Could chocolate cake really have lost the capacity to please them? Had they really considered it: no more chocolate cake? Such were the childish thoughts that used to rise up in me at the idea of suicide, although I also assumed that anyone considering it must be in possession of an incalculable maturity, a maturity in excess of anything I could (I hoped) ever comprehend. Yet now I thought of suicide often and it no longer seemed strange.

None of this worried me because Harriet knew it. It was all under control, I supposed. It was all according to plan.

"Walking Under the Earth," I wrote on a sheet of paper to describe my current life. I pulled a horizon line across the page and drew a stick-figure woman upside down, heels clamped against the bottom of the line, head deep underground. Trees were inverted, as was the house, all stuck to the bottom of the horizon line. Above, there was nothing. I'd never been this unhappy.

I recalled living up in New Hampshire. The reds and oranges of the autumn leaves had impelled me to race around snapping pictures. What to do about all this beauty? I invited my sister and her husband to fly up from the Bronx. We pushed Anita's wheelchair deep into the woods and stopped before various maples like Shinto temples. Anita wore yellow aviator Blublocker glasses and a checkerboard Icelandic coat, and gave me a house present of pistachios, which we stuffed our pockets with before another afternoon of trees. Anita's laugh filled the woods. The blackbirds went chattering. "Look!" I yelled, pointing to a brick red. How could one look enough? I squatted in front of a leaf the yellow of candle flame, my mind wheeling. How long would this color last? Two days? Three? "Look!" I said pointing. But it didn't alleviate the internal pressure. There wasn't enough time to see every beautiful thing.

Now I shook my head in amazement. How to care about such ephemera? Reading an article in the local newspaper, I wondered how the person had the energy to write their way all the way to the end. How did they stay interested in, say, reviewing a particular Portuguese restaurant? I could imagine writing a sentence or two, yes, but that was about it. The first draft of my own book was almost done, but I was incapable of writing so much as half a page of something new. Sometimes just listening to a person speak I marveled: how did they find the energy? How did they keep caring?

And yet even this effect must have been calculated. Harriet knows, I reminded myself, and is unconcerned. She must have planned on even this.

"I hate him," I muttered. I was standing in the kitchen, cutting a cucumber.

My husband sat in his father's big stuffed throne of a chair in the den. This chair was heavy as a fridge, and had glossy wood spheres the size of bowling balls to rest your hands on, and was brown. My father-in-law had fallen asleep in front of the TV in this chair when Paul was a boy. The afternoon I saw this gargantuan chair entering my house I had an urge to block the door and shout, "No, no, no, no!" But it was our housewarming gift. "I hope it gives you as much pleasure as it did me," said Paul's father as it was positioned in front of our TV, where it instantly ground four holes in the carpet.

"Thank you, Dad!" said my husband, who in fact liked the chair. He sat in it now, watching an old *Star Trek* episode, eating an eggplant grinder. He'd come home late from work, changed out of his suit, and collapsed.

I stood in the kitchen and thought of his head nodding. "Uh-huh, uh-huh," he'd said while we'd spoken, hurrying me. I'd been trying to tell about a flock of wild turkeys I'd seen in the yard. They'd seemed like a visitation, something really good for once, and I wanted to figure out a way to convey the exact soft brownness of their feathers. For some reason, it seemed extremely important to do so.

"Uh-huh," said Paul.

And I saw those birds fading, their pleasure just about gone. "I feel like you're telling me to shut up."

"I'm *agreeing* with you," he said. "This is the sound I make when I'm showing interest."

Uh-huh.

"I hate him," I now muttered. A thrill shivered through me.

The next day I found occasion to say it again. Within the space of a month I was murmuring this phrase several times a week, and it no longer brought a thrill, just bitterness. Still, it was easier to think of suicide than of leaving. I'd parted with so many people already, I told myself, I couldn't bear any more tumultuousness. Besides, my fantasies of death were always accompanied by miraculous rebirths. I'd hang myself and be reborn in the Midwest, in some new town. I'd meet interesting new people. I'd have great sex. I decided not to kill myself until my fantasies of suicide ended in death. "That's the one caveat," I explained to myself.

Harriet knew all about this, too, and seemed unconcerned. It must be according to plan.

One morning in the big blue house, I went to do laundry and saw a gleam flash across the basement floor: a pond the size of a Ping-Pong table! At its deepest it rose an inch. A metal box the size of a switchplate was dripping from the wall. When I set a kitchen pot under it, it filled up fast.

The water-pump person arrived within an hour dressed in a red flannel shirt and jeans. "Oh, there's nothing the matter," he announced cheerfully. He straightened up with a creak of his knees. "It's been a wet winter and the ground outside's saturated. This box will drip." He executed a mock salute and strolled out the bulkhead and over the emerald grass.

Crosby's General Store in the next town, I soon discovered, contained a marvelous variety of plastic cones and coils of clear hose. And after much experimenting at home, much balancing of tube and cup and pot and brick, I rigged a system that siphoned all the water from the dripping box straight into the sump. When I looked up, the high basement windows showed it was already blue dusk.

"Look at this!" I said to my husband that evening, smiling as I tugged him down the steps. He'd been at his high-stress job all day, but I was too eager to let him change out of his pinstripe suit. "Come on! There's something I want to show you."

He stood over my contraption. "Good," he said.

"Yeah?"

He nodded his head.

"Is that all? Don't you think it's clever?" I stared.

"Uh-huh."

But it had taken me hours—first of worry and then of tinkering! Fury stabbed through me, my heart the jagged top of an opened can. How could he be so niggardly? Why, he seemed to be vying with me—as if, if he complimented me, he would be detracting from his own meager, envious, siblingy self!

He sighed. Shifted from foot to foot. "I hate when you script me," he said. "It's so controlling."

I shook my head. "Oh, just forget it!"

"You have to stop," he moaned. "These past few months, it's like you just keep poking me with hot sticks. It's impossible for me to say the right thing. It's like living in an acid bath. You just keep biting my ears! Eating my head! One wrong word, and you lunge."

I glared over the dripping tubes and conduits. The smell of mold drifted up. Oh, why must he be so withholding? Why couldn't he be like my father, magnanimous? He was snatching something from me and didn't even know it. I thought of flat breasts, ruined, collapsed. He would do this to me and walk away, oblivious. I swallowed to soothe the ache in my throat. He was staring down with bloodshot, glowering eyes.

Tomorrow, as it happened, was my birthday. A Saturday. How awful for us both if we spent the day like this. I rushed upstairs. "You're there!" I cried when she answered her phone.

"I am."

"May I have three minutes?" I shut my eyes to focus on her.

"Yes, Bonnie."

It all spilled out, and then she said: "Someday you won't crave praise. Satisfaction at your accomplishments will reside in you."

"Thank you, Harriet. Oh, thank you!" The brown medallion wallpaper hung straighter on the walls. The galvanized tin trough in the yard gleamed as if positioned by a Zen artist. One day I won't crave praise, I thought. I shall be self-sufficient. An occasional act of cleverness by me shall be rejoiced in by me and that shall perfectly suffice.

Yet now it didn't. I'd fixed something. The day needed to count.

My puzzle-solving brain needed to count. Beautiful cone and curving tube! I wanted to be seen by my husband. Not as the old millstone, shambling apologist I'd so often been—my old self. Not as the depressive clasping her elbow, treading a few steps behind. Why, he wants me to remain a mess! I thought. A penguin waddling. A sidekick, a dwarf. He makes certain aspects of me invisible (cones, tubes) although he doesn't know it. When I share my work, he organizes the commas. I feel like the commas, toggles hooked, all loose ends lashed, while the body of the piece remains ignored. Something in me is crying out for him. He averts his eyes. Says uh-huh.

To praise, he contradicted. My husband explained this several times. If he thought an idea was good, he challenged it because it excited him to test it. He wanted to engage with it. So he looked for possible objections. "It's a compliment!" he said. But my idea felt permanently damaged after such an encounter. It limped, it could not be restored. Besides, what was this excitement which pricked him to challenge what was good in me? Could it be envy?

One Sunday afternoon I told him of a bold maneuver I planned in my writing—starting with a quote by Eudora Welty. The quote enabled me to formulate all sorts of critical points I'd lacked the courage to include before.

"But are you really going to be that critical about Iowa?" he asked. "Isn't that going too far?"

I didn't breathe for a moment.

Then I said, "Yes." And I silently vowed never to discuss my work with him again. We were sitting in the dark hot restaurant of an inn on Essex Street. My spoon clacked as I set it down in the empty sticky rum-raisin ice-cream dish. I shoved back my seat. No more, I promised myself. He's too destructive. I won't share what I'm really thinking with him. I'll share just superficial things.

It's surprising how easy it is to put such a vow into practice. In a matter of days one can be as self-contained as a deck of cards tucked in a box. He never inquired and I never offered to describe what occupied my mind all day.

* * *

During this time Paul was in his first job out of graduate school. This job consisted of responding to emergencies. The emergencies all involved big amounts of money and the maintenance of strict deadlines. Paul's job was so stressful that he asked me not to use a particular kitchen mug. This mug showed Mickey Mouse racing headlong away from a swarm of bees. It reminded him too much of work.

Paul also told me that sometimes, speeding home down Route 128, he opened his mouth and screamed. He felt better after. Even when he no longer drove home screaming, he recalled what it felt like, and that too provided relief. Sometimes when Paul said, "Uh-huh, uh-huh," I asked what he was thinking about.

"Work," he immediately said.

He always said "work." He said it as if he didn't imagine I would take offense.

And after a while I almost didn't.

One day about half a year later we were taking a long car drive. "You know, it's amazing that Stella doesn't mind if the people in the apartment building next door look right in her window," I said to Paul.

He nodded.

"She just waves at them over her breakfast bowl. I'd want to draw the curtains! She just has an incredible sense of safety. And yet sometimes I think she actually goads Jimmy into fighting with her. I think they're both attracted to her boundaries."

He nodded again.

"Do you think that's true?"

He shrugged.

"Are you interested in this?"

"Yeah."

"You know, I can't talk to you because you're not interested!"

"I *am* interested. I can tell you exactly what you're talking about."

"Just because you can do 'instant replay' doesn't mean you're listening." I sat staring ahead. And at that instant I made another vow: not to argue with him anymore. About anything. I was tired of trying to get him to show interest in what interested me, which these days was chiefly the psychological analysis of everything. The instant I start to be excited about something when talking to him—I told myself—I'll detach. Say, "whatever."

Sadness enveloped me. And I realized that arguing is based on hope. Give up even arguing and hope vanishes.

At a café in Harvard Square later that afternoon, in the midst of a discussion about new beginnings, my husband remarked to Juliet, "Oh, I love Bonnie's enthusiasm."

So why do you try to destroy it? I thought.

He met my gaze and, startled, glanced away.

"I felt so tense about coming up today, Harriet." My eyes were trained on the white plank of her door. "My work was going well. I didn't want to stop. Harriet, I'd like to be able to call and tell you I'm not coming to the session. Of course I'd pay for the session. But please don't wait for me."

"But of course I'll wait."

"I don't want you to! I want you to feel free to do something else."

"But, Bonnie, it's your session time."

"But I'd like to be able to give it back, sometimes! You should go out and eat an ice cream or something. Have a hot chocolate. I can't bear to think of you waiting. I'd have to come up!"

"But of course I'd wait," she said. "It's important for you to feel secure that I won't go anywhere during your time. I know you don't believe me, but I think it would upset you a great deal if you thought I was forgetting about you so easily. You'd get all churned up inside."

The white door had solidified into a giant beam of Turkish taffy, hard, dense. "If you say so," I said, clenching my teeth, feeling enslaved—feeling in fact as churned up and sick inside as she'd just described.

"I'll be here," she said serenely, "even if you show up for just the last five minutes. This is your time, Bonnie."

"Therapy induces craziness on the path to greater sanity," I announced buoyantly to my friend Gerald, a psychiatrist, stepping off the curb on East 72nd Street in New York.

He raised a blond eyebrow.

"It's like being inoculated," I persevered. "You get a little insane to spare yourself from being even more insane."

He smiled a pacific, enigmatic, perfectly handsome smile, so that I felt yet more crazed—and closer to Harriet, who understood precisely what I meant.

Yet this arched blond eyebrow was a thing of interest suddenly. I'd known Gerald for over ten years. And this arched brow, I now realized, embodied his characteristic stance in the world. A comfortable skepticism. An ironic distance. Why, I could even sardonically appreciate that the feeling of craziness Gerald induced might actually constitute a professional asset in a psychiatrist.

How exciting to notice such things! Other people were becoming increasingly more intricate. Not just in Harriet's office, but everywhere, things were acquiring significance.

"What seems to be the trouble?" inquired Miss X.

She was a couples' therapist whose skin gleamed like soap. The sleeves of her pink jumper stuck straight up in a gabled crease like a candy-striper's pinafore. The books on her wicker shelves were all paperbacks written in the last ten years.

I'd recently returned from three weeks at a writer's colony. "I don't want to be punished for my stay at MacDowell," I told myself on the drive home. When I turned in at our driveway I saw that the grass had grown so high it was a green meadow. The house looked like an abandoned house.

When I stepped inside Paul hugged me, and I noticed that he'd cleaned the living room. The predictable empty cans of Progresso soup and Goya pinto beans beside the easy chair were missing. The magazines were straightened. I sat down on the couch and he sat across from me, and I told him about my time away. I wanted him to understand all about it. But Paul stared at me rigidly, eyes big and flat. "Well?" I asked, when I was finished—for he'd remained silent.

"Sounds good!"

"Is that all?" My heart was breaking. It felt like two planks of side-walk, one pressing up, the other down.

"Look, what do you want me to say?" he groused. "Just tell me, and I'll say it!"

My eyesight blurred. "I don't know. It was just an important place. Look, what do you see when you look at this picture?" I grabbed out of my knapsack an Instamatic photo. It showed my Smith-Corona portable typewriter on the grass beside a bottle hold-ing yellow and orange and lavender wildflowers.

"I see that you have a good time away from me."

The next day, I dialed the number of this therapist.

Miss X's hands curled around her armrests like a gryphon's. She gazed calmly from one to the other of us behind glasses the color of pink lemonade.

"She's cut herself off from her three best friends," said my hus-band.

His words surprised me. I didn't see what this had to do with anything.

"I'm concerned she's going to do the same thing to me," he said.

Miss X looked at me. She said, "Your therapy is out of control."

"It is not out of control," I snapped. But my ears filled with the buzz of fear. "What does it mean, out of control?"

"You are acting out."

"Can't you speak English?"

She gazed at me. "You need to slow it down."

"I still don't understand," I said, although I did.

But she and her office seemed held together at that moment with toothpicks and Elmer's glue. If I inhaled, she'd whirl along the walls. I gazed at her and pitied her Popsicle-stick psychology. What did she really understand? Even her fee, seventy-five dollars a ses-sion, seemed weak-willed and pathetic.

"A marriage," she said, "is like two people who have oars for arms. Their arms are too long for them to be able to feed themselves. But each can feed the other. That's what you have to learn to do. When you refuse to feed each other, both starve."

"But people shouldn't have oars for arms!" I cried. "That's the problem. Healthy people can feed themselves. I don't want to replace my healthy arms with oars!"

"Don't you agree," she said, "that there are some needs a person can't meet by themselves?"

"There are some needs it's sad to have to meet by yourself," I said, looking at Paul, who was gazing disconsolately at the taupe rug. "What do you think of the oars?" I asked.

"I think lots of people starve," he said.

The word *happier* now frightened me when used in any context other than therapy. Paul said, "I think Mark would be happier living in New York," and my heart throbbed. I didn't want to believe a person could become happier except through therapy. This was because my therapy was making me so enormously unhappy.

But I reassured myself with the thought that I'd been an ignoramus before treatment. Vaseline seemed to have been smeared across my glasses. A girl in ninth grade had trod up to the Spanish teacher and whispered loudly that I was cheating on my test, which I certainly was. I could hear her words from where I sat. Her jade-green eyes slid over and gazed at me above her cupped hand. I stared at this smug blond tattler in bangs, and a hot awful feeling of admiration shot through me accompanied by a hatred as pure as kerosene. I decided to get rid of this blazing freight of emotions by becoming this girl's friend. I'd read this technique in a novel. If you dislike someone, become his or her friend.

And quite soon I *was* Jill's friend. It wasn't hard. With her upturned nose and sneering green eyes, she attracted few others. In fact I came to like Jill immensely. She knew the plots of all Katharine Hepburn's movies, and studied tap dancing, which required her to wear long black shoes with a heel. Sunday afternoons we rode the 100 bus to the Cloisters to wander through the medieval stone halls and listen to Gregorian chants, gazing at the marble knight and the unicorn in its green garden. We watched *The Lion in Winter* and read *Pygmalion* (Jill as Henry Higgins) while sprawled on a picnic blanket on line for Shakespeare in the Park. Jill often burst into the song from *My Fair Lady* that said if you spoke the way Liza Doolittle does instead of how you do "why, you might be selling flowers, too!" Her favorite joke was to cry, "The peasants are revolting!" and answer herself, "They certainly are!"

Jill was queen of a certain light teasing manner. I recalled innumerable afternoons watching the pink rubber tetherball in her backyard swing high into the sun (Jill was a clear foot taller than I, and adept at flinging the ball on its rope). We also played Hangman at her parents' little round kitchen table and an alphabet game that always began by guessing the same two words (nymph and lymph). I was already on Weight Watchers, and often Jill handed me a wineglass of tomato juice with a wedge of lemon squeezed into it. She gazed into my eyes as the cool glass hit my palm, then spun on her heel and mounted the stairs to her bedroom, her face holding an expression—cheeks mildly pinched in, lips pursed—of silent laughter. I followed her up the stairs. I couldn't imagine what the joke was. Its existence, though, was characteristic of Jill.

Jill ascending the stairs seemed to be in possession of a secret about me, and so I pursued her, hoping she'd open her palm and let me glimpse the secret—for certainly she had something, I felt it tugging me, flinging me after her. Perhaps it was the knowledge that I'd become her friend to rid myself of my shame at having cheated and of hating her. It was my anticipation that I would lose in any war with Jill. This bound me to her, as well as my delight in her style, which seemed sui generis.

I could see all this now, and marveled. My life did not feel good, but I could not imagine going back to the old blindness, the old fog, the smiling pursuit of someone splendid who reflexively held me in contempt. I wanted to believe I was now living the one best way. I wanted to believe that there was nothing else I needed to do in life except my work and going to treatment. I was fond of saying, "I don't see anybody really growing except through psychotherapy."

"When will you ever let me leave?" I nevertheless begged Harriet. "You always find more reasons for me to continue treatment."

She smiled. "Your very restlessness is a sign you have more work to do."

* * *

My new ability to see brought other rewards. I was evolving for the first time in my life an independent point of view. My husband's father sat on the couch without his shirt on, gesturing, holding forth. I noticed this. I'd known him thirteen years. He was a retired highway engineer, a job that had notoriously bored him. "Then I started working on I-84," he explained.

Upstairs in our bed in Paul's parents' house earlier that morning, I'd whispered to Paul that I'd felt silenced by his father's monologuing the night before.

"Do you realize, Dad," my husband now observed, walking through the living room in a robe, "that she can't have any opinion on what you're talking about?"

"That's why I'm talking about it!" his father replied. "As I was saying about I-84. . . ." And, without a hint of irony, he continued. He was a person who had been drastically ignored when he was a child. At the age of four he'd fainted and been carried off to the hospital where he was diagnosed as being near starvation. Neither his father nor mother had noticed his malnutrition. Now I saw the way he drank in attention as if it was hard to get enough. He was warm, funny, loving, with a grand need to talk and be heard.

My husband always had the sensation he hadn't given his parents enough. He wanted to bring them lavish gifts. On one occasion he brought his father a fancy cherry wood and glass kaleidoscope that he'd spent hours choosing. Paul's father opened the box, glanced in, and set it aside without pausing in his sentence. I saw him do this. There was a certain click that happened in me as if a bone had stuck in my throat. I'd never possessed this click before. It was like an uncomfortable gasp. It was akin to fear. I realized that my husband's father had in fact set aside all the gifts my husband gave him. The most he ever said was a flat "Thanks." My husband, in response, gave ever more extravagant gifts. After the kaleidoscope, it was a trip to England, then years of paying to snowplow his father's driveway. And all the while my husband's father clearly felt neglected.

In the past I got sleepy when I was with Paul's parents. I curled up on the living room sofa. My husband called it rude and urged me to stay awake. And indeed I'd been mystified by this grogginess. But now I perceived that there was often a placidly dismissive mood to his parents' reactions. It was as if they'd already heard everything I might say or as if they kept their lives safe by not allowing in too much raw contact. "And that shut him up!" was, I noticed, a favorite ending to an anecdote.

While we watched TV my husband's father explained to me how he'd wired the various appliances. Had I noticed the brown plastic casing by the doorway that cloaked the bare electrical cords? He'd installed it throughout the room. It occurred to me that my husband's disinclination to listen to me stemmed from how consumed he felt when his father talked at him. My husband himself must be suffering from a certain sensation of invisibility, I realized, glancing over to where he sat on the couch, leg jiggling. He was munching from a gigantic orange plastic bowl of salt-free pretzels, his knee bobbing while his father spoke. Did my talking to him feel like this? And Paul's disinclination to praise—certainly it was related to a childhood of feeling his reactions were coerced. Paul had actually explained this to me. His father especially needed a big, expressive response. I could just imagine the adolescent Paul staring out the car window, giving a curt nod—all that he could manage.

For all their volubility, though, I noticed Paul's parents remained oblique. In the kitchen, while Paul's mother and I did the dishes, she remarked: "My mother once told me when I was a little girl, 'Don't talk about yourself. Nobody's really interested.'"

She relayed her mother's words flatly, without the least irony; she seemed to believe that nobody is really interested. Yet in the family she was recognized as being "a people person." She'd studied sociology and worked for psychologists. She insisted upon the importance of therapy yet remained forever the woman stationed beyond the shut door, hearing the murmur inside.

People now seemed like safety pins, doubling back on themselves, hooked within. They seemed like the open closet of department store mirrors, those angled triptychs eternally tossing an image back and forth in their spread arms. A person was a Spanish question, beginning with an inverted question mark and ending with a right-side-up question mark, but with the question itself suppressed, just the twin marks clasped head to foot. The average personality was in lockup. It begged and begged you to enter, then shut the door in your face.

Now I noticed the elegant match between the man who hungrily expressed himself and the woman who concealed herself so ruthlessly. He said what came to mind, and she said, "Shh, softer" while she must have been suppressing the urge to say the words that would let her conclude, "And that shut him up." Perhaps they would be her own mother's harsh advice, from which she so carefully shielded him.

But this was precisely the sort of discussion that repulsed Paul. It made him feel crazy. It made him feel he was slipping into the childhood confusion, the cool embrace of the open mirrors. He'd majored in philosophy, attracted to its reverence for logic. Logic would be his way out of the nonsense of the family, he believed. The arbitrary prohibitions, the insatiable needs, all would give way before Hume, Russell, and G. E. Moore. Logic thrilled him. It forged a path. And, having found a way out of the emotional miasma of the family, he did not want to be tricked back in.

"You used to merge with others," says Harriet. "Now you are becoming separate. You have something of your own that you value. And you destroy it less and less."

In a ballroom of journalists, I do not wish to be a journalist. Reading someone else's printed short story, every word doesn't strike me as marvelous. When my friend Philip gives me advice after I ask for it, I can hear how the advice is characteristic of Philip, and that Becka's advice is characteristic of Becka, and that Paul's advice is characteristic of Paul.

Only Harriet's advice doesn't seem characteristic of a person, even when it falls into a familiar pattern. Only hers makes me want to take it on faith.

*   *   *

He doesn't love me, I decide one Thursday morning, slowly washing the dishes left over from yesterday's workshop. He wants me, he demands me, but my inner life is actually an inconvenience.

I set a clean saucer in the rack.

He acts annoyed when I'm sick. As if I'm faking. As if I'm trying to trick something from him he'd rather not give.

My fingers find another plate. The row of white saucers shines up like a skeleton. Porcelain ribs.

I feel, I decide, like the mother of a four-year-old. A four-year-old is not interested in his mother's internal life. A four-year-old is not terribly concerned about his mother's looks. It hardly matters if she had a good time when she was away; he's outraged she left. He wants her near. He wants her watching. He wants her performing her various nurturing functions.

I wipe my fingers on the dish towel, then walk into the living room and sit on the couch. The land outside looks like the battered suede of an old, forgotten shoe.

My sense of invisibility with my husband has increased from week to week. Home from Harriet, I sit in the car while my husband drives us to a movie, my face turned to gaze out the window. I feel ugly when I'm with him. Uninteresting. Deadened. The contrast with Harriet, of course, is intense. It is in fact the cause of all the trouble.

Gazing at the battered suede land, I imagine he does not care about my work—it is an inconvenience. And yet he chose a wife who has this need. He is attracted to this fight. He wants to commandeer the attentions of the distracted, oblique, bantering mother, the woman gazing into the distance.

But then the thought occurs to me—he is supporting me while I write! My advance is long gone. Yet he hasn't asked me to go out and get a job. What does that indicate about his desire for my happiness? Could there be a way I create this fight—somehow pulling the string on my husband to make him say "Uh-huh. Uh-huh," like some anti-therapist? It's true I've become incandescently sensitive to anything in him that sounds like disparagement. I seem to be trying to dig something out of him, to excavate something from him—acknowledgment. Only it doesn't please him; it makes him tense. I keep wishing he could be like a generous father admiring his daughter's traits, whereas I seem to appear to him as a jealous sibling, insulting, persecuting, nasty—as his own brother had been. I shut my eyes tight and open them. Perhaps to Paul I appear like an Anita, on the verge of making him seem a mess.

We met when he was a lanky, tall eighteen-year-old boy who'd run away to California and back, wearing denim shorts with a dozen clanking key chains hanging from it and a button-down shirt; I was an apologetic twenty-one-year-old girl in faded red painter's pants, hair falling into her eyes, ordering the cheapest thing. I still feel like a cheater when I take time on weekends to do my work. Paul, who has so little free time, waits. How to satisfy myself without feeling like I'm stealing from him? So I rise indignant, tall as Jill—no, taller! And thunder, "How dare you treat her like this?" When a month ago I treated myself the same way.

So, am I myself twin question marks mutually goggling, a room begging enter me, enter me—only to slam shut in my beloved's face? I certainly have a Jill inside, crooking a skeptical eyebrow. Paul seems beleaguered, armored. "I feel like that," Paul murmured during the Batman movie. Onscreen, Batman hunkered down in the Batmobile, defended, sheathed. Paul stares at me through slit eyes when I return from Harriet's. He looks as if at any moment I might utter a ridiculing comment, as if a smirk sits poised on my face. How interesting that he should see in me exactly what I'm fleeing!

Miss X's words ring in my ears—the sappy advice about the people with oars for arms. At the time I'd thought, but I've spent my whole life feeding others; I refuse to do it another instant!

I pick up the phone.

"Only got a sec," Paul warns.

"Want me to meet you in Gloucester? We can look at the boats."

"That'd be great."

"You can tell me what's going on with you."

"Cool."

"Do you have another second?"

"Actually, baby, I don't. I'm really sorry. I love you."

"You said it at work!"

He laughs. "I did!" He sounds surprised.

I cook up a skillet of chicken with lemon and dill, and microwave some big Idaho potatoes, and rinse off a pint of cherry tomatoes, and set it all in a basket. Then I shower and put on my red French dress. In Gloucester, the train pulls into the station and I see him leaning against the Camry, grinning. My heart lifts at the sight of him. He's so kind and handsome and smart! With crinkly eyes and a warm beautiful body in his gray suit. Not the person I've been thinking of at all, who coiled and coiled in my mind like black smoke.

"You look nice," he says.

"So do you."

He kisses me.

"Sexy kiss. Please."

He gives me one, and something inside me lurches. "Okay," I think, "Okay. This is good." I make myself not ask for another, which he might not want to give. I just hug him, hard.

If I fix my eyes on the thick yellow water glass while talking, I'm not distracted that Paul's head will start nodding uh-huh. We are sitting in the Big Boy in Danvers over hamburgers and apple pie and coffee. "Did I ever tell you about the fox in the writers' colony?" I ask.

"Nope."

"Everybody was seeing it all month. First this woman Maura, and then a performance artist named Elizabeth, and then everyone. They were so excited! I kept looking for it everywhere. It got to be the very end of my time. I didn't see it." The water glass spills yellow in all directions. "I was so disappointed. Then, that very last morning, as I was driving my car in a hurry to the cabin to empty out my stuff—there it was! Leaping right across the road! It looked so darn foxy!"

I smile, remembering that pointed snout, the fluffy, reddish tail. It feels good to tell him, even if it's weird to be staring at the glass.

"I'm glad you saw that fox."

I glance up. He's grinning. "Fox-seer!"

"Ha!" I say, smiling. I shrug. "It's just a little thing, really," which now it seems to be—as if restored to normal size.

"You saw the fox!" He grabs my hand and shakes it about.

"Yeah."

"Fox girl!"

I laugh, and get up and go kiss him on the mouth.

If I have to talk to water glasses, I'll talk to them.

It's early Sunday morning, and I've been up drinking coffee on the blue couch and reading Gertrude Stein's *Q.E.D.* The grass outside is shining a vibrant emerald. Maybe we should get a cat, I think. Fill up this big house. After a while I pad upstairs to where Paul's still sleeping. How warm and sweet his body looks, with his head on the pillow and the rest of him beneath the blue quilts. I like to stroke him between the eyes. I like to kiss him there, a sweet, fuzzy place. I push my loafers off and tuck myself under the blankets.

He flips to face me, and sleepily heaves an arm around me so we're nestled. I sigh, and suddenly feel acutely how lonely I've been with him. A metallic, chill sensation. I blink, and he pulls me close. Tears skitter down my cheek, pooling on the pillow. I'm glad he doesn't notice; it gratifies something in me. He doesn't know, he doesn't know, I think.

"Hey, you crying?" He's up and leaning over me. "Are you? You're crying!"

"I just want to."

"Why? What's wrong?"

I shake my head. "Just put your arms around me."

He does, lying down behind me and holding me close. After a little while the sheer pleasure from his warm arms and chest are so reassuring the tears dry up by themselves. I press back into him. "Nice," I say.

"Why were you crying?"

I shrug. "It's been so lonely."

"I know."

"I didn't actually feel like you loved me," I say.

"Me, either."

"I *have* been 'biting your ears,'" I offer.

His lips are on my neck.

"I never thought I'd say it, but it's true. I've been prickly and harsh. Overly sensitive. 'Eating your head.'"

"It's been scary around here," he says. "And sad."

"I didn't think you loved me, really."

"But I did," he says.

"Yeah, but—who I really am."

"I know who you really are. You think I don't, but I do."

I shrug.

"Shall I tell you?"

"Yes," I whisper.

"I'm holding in my arms an imp. A yukshee. A nerd. With coffee running through her veins. Who's smart."

"You do think I'm smart?"

"Yes. An Aries."

I smile. Neither of us believes in astrology.

"With terrible spelling," he continues. "And who never eats a vegetable. I have to beg you to eat a tomato! Who counts on her fingers and toes. I've seen those fingers twitching!"

The corners of my lips flick as if they want to start crying all over again.

"Who makes good observations."

"Really?"

"Um-hmm. Who was the pipsqueak of the family and had a very opinionated older sister."

"You think so?"

"Yes."

"Anita was opinionated?"

"Yes."

I nod and prop myself on one elbow. "Wasn't your older brother, too?"

"He liked to play head games."

"Sometimes I wonder if that has anything to do with why you went into business." I turn on my side to look at him. Then I sit up.

"I mean, so much of business seems to be head games, at least for the men you've worked for. And it's such a male environment, even though there are women in the company. A business really is like a bizarre family."

"But you know, sweetie, I went into business because I wanted to make things happen. To have an impact in the world."

"I actually know that about you."

I look out the window at the blue sky and treetops.

"It's like we've been divorced," Paul remarks.

I nod. I'd convinced myself I couldn't have all the pleasures of a marriage with Paul. I'd gotten used to feeling deprived and angry. How foolish! Why had I given up hope?

Paul is stroking my back. "It's been so sad."

I nod again.

"You acted like you despised me. I felt unwelcome in my own house."

I turn to him. "I'm so sorry."

He puts his arms around me and we lie there, hugging. "Do you want to have the house to yourself this morning so you can do some work?" he asks.

"If I did, what would you do?"

"That's my business. Just tell me what time you want to meet."

I shake my head. "I don't want to be apart today. It feels good to be close."

He nods and pulls me closer.

Do I want to take a music course at the local high school? It's called "Who's Afraid of Classical Music?" Paul is bent over the pulpy brochure. The cost is sixty-nine dollars. Yes, I say. I do.

The teacher turns out to be a retired Viennese audio engineer who lugs LPs to class in a green metal valise as big as a card table. Three weeks into the class, Paul raises his hand and offers the following rule of thumb: If it sounds like people bowing slowly to one another, it's Baroque. If it sounds like they're eating fabulous pastries, it's classical. And if it sounds like they're weeping or enlisting in the army, it's Romantic.

The teacher frowns, but the class claps and nods.

Sometimes during class Paul falls asleep in his crumpled blue suit and black wing tips, leaning on his hand. I murmur his name. He'd be disappointed to miss the one activity he looks forward to all week. He works eleven hours almost every weekday. Once, going to the store at night to get Parmesan cheese, and another time to buy a few limes, my car passed his. He was traveling in the opposite direction, driving home. I honked and waved, but he didn't notice. His eyes were opaque as buttons, staring straight ahead.

After class he and I have Sanka and chilled apple pie at a Greek diner and review our notes. I like to sit next to him on the orange vinyl bench. I like to grab his hand, which is freckled and warm. I kiss it and press it to my cheek. He smiles. "You seem to hate me less," he says.

CHAPTER TEN

My Gertrude Stein

Anita slept three feet away, I told Harriet. From across the ocean between us she described the glories she witnessed, the spectacle of a life worth living. She could look straight into the apartments across the street.

She saw a rumpled bed, a man and a woman drinking out of cocktail glasses in a tiny gold kitchen, a cat poised in the window like a vase, and a woman in a poofy plastic shower cap pulling on pantyhose and then throwing perfume between her legs. Anita narrated. I saw just a corner of cabinet and a piece of distant wall. Once I saw a door shut, but I could never see who shut it, even though I stared until even in my dreams I was seeing that shut door. From my view, everything across the street seemed molded of dust. If only I had Anita's bed!

"Star position is what I call this," she said. "It's how to sleep when the weather's hot."

Arms splayed, legs far as they'd divide, she looked voluminous, voluptuous.

Beyond her, the door to the terrace hung open on its chain. It was a humid night. The streetlight held a dusty smudge around it, an agglutination of air as if we were breathing chalk. Anita sighed. "What a breeze," she murmured.

"I didn't feel anything."

"No? There, that. Did you feel that?"

"No." I twisted in my sheets.

"Wait," she said. "Okay, now nothing. Nothing. Now there. It's—oh. It's exquisite. Like a cat brushing past. Like, like—no, now it's over."

"But I didn't feel anything," I moaned.

She stretched, more starlike.

"Let me have your bed. Just one night," I said.

"You chose your bed."

"Ages ago!"

"So what?"

When we first moved to Riverdale, the street had frightened me. In our old apartment the windows were far away, and a big blue tree guarded us like a risen moon. Here the city pressed close. The streetlight was an inquisition, and people walked under our window, jangling the change in their pockets. I wanted to be toward the room's inside, toward the hallways, the narrow ventricles winding to the kitchen, to my parents. I'd begged Anita to take that bed.

But now beside the open door I imagined she heard the tidal music of the street. I heard it, too, but like the ocean in a shell: miniaturized. She heard the real thing, car whoosh, laughter, the far-off haul of the 100 bus curving around the Henry Hudson Parkway, and the whispery road itself, an asphalt arrow pointing away. Anita's whole body pointed away, legs, arms, and even stomach, which rose to meet the world, and which had lots of the world inside it. She ate what she pleased. Jelly donuts, Godiva chocolates, tender slabs of farmer cheese, lavender wafers that tasted like soap, that tasted like churches, but which came in a beautiful package, all silver and purple. Anita was like an iguana or a baby, learning the world through her mouth. She advanced one tongue's length at a time. By now she was deep into Manhattan shops and mail-order catalogues, which she read with biblical attention, staring at the pictures in Lillian Vernon, ordering the stamp-thin ginger crisps, the Jordan almonds colored like sun-bleached gum balls and just as hard, the Danish cookies that crumbled to sugar at the first bite, spending her babysitting money with a wild hand.

I imagined grand futures for Anita. She had the aura of someone on TV. She spoke in such capacious sentences, with so many passionately expressed opinions and odd facts built in, that while she spoke I felt undeserving. Others should hear her. She should be a Personality like Julia Child or a special on the Hallmark Hall of Fame. She could tell the plot of a *Mannix* episode in more time than it took to watch it and yet she kept it interesting. She could describe what she'd seen on the street so that you felt you'd seen it, too. Above her flame-blue eyes, her bangs lay straight as a level. Anita cut them herself. But she let her ponytail bush out in a thicket behind her, as if what was over her shoulder did not exist. It was a snare, a rat's nest, a clotted glory. My grandmother threatened to snip it off; my mother whispered in a loud and mournful voice what a shame it was that such a pretty girl should have such an unruly head. Anita smiled. She sat in an orange flower-power muumuu sipping Swee-Touch-Nee and eating candied fruit slices with my friend's mothers, and giving her opinion about a daughter who ran off to get married or a son who needed the name of an excellent dermatologist. She was fifteen. It was just a matter of time before she lived beside the Seine.

Yet for all Anita's aplomb and appetite, I reflected with Harriet, it was I who left. I went off—I realized now—to find a place where I didn't covet someone else's bed or chair, where I was who I wanted to be. In fact, I wanted to be Anita. The real Anita stayed in the Bronx. She stayed more and more in her body. Her arms weakened; her legs stiffened into marble sculpture; she needed to be balanced over a walker or she'd collapse.

How to match the girls we were to the women we became? A sister's life interrogates yours, saying, Why do you live this way? Are you doing what's right? And when the sister has a disease, I realized now, she has it for you, so you don't have to have it, just the way she picked up heavy knapsacks when she was stronger than you, or took the bed beneath the windows when you begged, so you could feel safe.

"I weigh as much as the street Yankee Stadium is on," she told me from the hospital to which she'd recently moved. This was the hospital in the movie *Awakenings*, and there were yellowed clippings on many patients' walls showing Robin Williams here. Anita's roommate, Kathleen, was an extra. Kathleen has cerebral palsy, and a sign taped to the back of her chair: "Leave me the hell alone" below a picture of Edward Munch's *The Scream*.

"As much as the street Yankee Stadium is on?" I said. "How much is that?"

"One hundred sixty-eight."

"Oh."

"And now they're going to put Yankee Stadium in New Jersey. I think it's a shame. The Bronx has so many problems right now, it needs Yankee Stadium. Besides, what would Yankee Stadium do in New Jersey? It wouldn't be the same thing at all. It would be meaningless."

"You're right," I said. Anita came to Beth Abraham when she could hardly walk, and every day she's more static, while I keep traveling farther and farther from home.

"I hear you're going on vacation to Mexico," she said. "Send me a postcard."

"Okay. Hey, do you remember the postcard you sent me from Israel? It was an airplane, Anita! A Pan Am jet."

"I call that a good postcard," she responded. "You wanted to see travel, and travel is what I sent."

"Oooh, you're a smart one!"

"Jane Lilly is always telling me to join MENSA," she said. "She thinks I'm wasting myself."

"You are not wasting yourself. You are providing wonderful conversation to everyone around you."

"I'm glad you think so," she said.

I did.

When I started therapy in Princeton, Anita was the one topic I refused to talk about. I'd begun a novel about her and feared that if I told my story I wouldn't need to write it.

"Have you had the experience of things you shared being appropriated?" Harriet said, even then.

"No."

"You haven't had the experience of things you told about being taken away?"

"No."

Harriet's chin had a tendency to look fleshy and stubborn, like Anita's. Occasionally I heard the ball of her palm rubbing callously against the page. This reminded me of Anita, too: an insensitive body pursuing its own course.

※ ※ ※

Anita sewed little books. Palm-sized, they were cheap typing paper stitched with three bold strokes. Into these books she set fabulous stories about sisters and fireworks and pounding drums. You opened the book and stepped in.

I copied her books and called them mine. "By Bonita Friedman," I wrote. I folded the same kind of paper, then sewed it the way Anita taught, with a long needle that hurt my thumb when I shoved it through the wadded sheets. I drew the fireworks she drew, and the two sisters walking, their hands like five-pronged forks entwined, their skirts like little bells, and their hair a flip. Crayon smell filled the room, or else the besotting scent of markers—you had to use orange with such care: it soaked everything.

Some days Anita drew her stories on spools of adding-machine paper she bought for thirty-five cents at the temple bazaar. Those days I drew scrolls, too, persuaded by watching Anita that really these were better than books, these tales taped to a pencil at one end and rolling around and around, girls following fireworks following pigeons and alley cats and cocktail glasses and drums and more girls still holding hands until they all lived in a realm you could enter anywhere, a great big bolster like a thicker and thicker epithelium made of a tissue of stories.

In fact, lacking adding-machine paper, we actually used toilet paper, which required an agony of tenderness and much precise administering of that orange, which bled like methiolate. The result was a sort of saturated snowball of color that to the uninitiated might look like a collapsed mess, but which, to Anita and me, was visual shorthand for stories themselves, better than even *Harriet the Spy*. Once finished, the tissue scrolls were too fragile to open: they nested like eggs in Anita's drawer. Glimpsing one imparted an instant's delirium, my first contact high.

While we worked, Anita sat on the scabby yellow Windsor chair. I sat at her elbow on an overturned wastebasket that pictured Bohack-brand vegetables. Where did Anita's stories come from? I wondered. How did she know how to draw? Somehow she saw that fireworks were airborne spiders, and that curtains hung in windows like a central part in a chunky girl's hair. Even her handwriting, always print, was unstoppably expressive, a parade of characters tumbling across the page, her plump lowercase *a*'s Winston Churchills propped by a cane, her *m*'s the top of the Ten Commandments. I watched the letters appear out the tip of her pen. What fun to be her, I imagined. Collections assembled around her. In her big white Formica desk stood sky blue letters from pen pals, each marked "Answered," pamphlets from Weight Watchers shaped like loan coupon books, wool "god's eyes," gold-plated charms for a charm bracelet. There was even an envelope of phosphorescent pollen. This was shimmery yellow green, an exhalation of the trees, which Anita had swept from a certain porch. I'd seen Anita's heels glowing like night-lights. "Anita!" I'd said. She looked and laughed. "Pine tree pollen," she announced, and swept it up in one of the envelopes she carried in her pocket as nature counselor.

That envelope now lay in a coil, bound by a rubber band, in her top drawer. I seldom saw it. Anita forbade me to investigate her desk without permission, which she rarely gave. The insides of her desk were private. A feminine scent of bath powder sifted up when you opened a drawer, and I once discovered a fascinating lumpy package that looked as if it should unfold but wouldn't: a sanitary napkin, Anita later explained.

I knew the inside of Anita was like the inside of all these things, of the desk, the books. The inside of her was like the sky on Independence Day, lit with the fireworks she loved, or the black crayon drawings she taught me to scratch with a pin, revealing rainbows of nighttime carnival underneath. She was the first person I met who had an actual internal life. How I wished I were she!

What is it to grow up wanting someone else's eyes and fingers and mouth and mind? I erased so much of what I wrote in second grade, my teacher cracked the tops off my pencils. At home, I sat very close to Anita. I thought if I copied her long enough, I would learn how to create.

Anita seemed to copy no one. She went off to Israel, and came back with a tingle in her elbow that wouldn't go away. This tingle was the beginning of her body erasing herself, the myelin sheaths around her nerve endings degrading, forming obdurate scar tissue —although this took a while to find out. I was there the day the doctor stuck a needle in Anita's palm and she felt nothing. I saw the needle jab, and Anita, with her eyes closed, waiting for a feeling to start.

"Do you feel anything now?" asked the doctor.

"No. Not yet," Anita said.

The doctor pushed the needle against another part of her hand. "And now?"

"I don't feel a thing. Are you touching me? I don't feel anything at all. I can't feel a thing."

I also saw Anita, with her eyes closed and her arms out, attempt to walk straight across the examining room. She took one baby step and then another, and the more she walked, the more she diverged.

"Anita," I said, and she opened her eyes.

She was in the wrong part of the room.

"Here is your pocketbook," I said. "I want to go home."

We rode the number 1 subway together to our jobs every morning. Anita's blue Bronx Music Society tote was now stuffed with brochures she'd sent away for. She turned the pages slowly—laetrile therapies, Swiss spa therapies, thermal therapies, all costing tens of thousands of dollars. Anita read the testimonials and studied the pulpy photos of men in lab coats.

"It's bogus," I said. "It makes me so angry. They're just trying to prey on your fear."

"Maybe there's something to it."

"I really doubt it."

"But maybe there is." And she tucked the brochures back into her satchel.

"They say if it begins mildly, it will continue mildly," I said, quoting something one of the doctors had said about the progress of her disease.

"Yes, they say that."

"It began mildly."

She took my hand in her small one. "Yes."

* * *

Where Anita lives now, men and women loll in wheelchairs. Pieces of them are missing. Some have a bandaged stump where a leg should be. Others are too skinny, and remain collapsed sideways in their wheelchairs. Their eyes follow you down the linoleum, past the café where angels—volunteers—serve weak coffee and day-old chocolate chip cookies, and where many wheelchairs are lined up in late autumn, so that people can gaze out at the treeless courtyard, the peeling white gazebo, the two patchy street cats, black and white, climbing the wood like squirrels, and then dashing across the pavement. "Look! Look at that cat! She's so fast!" a few patients murmur admiringly. After the cats are gone, they continue to gaze into the stark yard.

People here are friendly. If you ask one patient where the elevator is, three or four will answer. They all point you down the hallway, elaborate what you will pass on the way, and many smile encouragingly, and, like parents, watch your progress. To each other they don't say much, though. Maybe this is always the way with people together from dusk to dawn.

The home has a compelling, miraculous atmosphere. The heat is amniotic. You're on the verge of a sweat. The granules in an hourglass are floating up and down throughout the corridors. Time has assumed a gauzy detachment, a free-floating, deep-space granular air—as if all the Jean Naté Anita ever powdered is rising in a gust and subsiding, as if you are seeing the very molecules of the earth recombining, decaying, recombining again. "Dr. Hall, report to the third floor, please. Security, pick up line two." The building makes announcements to itself. Even in the bathrooms, broadcasts permeate. One feels that in here no doors really matter. Nurses and TVs and PA systems can enter even one's dreams.

During Anita's birthday party her new roommate, Rhea, left her TV tuned to Sunday afternoon football, although she didn't watch. A woman in her late seventies, Rhea sat in a pink robe and slippers, an old *Newsweek* lying in her lap. "Thank you, darling," she said when I gave her a piece of cake, and "No thank you, darling," when

I offered coffee. Mostly, she daydreamed. Meanwhile, the rapid, monotone male voice on the set announced plays, cheers erupted like static, and flickering shots showed bent men running, charging, poising themselves in configuration. We licked our frosting and Anita opened her cards bathed by the sportscaster's excited, distant voice.

When my phone rings at home, and the stranger at the other end firmly advises what to add to my guacamole or what's coming up on *Entertainment Tonight,* I know it's Anita calling. "And now the latest on President Clinton's summit trip," I hear, and Anita materializes in the foreground: "Bon? How are you?" It's as if she's reporting live from the scene, as if the events of the day are clamoring for Anita's attention, but she's decided for the moment to ignore them.

Anita asks me to take home Mishka, the Olympic teddy bear I brought her. She didn't ask me to bring him, she says, and wishes I hadn't. This is a hospital, and ought to look like one. She's leaving as soon as she's strong enough, she says. Twice a week she has physical therapy.

Twice a week seems very little to me, almost a token amount. But, wouldn't it be wonderful if she could get stronger? Who's to say it won't happen? Who's to say it out loud? Maybe a miracle will happen. Maybe a doctor will discover how to make nerves grow back.

"I'll take Mishka next time I come," I say.

"Good. I want him home, next to the piano. And take home the poster of orange groves, too. The more you bring now, the less we'll have to occupy our arms with later."

"You don't want it there to cheer you up?"

"It does not cheer me up to have it here."

When the elevator door opens on the sixth floor of Beth Abraham, I usually find Anita sitting outside her bedroom door. She wears cherry red or navy blue cotton housedresses with snaps down the front, which my mother buys at Kress's, and reads *Ellery Queen's Mystery Magazine,* holding the magazine three inches from her face.

"Let's get your coat," I announce.

"Bonnie!"

"Where's your hat? Do you want your purse?"

"I had no idea you were coming today! I want a kiss." She tilts her face to the side, and I kiss her.

"Now, where's your other glove?" I say. "I've signed you out. I've sprung you! Let's get some fresh air."

"Slow down!"

"Oh, it's not cold out. You don't need your other glove. Let's go."

Nothing feels as good as taking Anita out of here.

I'm uneasy about what's happened in therapy. I often still feel estranged from my husband and parents, and even from my own self. Paper has been inserted between the layers of me. I feel detached.

"You are taking your happiness away from your own self. Don't you see? It's intrapsychic."

I laugh. "Paul says, 'Intrapsychic is just another way of saying, It's in yo' own head!'"

Harriet remains silent.

I don't like what's happened to my feelings about Anita, either. I used to think of her with wild affection and pity. She was overweight in adolescence, and I recall watching from the bedroom window as she toiled up the street in her oatmeal-cloth coat, moving like a sixty-year-old woman although she was seventeen. How that sight contracted my heart!

Now, though, my view of her has flattened. Was she domineering, or is this simply a puny, resentful, younger sister way of seeing her?

"You know, Harriet, I sometimes feel as if you've broken into me. But the way someone breaks into a house. I have a friend who says that whenever she falls in love she dreams of a house broken into. I feel invaded. I would love to get rid of you."

"Maybe you've never been close to someone who would tolerate your desire to leave. You had to stay and do what the other wanted in order to feel safe. But you felt rigid."

I laugh. "Yes! Keep talking! When you were speaking I felt—oh, such joy! Such wild joy."

We are silent. The sun flings a golden carpet across the floor. It swirls with dust, like a sparkling scrim curtain rising. For an instant my cheek is cooled by a delicious breeze, and I'm sure she feels it.

Anita fell, and I became the star. What sort of joy can there be in this? My handwriting looks like what hers used to. Her handwriting looks like a child's now. I found her once in the hospital's empty dining room, writing a postcard against the paper tablecloth. She was writing to Jane Lilly. Nine or ten of her arduously shaped words would fit on the whole card. She laid her pen down in midsentence. It took so long to write each word, she would finish the card later.

Just going to the bathroom is an expedition now. Anita has become mindful of small pleasures. "Mom brought me a basket of strawberries and two cans of Coca-Cola when she came yesterday," she tells me. "When I'm done drinking them, I'll rinse out the cans and save them for Mark." Anita had suspected an orderly had taken some of her cans. Now she keeps them locked in her cabinet.

"Her horizons have narrowed to a pinpoint," my mother once said.

Mine have expanded. I have a bed by the road, a night view of stories. The black field of my computer screen kindles with tangerine letters, like the art Anita taught me, black crayon scratched to rainbows underneath. But these glories don't feel entirely mine. I'd wanted to become Anita, but I'm me, sitting in her place. How can I help but feel fraudulent? In her sleep, Anita can still walk. In my sleep, I'm still on the Bohack garbage can.

"My body is attacking itself," Anita said over the phone recently. I nodded, twisting the cord between my fingers.

"When people ask me how come you're here," she said, "I tell them, 'Because I donated my blood to the floor.' The first time was on my birthday. The insurance company came, picked me up, and took me to ER. They stitched up this part of my head so the blood would stop. After the second time, I was brought here. Two days ago I saw the neurologist. He said, 'I haven't seen you in a year.' 'You haven't cured me in a year, either,' I told him. We talked. What doctors generally do is ask questions. You give them answers."

"I've noticed that, too," I said.

"Well, there are a lot of things they still don't know. Speaking of which, did I tell you there's a man here that wants to feel me up? I told him, no. You are my boyfriend but Mark is my husband."

"Anita, don't let him! Unless you want him to."

"I don't want him to. But, you know, we all get old at the same rate. One day at a time."

"Meaning?"

"I'm happy for the attention, I suppose."

Once upon a time I wanted Anita's attention. I craved to see the world from her perspective. When she went to Israel after college, all her furniture became mine. The bed had a trough. The desk was stuffy. Steam pumped from behind it in a way that gave me a headache. I studied into the night. Sometimes a motion reflected in the night glass jolted me. Was the door opening? Was it Anita coming back early?

I sat for hours on my ankles, bending my head beneath the halo of her Lightolier lamp, desperate to forge a mind. I felt as if I was pushing books into my head. I wanted to shove a whole library in my head, and was disappointed by my memory. Certain facts I'd known in October had vanished by April. I had to put them back in again. Summer came, and I spent it exiled among pine trees at a Jewish sleepaway camp. I sat on a big rock and ate fizzy candy and fake vanilla ice-cream bars bought from the canteen, and by September my head was empty again. I gazed at the apartments across the street. They still seemed uninhabited.

Anita, meanwhile, was walking in orange groves, sipping ginger in her coffee, cutting purple cabbage into salads heaped with fresh feta cheese she served her new friends, speaking Hebrew at the Ulpan and practicing Italian to sing arias at the Ruben Academy. She wrote home on the translucent blue paper I'd always admired, the paper that was a layer of sky you could hold in your hand. Anita plucked some sky, covered it with her adventures, and sealed it all around with a lick of her tongue. The return address was in hieroglyphs more expressive than anything I'd ever imagined. Her bet was a serene dove, gazing. Her aleph an upright person who could also bend. "Answered," I wrote on her envelope before tucking it in her drawer. Whatever spot I occupied, I wasn't in the desirable place.

I once house-sat for a man in New Hampshire whose house turned out to be full of guns. Every book on his shelves was about war, as were the videotapes and magazines. In the barn, beside the Ford Taurus, was a genuine World War II Jeep. "He trained to go to Korea, but never went," his son explained. "He was too young, and the hostilities were over by the time he was prepared." He's been fixated on fighting ever since.

I didn't train for war. Nor did I really train for achievement. My training, I now understood, was in appreciation. Like Alice Toklas, that's what I felt I did best. I was good at admiring others' art—Anita's illustrations, the beautiful light blue and dark blue afghan, which, before she went to Israel, flowed from her needles in opulent woolen waves. I loved to hold my hands apart as she spooled a hank of fresh wool into a ball. I loved to gaze at the tips of her needles, which made a rubbing clacking sound and turned like the mouth of an origami fortune-ball, opening with unconscious assurance in this direction and that. More than anything, it was that assurance I craved. "Anita, in Hebrew, means 'you answered,'" Anita once told me. "Ah. Nee-ta." She seemed the answer to me.

What if your job were to describe what it is like to eat a kiwi? Well, watching someone else eat a kiwi, I can imagine the lush strawberry-mangoish flavor in their mouth. I can imagine it so vividly that my own mouth waters with the sweet green taste. I can also imagine sitting alone behind the living room curtain of my childhood, and savoring a kiwi by myself. But to stand up front and eat that kiwi! To describe that taste for others!—to think the way that kiwi tastes to my mouth is significant, and to trust that the way I knit language can do it justice—there I falter. There I murmur, "You taste it, Anita. See what you think. You tell it, Anita. You are good at telling."

I carry her in my mind as the real one, the original, the aleph to my bet, the word to which I am the rhyme, the person whose vision is clear while mine blurs with distortion. She was the original of those women—Janice, Kate—whose presence has become anathema to me, kryptonite, the very idea of whom transforms me into a muddle-headed girl in tights that are wrinkly at the knee, hair sporting a clump of dried Wheatena, shirt untucked, shabby, a mess! But I never knew she made me feel that way!

After she went to Israel, I sat in Anita's chair and slept in Anita's bed. Goldilocks broke all the family furniture except what fit her. Yet I wanted Anita to persist.

Harriet suggests that this is the dream that goes unfulfilled: that I can break her and she'll remain, that I can topple her and she'll still be triumphant, that I can rip and punch and bite her and she'll know this is the demon me, the puny me, not the me who loves her, who really loves her—not politely, not for show, but savagely.

I want to tell Anita, my secret desire was that you could be even stronger than you were. I wanted to reveal everything to you. I wanted to bring in the exiled me, the pariah me, from where it was banished under my bed, in the farthest corners of my terrifying closet, in the door that stayed shut even in my dreams because I could not imagine it opening, because even my drowsing self knew I could not keep sleeping if that door opened. I wanted to bring in the part of me that resented and even hated you and have you see it and still let me have your smile. Your smile! It lit me like a bulb in a lampshade. If only I could harvest that smile, and dry it, and put it in a box! Oh, a little box like a matchbox, and from time to time when I'm sad and desolate, when the sky is all grainy ash, slide open that little box and take a pinch of you, and have my whole being blossom.

Or did you already know my heart when I didn't? Was it sweet as the apple the envious queen sent? Was the knowledge that apple held so appalling you went rigid? Do we always hate those we love? Hate them because we can never leave them? Hate them because they have so much power over us? Hate them because their heels glow like night-lights and their eyes are boxes of sun? It felt like your life or mine, and mine won. You fell and fell, and now you can't keep from falling. If only I were far away! Then I wouldn't see you lean against a walker, having your heavy feet lifted for you.

You once told me that you console yourself with the thought that because you have this disease I probably won't ever get it; the chances seem diminished. This way your life is of some use. I'm in your prayers. When the nurse leaves, and your door is swung open to the hospital corridor, you ask God to keep me safe. Mark, our parents, our brothers and their families, me. Could I ever really have hated you? Wasn't it you who taught me to scratch through love's darkness to find the carnival colors pulsing underneath? The blaze in the jack-o'-lantern, the apartments where phosphorescent strangers shone with loneliness, the glaring sense of personal bizarreness, the wild, wild desire to run away from here.

I try to remember ways Anita was mean. Surely she must have been mean, otherwise why would I be so attracted to grumpy women, to demanding landladies and housemates with peroxide hair and an unpleasant manner, to middle-aged students in white big-pocketed blouses who declare that their problems are unsolvable?

Such women compel me, I've discovered. I bring them valentines, chocolate cakes, compliments on a blue wool coat or scarf, sincere reveries on the talents they display and to which they seem callous—mistaking their happiness for my happiness, thinking if only they could be happy with me then we both could be happy. They seem to have devoured my happiness with their unhappiness. With what vigor they insist on their dissatisfaction! If I could give them their own joy, then we could each have ours, like each person having her own chicken pot pie, and nobody grabbing anyone else's.

The fat women, the clench-faced women, the stubborn women, the scary women—all draw me. I think, Oh, I know how to make her happy, and try what worked with Anita: the Bohack wastebasket, the oddly pleasurable groveling, the acknowledgment of strengths, the reflection of what, in fact, is spectacular in this woman. How safe I feel! When the lion is smiling, she is not eating you. When the lion is letting you pull the splinter from her paw, she is not slashing. Yet I can come up with just one memory of Anita's being nasty to me. It is an almost inconsequential moment.

One childhood summer morning she tripped on the bungalow's concrete steps and went sprawling.

"Are you hurt?" I asked, anxious.

"Of course, you idiot."

Finis.

Although I recall, too, the shamed way I trailed after her like a kicked dog, wondering why I was such a jerk, why, why, I hadn't thought of something intelligent and helpful to say.

"Anita was trouble," my friend Daniel remarked.

"How do you know?" I asked, excited.

"But it's what you say all the time!"

"It's hard to love you," Anita said to me when I was nineteen. I stumble across this remark in a peeling cardboard diary from 1977. We both seemed to believe she was saying something about only me. At the time I was going off to live with my boyfriend. She was single and not dating.

"You're a snob," she apparently said a few weeks later. And, once I'd returned to college she wrote to me: "You are the ultimate achievement of the Friedman family"—a shocking remark, considering that it was my brothers and Anita herself who had always seemed spectacular. But Anita had gone to City College. There was a class division in our family. My brothers both attended private colleges, and when it was my turn I wanted that, too. How must she have felt about her bratty little sister, given an expensive education, living with her boyfriend? I've never thought of it from this point of view before.

Anita had cracked big sticks across her knee to stoke a campfire when she was thirteen. She banked the logs until the fire tipped back its head and roared. She suspected our mother disliked her, that everyone else was her favorite. She suspected our father thwarted her, preferring to satisfy our brothers' ambitions. She was deposed, and deposed again by a torrent of siblings.

I thought of her with her thicket hair, her enraged impulsiveness, her pointed tactlessness. She was asking for something with her mouth and hands and stomach and stomping, tantruming feet—but what? The wilder she got, the more my mother shunned her. She saw in her first daughter her tyrannical mother. What she couldn't confront in her mother, she left unanswered in her daughter. Scalding tears, doors flung shut, hungers that no quantities of food could satisfy, something avid and wanting worked its way through Anita, and her way of reaching out was pushing away.

I walked around Levitan's Bungalow Colony with her when she returned from months of camp—my heroine! Suntanned, reeking of wood smoke and pine sap, the muscles in her legs like bowling balls, her hair a warren, she said, "Oh, how could she do this to me? Look how fat I've got! It was her—I was doing so well! I'd lost so much weight on Weight Watchers, but she said I had to go. And look at me now. All they feed you are starches! There's a loaf of bread at every meal. They pass it around, they keep filling the basket. Yellow margarine as soft as mayonnaise. Spaghetti, white ice cream, sloppy Joes on hamburger buns, Kool-Aid in a tin pitcher. It tastes good in that pitcher! And I was thirsty. Empty calories. Empty, empty, stupid calories. She did this to me," she said, punching her leg.

I skipped alongside to keep up, marveling at her words, struck by her beauty. "What are you doing a little jig about?" she said. "What's the matter with you?"

"But Anita—you look, you look great."

She snorted. "If everyone were as blind as you."

"No, Anita. You do. I'm so happy you're home!"

She laughed. "You're her favorite child. That's always been obvious."

"But that's just not true! We both are. That's what she always says."

"Blind, blind, blind," Anita replied, but she grabbed my hand nonetheless, and swung it while she sang a new Girl Scout song:

Like snow-white sailing boats on a blue sea,
High in the heavens are clouds floating free.
If I could fly away,
If I might fly away,
Sailing and sailing
What pleasure would be!

I try to reconcile the strong Anita to the weak one, the adored Anita to the despised one, the Anita who really lives, and the one I seem to be forever inventing. Nothing matches. Always, I feel I'm lying. Everything is too absolute, but I don't believe the truth lies somewhere in the middle. The truth rarely lies somewhere in the middle. Is it true I wanted her to fall? As often as I say it, I know it's a lie. And as often as I say she wasn't oppressive, I disbelieve it. She is a thimble and Twin Towers, vague as a photo of a photo of a photo, and clear as lightning—a forty-two-year-old woman who told me on Friday she painted a jewelry box in occupational therapy. "I painted one side of it pink, and then on another side I used yellow," she said. Could this be the person who had such a drastic effect on me? I would like to kiss her too hard, a kiss that lets me feel her teeth underneath.

Somehow we are forever sitting side by side and caressing one another in the bodies we once had. This is the scroll-story constantly uncoiling, the truth as it persists, a memory that captures the big reality. Anita stretches her arm out to expose the silken bruised blue of her inner elbow, where the vein leaps toward the surface and the body is most sensitive. "Right there," she murmurs. "Ah. Nice. Good, Bonnie."

Or it is New Year's Eve, and I am trying to untangle the brier patch of Anita's hair. I dip my comb in water and work as carefully as I can. The knots are hungry spiders with hard centers. Anita's eyes are tearing. "Shhh," she says, as if I'm being loud, not rough. "Shhh."

"Okay," I say, dipping my comb. There's more knots than hair. I sink the comb's teeth into the edge of a knot and pull, holding the top of her hair with my other hand. "Just think—by next year, your hair will be smooth. Anita, this time don't let the knots grow back."

"Shhh," she says.

"No, listen, Anita. You don't have to go through this again. Don't let the knots come back. They always want to come back, but this time, don't let them."

"I can't help it," says Anita.

"Of course you can. Just remember to brush behind you. Just remember people can see that, too."

"I don't want to think about people seeing me all the time. That's their business. I can't live like that."

"Of course you can. It's so easy. Just—"

"How do you know? You don't know anything, Bon! You live in this world like a blind person. You can't even see what's in front of your own nose."

I see your knots, I think, but remain silent.

"Ouch! That's exactly what I mean!" she says. "Look at what you're doing! Try to see it. Look inside each knot."

Her hair floods reddish brown in the lamplight and swarms with knots. For a moment, it is an impossible task: untangle this by midnight. But then I take a breath. The comb's long teeth plunge slowly.

"That's better," Anita murmurs.

I work as kindly as I can, and Anita knows it's always an accident when my hand slips.

CHAPTER ELEVEN

My Paris

"Paul has two weeks of vacation and he's asked me to take a trip with him to Paris."

Harriet was silent. She recrossed her legs below her blue-black skirt.

"I'd like to go, if it weren't too big a disruption of our work."

"How big a disruption do you think it would be?" asked Harriet tonelessly.

"A big one, I guess," I said. "But he really wants to go. And he works so hard."

"I'm sure Paul works hard," she replied. "I don't see what that has to do with your interrupting your treatment."

"Yeah." My insides were twisting.

"What do you want to go to France for?" she burst out. "To see the Eiffel Tower?" Her voice dripped with sarcasm.

"It seems shallow, doesn't it?" I said. Then I added in a low voice: "I was going to say that I wanted to try the food and see the art, and just experience the atmosphere of the place."

We'd be there in early spring. It had been a snowless winter of cinder-block skies and Massachusetts landscapes that looked like the back of a junkyard—tangled branches, rusty seeping things. "I was in Paris once when I was in college," I said, "for just two days. It was wet and cold. It wasn't the romantic place I thought it would be."

"And you think now it will be better?"

"Maybe," I said.

She was silent, listening.

"But I guess it sounds superficial, compared to maintaining the momentum of our work."

"It's your decision, Bonnie," she said. "But yes, the work we're doing in your treatment does require maintaining a certain velocity and intensity. And it does recalibrate things for you to go off."

"I know," I said softly.

"But if you want to go, we'll figure out how you can."

"That's so nice of you, Harriet!" I exclaimed. I felt like leaping up and kissing her. After a moment, I added softly, "It really is."

And staring at her poster of the Mediterranean, it suddenly occurred to me: but this is exactly how to get to Paris! Not by an airplane. Not by a ship. If I stay on the couch long enough, I'll find myself in my own Paris, where food tastes more delicious, and the sun glows more warmly on my arms because I'm happier and more present in the moment and more at peace. It's precisely by staying here that I'll really arrive in Paris. I smiled, gazing into the depths of the painted sea.

"What are you thinking?" asked Harriet.

"That you are my Paris."

She smiled.

"It's true!" I said. "This is one of the great experiences of my life. I know that, Harriet. I'm enjoying the prime of Miss Harriet Sing."

I turned back. She blushed, and looked radiant in her starched white pleated blouse with its fabric crackling like parchment paper, her cheeks flushed pink.

"I'm building a Paris for myself right here," I said, recalling the sensation of beauty that illuminated everything late in a session, when I was done speaking and she provided an interpretation, and it seemed the whole world was lit like a Tiffany lamp, everything shining and linked. "I'm in Paris."

"What a lovely way to put it, Bonnie," she said.

CHAPTER TWELVE

The City of Envy

Envy framed my sessions. I walked in sick from bingeing on the faces of successful writers grinning up from *People* and *Vogue* found in the waiting room. After my session, I wandered straight to the bookstore to look at journals containing stories by peers.

In fact, even during my session envy presided over me, captured in a shiny steel frame, a Native American with bristle-black hair and turquoise earrings goading her pony to fly. This woman spoke of a certain rival. I turned my back to her, leaning on one hip. It felt as if Harriet imposed her on me—as if, if Harriet really cared about me, she would take the woman down, as I'd asked. It was true that both before and after my sessions I sought out envy as if in a propitiatory ritual. But the imposition of this envied figure here, right here, galloping over me on the couch, struck me as outrageous. Wasn't this supposed to be my space and time?

"I think it's actually misguided of you not to take her down," I told Harriet. It was an early June day three and a half years into treatment. "I'm sure she bothers other patients."

Harriet was silent a moment, then said, "But do you always go to the bookstore after your sessions?"

I blinked at the change of topic. "Yes."

"And don't you think that's remarkable?"

"There aren't any bookstores in my town."

She recrossed her ankles.

"I'm always interested in seeing what new books have been published," I explained, "and if someone I knew from Iowa has a new story out."

"And you don't find it curious that these questions rise to your mind right after a session?"

"But the bookstore's right here!"

Again she allowed a silence to unfurl.

"Maybe it is significant," I conceded, pondering for the first time the physical sensations that possessed me at the magazine rack and while walking toward it.

For after a session I felt happy in a strange way. It was as if locked within me stood a garden with all sorts of stringed instruments that had just been blown across, zithers and guitars and recumbent pianos, and the music was still echoing in my ears. Every last event in life chimed with internal rhymes—if the parking spot before her office happened to be taken, if the coffee in the Texaco station was bitter and too strong. A pleasant disorientation charmed me and I felt connected with something good about which I nevertheless felt suspicious. Harriet's separateness from the rest of my life made me wary. It was like the covert pleasure of a drug. Could I trust the joy she imparted? Was it based on anything real? The street shone a steeple white after the cloistral shade of her office. The sky scrolled Wedgwood blue. My feet carried me along to the bookstore as if in a dream I hated to be roused from, and here in my hands was the rival's book to rouse me.

"Do you always go to the bookstore after your session?"

Harriet's question lingered in my mind, slowly awakening me to envy's lure. I began to notice envy's addictive qualities, its paradoxical satisfactions. I'd written an essay on envy once, and it became the cornerstone of the book I was finishing. But that essay now struck me as just an introduction to this feral predator. It was as if before I'd just glimpsed the clothes the bogeyman wore, whereas now it was possible to track his comings and goings and provide a precise description of his face.

I wrote out my new understanding one hot afternoon at my desk overlooking the high Boxford meadow with its blaze of black-eyed Susans and loosestrife. I took as a reference point the very first life I made for myself as an adult:

I came up to Boston to become a writer when I was twenty-one. I rented a cheap room on Garrison Street, which was then a little block ending in a rent-by-the-week hotel with bordello terraces. A red-haired

actress occupied the biggest room in the apartment and the one far-
thest from the street. She woke at noon and toasted an English muf-
fin with peanut butter on it. The other apartment-mate, in the mid-
dle room, was a dancer. She lived downstairs with her boyfriend, so
the house was quiet all morning long. I sat at a big industrial metal
desk that engulfed half the room and wrote until I smelled the peanut
butter melting. Then my alarm clock erupted, and I rushed out the
door.

I was working on an interminable novel about a ménage-à-trois.
This novel would haul me in every morning like the embrace of a big
ape; I would get lost in it. It went on and on, page after page of yellow
legal pad full of all my favorite words and emotions.

Since I'd never written a novel before I had no idea how long a
novel should be. All I knew was that novels were very, very big. So I
had no qualms about getting enthralled in my story. The peanut but-
ter smell drifted in, my alarm clock buzzed, and I ran out the doorway
toward the Copley Square T.

I had to walk through the Prudential Center, a great big gateway to
the city. Every afternoon I felt an urge to go into Brentano's to look at
a particular book, and I almost always surrendered to this urge.

The book was by a woman my age and had just come out to rave re-
views. This woman was now famous. And her book looked beautiful:
set in the Caribbean, it seemed awash in sunlight and opulent trop-
ical flowers in colors like fuchsia and orange and egg-yolk yellow.
On the back was the author's photo. How composed and lovely she
seemed!

As I slid the book back on the shelf, my hand felt numb and tingly.
My whole body seemed robotic, hollow, scooped out by envy. I felt . . .
unreal. Then I continued on my way to work. All the excited, thrilled
feelings from my own writing were banished. When I set my shoe on
the sidewalk it was just a strange, dull, faraway shoe. Soon I was en-
closed in my airless office, filing away insurance forms.

What is envy? Why does it have such a violent impact? And why
did I, for instance, experience such a strong desire to go in and look at
a book guaranteed to give me a bad feeling? Every compulsion, after
all, has its reason.

When I read the book I envied, it was because I wanted information on who was out there and how good she was. I would read fast, feeling ill, with my body braced as if to say I can take it, I'm taking it. And while I was reading, a switch happened. Instead of being adrift in the mood my own novel was conveying, instead of being immersed in its story and vocabulary, instantly my own work became flat and strange, boxed and distant.

It was like having a crush on someone else's husband. The more I admired this other book, the more my own seemed dull and limited. When I looked askance at my own book, with envious eyes, it shrank, while this other woman's book became saturated with all sorts of beauty.

Envy is being unable to digest the satisfying things that do come one's way. The smell of peanut butter drifted into my room, alarms went off, and out I ran. The aroma of the delicious, caloric, rich food I didn't allow myself set me running.

Envy feels, most of all, like somebody has stolen something from us. I was meant to be the special daughter—but look, someone else has swiped my position. I was the girl who loved Virginia Woolf; but look, whole seas of other girls did, too. Freud wrote about the desire to topple the father. For me, it had to do with the sister who, like Goldilocks, sat in my chair and slept in my room, a few inches from my own bed. I wanted to swipe back what I felt she'd stolen. The feeling of specialness, of imaginative celluloid green spangles and silver triangles and sequins, restored to me. The coat of many colors, all mine.

The hollowness of envy is due to the feeling of something being swiped: one's own inner self—gone! You are just air in a dark dress. No longer can you love what was inside—your own idiosyncratic images and gardens. It is charred, scorched, written in soot. One incinerates one's own self, striding up the street on the way from the bookstore, because to whom could one talk about this voracious envy? How could you ever share it? It's bound to set off alarms. "You want that?" the other person will ask. "You feel envious because you want that? Well, who are you to aim so high? Shut up about your ambitions! After all, here I am in the office next door, filing life insurance policies."

When I stopped in at the Prudential bookstore (my gateway to the city was a monolith to the desire to be prudent—a tower built of insurance premiums) what was I looking for?

I was most susceptible to my urge to go into the bookstore when I was feeling good from writing. The good feeling from writing gave me a sense of being strong, and I felt I ought to do something with my strength. Now that I was strong I had no excuse for not looking at that other woman's book. It was an attraction like magnets: I felt positive, the book was negative to me, but I felt an almost Puritan obligation to learn from it what I could.

What I wanted to learn from it was, do I have a right to feel good about myself? Am I being a fool to feel good, considering what I just wrote?

Because in fact, striding out the door to my afternoon job I felt good, elated, euphoric, almost heliumish. This is certainly one of the secret pleasures of writing. A friend of mine once said that after she wrote, she noticed things like the way the grass is sprouting between the dust tracks on an old road. That's how she knows if she's had a good writing day: the hay color on the tipped stalks is more vibrant. The way the unmown green path sways slightly between the beaten tracks is more particular, something she's never seen exactly this way before.

When I was a girl we talked about other girls who were "really conceited." I didn't want to look like a fool or conceited, arms flung out like Ethel Merman, hogging the stage. My urge to look at another woman's book was due to my absolute need to get rid of my own strength. At the MacDowell Colony a woman who was an architect, playwright, performance artist, and scholar told me before hopping on her emerald bike and cycling away, "I think I do so many different things so nobody will envy me." That is, if she spreads herself thin enough, and she was extremely thin, she would never attract envy. A friend of mine's mother used to tell her growing up, "Don't take yourself too seriously." But how should one take oneself? As a joke? As a bit of decoration for the world?

The first time I ever acted was as the Cheshire cat. I was supposed to be invisible, except for my smile. Everyone else in the cast had a cos-

tume. I wore the bright goldenrod Camp Len-How T-shirt and blue shorts, and walked across the grass stage grinning as broadly as I could. "Smile bigger!" whispered my counselor very loudly. I was embarrassed. This was as big as I could possibly smile. My cheeks were cracking.

Writing has to do with giving up the Cheshire cat smile. That is another of its secret pleasures. But it's scary. A lot of us since we were children were coached "Smile bigger! Don't take yourself so seriously! Don't you dare inflict on me the pain of envying you! When you get good, spread yourself thinner! Don't be too substantial. Because if you are, I'll knock you down. So keep smiling, just the way I am."

I stopped in at the envy store to protect myself. I destroyed myself to protect myself. I made myself unreal to counteract the vivid aliveness I felt from writing and which I associated with being foolish and exposed—the child with her hand up, oh call on me, call on me, desire all over her face.

It's our own desire we mostly feel ashamed of, after all. Why? Because it's at that moment we are most unguarded, most on the cusp of pleasure, strolling along, noticing the stalks of crabgrass pushing up between the cracks of the pavement, the blue wild carrot in a little tuft by the apartment building wall, that we are afraid we're being foolish, in love with life, with our own lives, as if there's something better to love, as if we weren't meant to love all this.

I set my pen down and blinked at the skeins of purple loosestrife in the high meadow.

What interested me most in examining the journey into the city, I suddenly realized, was the moment of transformation, of lingering in the gateway until I'd switched from being infused with the feeling of my own book to feeling a distinct deadness that allowed me to step out among other people.

Why dispatch with one's good feeling? After all, feeling at least minimally good is what enables us to write or paint or return phone calls or simply get out of bed. Some of us take excellent care of our good feeling, I thought. But others obey a compulsion to destroy what we've hungered for, as if we were phobic about it, as if this thing that we imagine would make life most worthwhile—a particular joy and confidence—is too frightening. We treat our gold like poison. Why?

The question itself was a discovery from which it seemed important not to hasten with too quick an answer, like slamming the cage shut on a lion. I wanted to get quite close to the lion. I wanted to see how his whiskers were attached to his cheeks and to smell his breath. What had he been eating? How old was he? Why did he so transfix?

Then one evening a week later I realized I had a different story concerning envy. It had to do with Kate. This story had a happy ending and pointed in a new direction:

When I was eighteen years old, I lived in Spain. One day I heard a woman step through a door saying, "I am a writer." I caught the door and rushed in behind her. It was as if she'd sprayed perfume in the air; I must pursue her. I was so many years from being able to say the same thing myself. How did one become able to claim this identity? Soon this woman and I became best friends.

Kate flew off to the Iowa Writers' Workshop a few years later and a letter arrived back written in blue ink like a flash flood. She was living in a storefront among cornfields fifteen miles out of Iowa City. She had an old green Nova she drove barefoot. Sundays she hosted a brunch to which poets came. She baked scones and brewed strong coffee, and all the poets brought something to eat. Her writing had improved by a quantum leap, she said. I should come, too.

But what did this mean, for a person's writing to improve by a quantum leap? I had no idea. I didn't even understand yet that there were better and worse things in writing. And partly because I didn't understand it, I was entranced by this idea of a quantum leap. I believed that the only place where you could get the leap was Iowa.

When I arrived the next year, I unpacked my suitcase into a studio apartment that Kate had found. It had a tan vinyl couch imprinted with paisleys and a blue-and-brown rug stiff as a toothbrush and a big glorious view of a grassy playing field. That first weekend Kate took me shopping. The supermarkets were far from town, and I didn't have a car. Strolling the aisles of the Hy-Vee, we turned a corner.

"Mugs!" cried Kate. She stopped before a display. "You can use some. They're only ninety-nine cents."

"But they're all so ugly!" They were mustard and burnt brick and black and a wretched olive.

"Oh, do you think so?" she said, smiling. "Well, if you were going to choose one, which would it be?"

I shrugged, considering the awful colors. At last I chose a Mexicanish yellowy orange.

"Ah," she said. Then she lifted her hand, and set it down on a sky blue mug, which instantly was the most beautiful mug I'd ever seen. Robin's egg blue, the exact color of Kate's eyes. I bought it immediately.

Every morning before I wrote I fixed a pot of coffee. Then I opened the cupboard and there was the exquisite blue cup saying to me: "Kate's aesthetic is better than yours. Her sensibility is more refined. Yours is earthy, clumsy, ethnic." And the novel I was about to work on that morning seemed as garish as the yellowy-orange mug which my hand had reached for first. My story was set in the Bronx, and was full of fire escapes and claustrophobic apartments, which seemed somehow less worthwhile than the gardens of Kate's Fairfield, Connecticut.

One morning, eight years later, I mentioned all this to my friend Mark, with whom I was talking by phone. "It's so beautiful," I said. "And I still get a kick out of the fact it cost only ninety-nine cents."

"But, darling," he said, "you can't afford that mug!"

So I carried that mug outside of the house. This was the first house I'd ever owned even in part. I lifted that mug high in the air and flung my arm down as hard as I could and let go. The cup shattered into dozens of pieces. Instantly my spirit felt free.

Then I plucked up all the pieces I could find so as not to puncture my car tires when I drove in or out. But every now and then I saw a blue needle glinting in the lawn, and what that needle told me was: "Your own way is good. Your own stories are valid. No more idolatry!"

One day a few months later I stepped out of my car and found my-

self staring at a sliver of sky implanted in the lush green grass. It oc-
curred to me: Where did the beauty of Kate's mug come from in the
first place? Who put it there? And if one can find the good in others'
possessions, isn't it possible to find the good in one's own? How to
begin?

I walked across the grass and plucked that needle up and set it on
my desk. Its blue seemed as exquisite as ever. But it was mine now as
well as Kate's. I was stitched into the story, too. The needle lay like
a piece of the empyrean, as if the heavens were a mosaic of which
I'd chipped a sliver. Begin right here with this, I told myself, and I
thought about how I'd pursued Kate and how she'd welcomed my pur-
suit, which started in the Bronx among fire escapes, and whose end
was nowhere in sight.

Something bothered me about the story, I realized, describing it to
Harriet. It culminated in an act of violence, as if I wanted to smash
Kate. Well, I certainly wanted to smash Kate's hold on me. And it
suddenly occurred to me that my urge to break Harriet's hold was
identical when I walked to the bookstore after my session: it was a
desire to be restored to myself, to gain myself back even at the cost of
having to surrender magical pleasure.

"You know, you actually remind me of Kate's beautiful cup, Harriet," I told her. It was an afternoon in late July. I was sitting in the
Boxford kitchen, the phone to my ear. "The cup you remind me of
is lovely, but it would have a lip like a blade."

"Really?" said Harriet.

"Oh yes. Sip from it and you bleed."

"But why?" asked Harriet. "Why does it hurt you to accept from
me?"

"Isn't it obvious?"

I listened to her breathing on the other end of the line. "It's what
you're always telling me."

Still she was quiet, listening.

"You've been right all along," I remarked. "Now, what is it you always say?"

"Are you teasing me, Bonnie?"

"I just want you to say it."

"What?"

I laughed. "Envy."

"But why would you be envious?" she asked.

"Because I still need you so much," I said. "Because when you give to me it makes me feel my need for you even more. It makes me feel out of control. Think of why the anorexic likes to preside in the kitchen and bake her family all sorts of cookies and cakes."

"You would like to cook for me," she said.

Tears sprang to my eyes. I loved her! "Yes."

What was really so very compelling in my rivals' pages? After a good session with Harriet I felt as if I'd acquired a protective bliss and a euphoric mental distance. The rival's work sliced through the anesthesia-rich happiness. It cut. And it took from me a joy that seemed suspicious, illicit, misleading, foolish, and dangerous.

While I stood at the rack before locating a rival's work, a certain impatience grew. An anxious restlessness. For in fact the joy with which Harriet imbued me made me feel dazed, ever-so-slightly numb, like the novocaine shot that makes your mouth a blow-up mouth, a rubber mouth, a mouth belonging—it seems—to some-one else. Who? The dentist? And so one bites that mouth, first ten-tatively, then a bit more savagely. From far away comes a tintin-nabulation of pain. It's as if the wall is having the sensation. Then the pain steps closer. At last it is somewhere near the vicinity of your mouth, although it is still a bloated mouth, an obscene dream of a mouth, yet at least this mouth is attached to you, although with strings of pain. After Harriet, my whole being was somehow that big fat mouth. Although I didn't quite realize, of course, that I felt this way.

Still, reality was what I wanted, not delirium. I stood in Harriet's Oz, missing home. "Let me see . . ." I muttered as my hands moved about in the book rack.

An atmosphere of curiosity possessed me. I was finding some-thing out. I was discovering something. What would happen if I brought my joy to the bad place? Could the joy withstand it? Was Harriet's viewpoint strong enough? Could it endure exposure to my rivals?

My question was sincere, and yet I was carrying it to a place where it could receive only a single mechanical answer. I seemed not to know what that answer would be. But how could the answer I found here be anything but "no"? That's all rivals' work ever said to me. If a particular work struck me as mediocre, I continued to search until I found the sparkling story or book that provided the sensation toward which I quested. Yet I actually seemed to believe that for once I might hear "yes." It was, in fact, my *real* wish— past the urge to hear no, the fantasy of yes. Ah, the repetition compulsion in all its regalia of feather boas and body piercings: rushing to the place of No craving to find Yes.

And I was also punishing Harriet for ending the session exactly how I'd craved, with a display of interpretive fireworks. Days and days stood between this session and the next. Sweet bewilderment, after a good session; a tide recedes, marvels slip away. At least, in pain, my body was *mine*. My enemies' books returned me to myself. Stuck on them, I was as I'd long known myself to be: the child wearing trees caught in a blue storm. To feel better was to feel alien. Harriet filled me with an odd joy I reflexively expelled. She was a surrogate mother, a taboo mother, feeding me what my own mother chose not to, traif notions. Would a good daughter run to a cheater mother? I gulped what she gave and spit it right out.

My rivals exorcised Harriet. I sought my multiple small idols to cast this big idol out. *This* is real, I instructed myself as I held a rival's book in my hand. "Account for *this*," I silently declared to Harriet, as if the envied object would transfix her as it transfixed me, as if the glorious sight of it must surely convince her that I was stupid, worthless, that in fact *it* was more important than I was (the implicit message of treatment: the person is more important than whether or not he or she produces ideal behavior). Could she behold the rival's object and find me undiminished? Could she look at someone else's perfect magic and still find me good? I behaved toward my rival's book as if it were a cross raised high, the very sight of which would convert Harriet and make her to declare, "You're right!"

Although in fact I would have been sickened by her defeat.

To my surprise, Harriet remarked: "It's so hard for you to talk about envy." I stared at her. Was she out of her mind? The days by now were so long they seemed to last forever, the hours taped into a brilliant Mobius strip. Paul and I ate supper beneath a gluey-white August sun impaled straight up in the sky.

"Hard for me to talk envy!" I said to Harriet. "Sometimes I think it's all I talk about."

"Envy between us."

I nodded. "It's funny—I felt so much envy yesterday I had to go to bed early. I couldn't stand it. You wouldn't think that the week my work was chosen to be in two different anthologies"—as it had—"I'd feel like this. Strange, isn't it?"

"Tell me about the envy you felt last night."

"Well, in the evening I was sitting in the bedroom with the air conditioner on while Paul worked. I was reading the *New York Times*, an article about what they called 'starter marriages.' They quoted a woman my age who has a novel out. She decided to get a divorce after she went to MacDowell and realized she was happier there than she'd ever been with her husband. She said she'd been resolute about getting a divorce even though it's suing your own family. It seemed so impulsive of her, to pursue this divorce. And that was one of the things I envied about her, that she just went by her gut."

An image flashed into my mind, a girl, a child, masturbating. I blushed, and told it to Harriet, adding: "I don't see what this has to do with envy."

"Tell me more about the image."

"Well, it's of a girl touching herself between the legs. But she's appalled. Her genitals seem excessive. Too womanish. As if she's gotten someone else's body part."

"The experience of being engorged—you resist it," said Harriet. "This is how come you feel such envy. Envy flourishes in you because you don't let yourself feel excited. Imagine how you'd feel if Kate were going to be in these two different anthologies."

I laughed. "Oh, I'd want to kill myself."

"The only way you can feel this excitement is vicariously: by imagining Kate's excitement. But you're Kate."

I shook my head. "How? How am I Kate?"

"You're going to be in these two books."

"My pleasure sent my mother running, once," I said. "It feels connected to all this."

She turned her peacock-blue eyes to me. "When?"

"In nursery school. My mother was visiting—the mothers took turns—and the teacher asked us children to march in a circle in a parade. Instruments were distributed—the yellow plastic recorder, the xylophone, even the beagle that wheeled its legs and quacked. The worst instrument, I thought, was the triangle: so boring. But worse even than that—not really an instrument even—were the grooved red sticks. These were distributed when the teacher ran out of real instruments. We started marching. Children were striking the triangles, shaking the tambourines, and I was hitting my two red sticks together, when suddenly my mother said, 'It hurts my ears.' She covered her ears and ran out of the room. I felt stricken. I wanted to protect my mother."

"From your pleasure."

"From the loudness."

"Ah."

I was thinking, however, of how my own mother truly felt devoured. The more her children consumed, the more fragile was the structure of her very own self. Our eyes were chisels and our mouths saws. We'd chewed down to the very frame. To preserve our mother, she must push us away. We must try triply hard to be good. Take as little as possible. Take less.

"One other time comes to mind when my pleasure hurt my mother," I said. She'd been reading aloud to me—the one time I can recall, in fact, when she ever did. We'd walked to the Francis Martin library and checked out *The Cat in the Hat*. At home we sat close on the couch and she turned to the first page and began. What joy! I could scarcely believe it: all this attention, for me. She read five pages, then exclaimed, "My throat's so dry! Oh, you have no idea how it dries your throat to read out loud." She stood and walked swiftly out of the room. The white door swung back and forth on its hinges. But I'd so enjoyed the reading aloud! Now I gazed at the flipped-open book, horrified. I considered the red, painful, raw throat about which I could have no idea. Poor throat! Why did reading aloud have to cost it so much? Even when my mother settled herself beside me, delight refused to return. A gong of worry had been set ringing.

My pleasure seemed "too much," I thought, lying on the couch. It parched my mother, made her disappear. Joy itself was dangerous. A burglary. So when I felt too good, I resorted to the stinging whip of envy. It returned me to an ancient mood. It restored my mother to me.

Envy felt like the most real thing I could bring Harriet. It was as intense as sex and even more commanding. I assumed that the people whose photos gleamed from flyleaves lived in a state of immersion, not absentia. That's what I really craved: the life where pleasure swelled you past your boundaries and nothing cut you down to size.

So it seemed crucial that Harriet could show herself proof against what mesmerized. If she could show that the sky blue mug doesn't warrant adulation, Kate's blue eyes flashing and cutting with their gloating glance: "Oh, really? Which would you chose?"

"You, Kate. I would chose to be you." If only Harriet could gaze at what transfixed and point out the mechanism that held me captive! If she could help to break my reverie! Then life would seem more important than performance. Happiness would seem safe no matter how beautiful the idols. One day the thing that said no would say yes, I believed. You never knew when that day might be.

"What does envy turn into?" I asked Harriet.

"Gratitude," she said.

* * *

One September afternoon as I was pushing off my sneakers I glanced up at the woman galloping across the wall. Hello, old friend! I thought with a sad smile. Are your ankles tired from pressing into your pony? Does your back hurt from leaning forward through all eternity? Is it cold and airless behind your pane of glass? Do you ever wish to breathe more freely? What a lot of work you've had to do, to carry all my envy.

Even my dragons are meant for me, I realized now. Their scales have my name on each panel. Their jackhammer roars bring a message to my ears. Even what seems to interrupt the story is actually part of it. Every place one disappears is significant.

I no longer rushed to the bookstore after my session. When I did step in, it no longer affected me as it had. Simply knowing its purpose for me had modified its purpose. Now what I read often made my palms eager to grab a pen and start writing. And I perceived that there was an everlastingness to my old envy. Each week the newspaper fetched up another rival. If it wasn't this one it was that. An unreality inflected all those I'd once envied, as if I'd half-invented them. I had something colorful of my own, my own iridescent Picasso room, my own intricate pavilion hung with fringed Tunisian curtains around a four-poster bed.

The people I admired were no longer set against the sky. I had my own way now, which wasn't theirs. It was neither good nor bad: it was real. Sometimes I strode up to the high meadow and lay down amid the wildflowers. It was September and everything up here rallied forth in one last sultry blaze—the black-eyed Susans with their tattered gold tutus, the Queen Anne's lace unraveling across the field. The world was extravagant with beauty. It wanted to be seen, but if it wasn't, that was fine, because there was always too much beauty to be seen, anyway.

Lying on my back, I realized that I just simply envied less. When once I would have lost a day to envy, now it passed in ten minutes. This was a change that, if Harriet had ever promised it, would have seemed preposterous, like being told I'd no longer itch when rubbed with poison ivy. These days I scarcely ever raced through tunnels of self-estrangement. Kindness appeared in many places. I could count up the gifts others gave freely all the time, at the supermarket, at the newsstand, in a feta cheese market on Atlantic Avenue in Brooklyn, at a tollbooth in Vermont. Is this real, is this real? I asked myself. And it was.

CHAPTER THIRTEEN

Please Get Up

One March afternoon when every inadvertent brush against the bushes released a glittering cascade, I noticed a white Airborne Express envelope peeping out from the side door. I set down my groceries. Could it be? Out of the envelope slid two hard-bound copies of my book. Wrapped in a beautiful spooky cover. My eyes raced over a page or two, and I dashed to the phone to dial Paul. And all that afternoon I stood or sat with that book in my hand. Even while putting on a sleeveless black silk dress, I didn't release it; I set the book in my mouth, between in-bent lips, while I rucked up my dress and zipped.

"Congratulations, sweetie!" called Paul as he stepped in the house around six P.M. I clattered down the steps. He stood in the doorway holding a bouquet of irises, blue with egg-yellow centers.

"Oh," I said. "That's *so* nice!"

"You did it!" he said with a smile.

We drove out to the Steep Hill Grill where Paul ordered a whole bottle of champagne. The air itself seemed resinous, silty as halvah, and shimmering ever so slightly like the last instant on a carousel.

In the attic doorway two days later I stood smiling, biting my lips. Harriet was already in her chair, opening her yellow notebook. "Hello, Bonnie," she said in her usual calm manner.

With a flourish, I drew my hand from behind my back.

"Your book!" She grinned, and accepted it.

She gazed at the cover art. She carefully read the flap copy. I set the tip of my tongue between my teeth, waiting for her to arrive at the page where I'd inscribed: "All this would have been impossible without you." Finally her eyes lifted, and I was shocked to see them shine. Oh—so what we've done together has been real, I thought.

I've touched her. "Thank you, Bonnie," she said, wiping her smiling face with her hands. She set the book on the windowsill, near two silver cuff links with long pins.

"We've come so far together," I said, once I lay down.

"Yes."

The chickens looked shaped out of some framboise-infused whipped cream. "So much has come true because of this therapy."

I looked behind me. She was silent, nodding.

That weekend Paul and I drove to New York. My agent had advised me to visit bookstores and ask those not carrying my book to please order it. Early Saturday we stepped into the Shakespeare and Company on Broadway near Zabar's. "We have ten copies," announced the clerk after checking her computer. We found them stowed in a corner on the upper floor, under "Writing."

"Can't we please put the books downstairs?" asked Paul.

"I'll ask my supervisor." The clerk swept up the entire stack and toted it to a back room. She set it on a cluttered shelf, and shut the door upon it. "Tomorrow," she said.

Next we strode to the flagship Barnes and Noble at 82nd Street. Here too the book was consigned to the distant writing section — "as the publisher requested," a woman with a long yellow braid informed us.

"What? The publisher tells you where to put the book?"

"Exactly," she said. "They program it into the computer system. That way it's the same in every store."

Paul and I gazed at each other and shook our heads.

We'd just crossed the windy width of Broadway and were tacking east when the words "Oh, I feel terrible" came from my mouth. My knees did something funny. I found myself sitting on the pavement.

Paul stared. "What are you doing? Are you okay? Get up."

But the pavement was swimming around me. What an idiot, to spend so much time on a book no one's going to find, let alone read! What a lot of trouble for nothing! For it had somehow never occurred to me I was writing a book about writing. I'd imagined I was

writing a book of essays about life. What a nitwit! All that agoniz-
ing—for what? "I feel terrible," I moaned.

"Get up!" said Paul.

I was shaking my head.

"We're going right back! You are not going to give up! Now please
get up!" And he clasped his hand around mine and helped me to
my feet.

"What's the use?" I whispered, and trailed Paul, my face taut red
with shame at having to return.

Paul marched straight up to the blond clerk, introduced me, and
said: "Don't you think everyone who steps into a bookstore dreams
of being a writer? A mistake was made in assigning this book to the
fifth floor. Don't you think it ought to be downstairs?"

The woman picked up the phone and murmured to someone.
She glanced over at us. "Yes. Yes. All right," she said. She set the
phone back. "We can reposition it."

I smiled weakly at Paul. He raised his eyebrows. But on the pavement, he broke into a grin. "That's more like it! Now let's go back to
Shakespeare and Company."

By the time we left that store, the manager had offered to put one
book right in the window. We stood out on Broadway amid the bus-
tle and honks, the parade of strollers and bagel-eaters and a man in
a tux, and watched. "Thank you!" we called to the clerk.

"I don't know how I can thank *you*," I said to Paul.

"Tell me the next store on the list."

One Friday afternoon we checked out six books-on-tape from the
Boxford library, loaded the car with tuna sandwiches and apples and
a big thermos of coffee, and drove off for the book tour Paul had
planned. In Indianapolis, ninety-two people turned up; in Cleve-
land, eighty-seven. In Cincinnati, due to a flyer misprint, just one
person sat in a folding chair. She worked for the bookstore; this was
her day off. "Why don't I give you a private reading?" I asked. "Why
not?" she said. I sat beside her and read to her softly, and she nodded, curling her reddish hair behind her ear and smiling. One per-

son is an infinitude. Who did who the bigger favor? I was sure it was she.

"I won't ever forget you pulling me up off the pavement," I said to Paul.

Nor would I forget that in the months ahead he came to every single event. Even at a last-minute reading at 2:30 on a Wednesday afternoon at a Borders in suburban Rhode Island, Paul turned up, smiling in the back row. Gratitude overwhelmed me.

CHAPTER FOURTEEN

The Secret Smile

Something good was certainly happening. Food seemed more fabulous, especially healthy food. Cherry tomatoes and squadrons of juicy orange baby carrots, buttery leeks and snow peas and great jungles of kale shoved in a pot and steamed with garlic—why, I seemed to have just emerged from a winter of potatoes. Kohlrabi (I was working my way down the produce aisle), which cooked up into a quiver of splinters. Still: interesting. I envisioned a book that celebrated ordinary foods: the warm hard-boiled egg sliced in quarters and crumbly as halvah, slipping about on a saucer, a quartet of white gondolas. The blue-black crinkles of peppercorns, webby as tripe, dented, miniature asteroids, no two alike.

I scrubbed the windows with ammonia and waxed the floors. Everything glowed. One Sunday I sat cross-legged in my closet and sorted old shoes—vinyl loafers that Paul toted home from an ad shoot and which looked like big Ken-doll shoes (I'd adopted them for chores), cracked army boots, blue velvet high heels rubbed to a pearly gloss at the big toe, two right-foot black wing tips whose soles curled down like a sheaf of elephant tongues—all set in a grocery bag for the Salvation Army. It was as if I used to believe my efforts had the value of prayers to distracted gods, whereas now the world was responsive and my actions could make a difference.

One late summer dusk I lifted my head from *Nicholas Nickleby* and thought of Kate. I'd seen her in just such a position dozens of times—on a couch with a novel open in her hands, and I'd always coveted what I'd imagined was her rich sense of inner pleasure. Now for a moment the pleasure was mine. I have something another person could envy, I thought. A unique sensation, although of course I'd been reading novels almost my whole life and sitting on couches.

My eyes took in the sky blue couch fabric woven with pink bouquets, the heap of yellowed pages arching off the concave spine of the paperback. So many beautiful textures the world possessed.

"I saw where you got your Athena," I said to Harriet a few weeks later.

"Where?"

"Freud's house. Paul and I went to Maresfield Gardens. And I was standing in the gift shop—and there was your Athena! Among the antiquities of Freud's they'd copied. It made me so happy to see her there. Although it sounds funny to say, 'I saw your Athena.' Sounds like 'I saw your vagina.'"

"You had a very private viewing of me."

"I suppose."

And I thought, maybe that's what my gift to her will be when I'm all done: a wonderful antiquity from out of the gift shop catalogue. The Egyptian cat, perhaps, or the Victorian sphinx. And I exchanged a warm smile with the bronze Athena.

One October evening soon after this I noticed that I was no longer lonely. I'd been lonely for years, since my first fight with Stella—an incessant cauterizing chill. Gone!

I stood in the kitchen patting spinach leaves with a white tea towel. A piano quintet was on the radio and I could follow the progress of the melody. There it was! There! I recalled a night in Boxford when I'd lain in my orange coat on the couch clasping the writhing cat. She slipped off and I wept for no reason I understood. How long ago! The world no longer seemed frightening. It was no longer a ride in a dilapidated amusement park—the Teacups perhaps, but a black-market version, the cups pitching and clanking, my seat jerking to a stop then heaving in the opposite direction. No more. Now the cups smoothly executed their mysterious gyrations, looping in a minuet, sketching figure eights.

"I won't let the fact that the lawn next door is being mowed take away from the pleasure of talking with you," I announced that Friday, plugging my finger in my ear against the sound of the racketing machine. "I used to be so distractible!"

"You have less conflict in yourself about having your pleasure," she said.

"Could be," I agreed.

Paul and I had moved to Connecticut, where Paul had accepted a new job. The old one had managed to become routine without losing any of its stress. This Connecticut town wasn't made of forests. The houses sat in the midst of lawns like teapots on fresh tablecloths. Our new house was just an hour and a half from Manhattan, an hour from the Bronx. Sun skated through its rooms. It wasn't a brooding colonial like the last one, but a glassy raised ranch. So much light deluged in I had to cover the furniture so it wouldn't bleach. Our old house had always seemed to belong to the man who owned it before us. He knew the precise shade of Minwax needed to darken the color of the newel post and where the pets lay buried in the yard. This new house seemed entirely ours.

"You analyzed this so well," I told Paul one night, helping him to another piece of ginger-pineapple chicken and another half a sweet potato. Unpacked boxes still stood in the corners.

"I wanted you to have the house of your dreams, baby. But that other house had no garage or deck, and its living room looked straight into the neighbor's."

"Yup." I nodded my head, munching happily. He was right about that other house. It was a relief we hadn't bought it. "Really, Paul, you have an incredible ability to analyze a situation and see a good thing."

"Well, it's what I do for a living."

"Well, you do it really well."

He smiled back at me with those crinkly blue eyes.

"That's nice of you to say," he said, quoting my father with a smile.

Tree frogs throbbed in the backyard, an overlapping, flying saucer sound, one probing cry expanding inside the next. It occurred to me that the world was real to Paul in an altogether different way from how it was real to me. He believed that the information he read on a piece of paper could be used to change his own circumstances and other people's, too, whereas what I read on paper I expected to affect only other pieces of paper. Life often seemed like a mammoth sloppy play with lots of extra pages stuck in, intended to spawn neater novels. Things weren't quite real for me until they'd been reduced to ink. Things were real to Paul every day.

In Connecticut I jumped out of bed at six-thirty. "Come on out!" I yelled to Paul as he brushed his teeth in his fuzzy brown robe. I had coffee and the newspaper and fried eggs and sliced tomatoes and the radio all set up on the big round green metal table out on the deck. The neighbor's Russian blue cat slunk out of the woods, her belly brushing the long grasses. Often a floury thumbprint of moon was fading into the sky.

I had driven north to find a self, and I found her. There she sat in a stiff blue dress and glossy boots. But our new house made her a four-hour drive away. Perhaps I should find a new therapist, one in Manhattan.

"Switching therapists is like switching mothers," said Harriet.

I pictured a sympathetic woman blinking at me through oversized glasses. A nurse's uniform sticks up stiff as meringue on her arms and binds her body while she gazes at me below a rumpled brow, trying to understand what I'm trying to convey: the magical connection I'd had with Harriet. Who precisely was this coarse-skinned woman who sprang to mind at the idea of a new therapist? Anita stating perfectly rational, laudable sentences that made me less and less intelligible. Some dull nurse, trying hard but failing. She reminded me of certain nice ladies who'd been neighbors in Iowa, offering sugary cakes and weak coffee, their pocketbooks like little churches upon their knees. I felt overly intense in their company. Too hot and hairy. They'd corrugate their brows as they tried to understand me, but the more they tried to understand the more the words in my sentences spun like windmills. No, I would only be more sick in such a person's company. "It would take a long time to switch mothers," I said to Harriet.

"Yes."

"And you'd miss the old mother."

"You would."

So I made my peace with the long trip. I drove four hours to Harriet every other Friday for a two-hour session. In between, we spoke twice on the phone. I borrowed the longest books-on-tape the library had: *The Mayor of Casterbridge, Daniel Deronda, The Return of the Native*, dark blue boxes jammed with cassettes. I reached home so tired I hallucinated music coming from behind the curtains. So far I'd been in therapy five years.

More and more these days I collected glinting scraps to bring Harriet: observations I hadn't been capable of before, tributes to our work. For instance, before we visited my friend Becka, Paul and I impulsively stopped into a bakery and bought her a heart-shaped chocolate cake. She always ordered chocolate desserts in restaurants and savored them. "Thank you," she said when she peeked into the box. Then she strode the corridors of her rickety house all the way to the distant kitchen. At the far end of the kitchen stood an old yellowing refrigerator with curved edges. In an instant, the door was flung shut on that cake.

Once upon a time I would have merely felt disappointed. How fast she'd made that cake disappear! But now I thought: perhaps she needs to save the cake for later, to guarantee it remains hers, even if it means inadvertently spoiling it. After all, Becka stockpiles lots of things: tampons, coffee, jelly beans, Necco wafers. She laughingly calls herself a "hoarder."

"Maybe it's like me sticking the valentine purse in my drawer," I said to Harriet. "You know, it makes me happy to have actually perceived the moment Becka shut the door on that cake. Before I met you that moment would have been lost. I would have been too engulfed in my own response to really perceive Becka, to observe what exactly she physically did."

I glanced back at Harriet. She was going away on vacation. "You've given me so much," I said.

"And you no longer stick it in a fridge."

During Harriet's vacation, Becka came down from Boston to visit. My husband and I met her train. "Let's carry her bags," I suggested, bouncing on my toes as we waited on the platform. How cherished it made me feel when my friend Juliet took my bags! At last Becka emerged from the train, an orange knapsack strapped to her back. She heaved alongside her a giant oatmeal-cloth suitcase.

"Let me," said Paul, reaching for the suitcase.

"It's all right," said Becka.

"We'll carry it!" I said.

"Look, it's attached," said Becka sarcastically. She nodded toward her hand, which held the suitcase's handle.

I dropped a few steps behind. My right hand cradled my left elbow, and my eyes studied the pavement. How colossally stupid I felt!

But then I noticed. What an ancient sensation: precisely how I felt trudging behind my brothers to P.S. 26 in the Bronx. How quickly I'd been converted into a shambling, shamed child!

I shook my head and stepped up beside Becka, marveling at the shift a single remark can bring, and thinking how extraordinary—how very *interesting*—it was to fetch oneself back from a state of disappearance. Why, Becka had in fact *hoarded* her suitcase. And she'd responded with worry and aggression to my excitement. Had my excitement somehow seemed threatening?

At the Starbucks near the station, my husband said, "Please let me treat."

"Thank you," said Becka.

He and I ordered coffee. Becka ordered a double hot chocolate. When it arrived, she requested whipped cream with cocoa powder. "As if the double hot chocolate weren't enough," she said in a self-mocking tone as she accepted the oversized cup.

Her mix of stubborn desire and embarrassment struck me for the first time. Becka wanted all the good things, and why not? Even when someone was treating, she needed not to feel deprived. It was one of her guiding passions, amounting almost to a constraint. For years she'd been unable to lose the pounds she often said she wanted to lose, and she remained a large woman. In our high school English class, Becka had written compositions in pencil on double-spaced paper. Her physicist father wrote in the lines in between, corrections, suggestions about phrasing. "Stopping By Woods on a

Snowy Evening." What did it mean? Whose woods these are I think I know. . . . Her father's writing was a subscript and superscript to her own, gradually outpacing hers. Years later, she resigned from archaeology grad school with eight incompletes, all for unwritten papers.

"My problem is I can't organize my thoughts," she explained, but I believed she organized too soon, before her thoughts had half-emerged, when they were still knobby shoulders and staring eyes, and not yet ambulatory creatures. Her need for organization raged until all she had was perfect white potentiality and no grubby words. Her father's subscript and superscript ran invisibly ahead, and she added nothing to impede it, no tongue in its brass bell, granting it silent communion with itself. Without her raw material there was nothing to correct.

And yet the ferment of her mind! Her stubborn, precise appetite! In the morning in high school when I slept over she filled a tall glass with ice cubes and instant hot coffee, and a cup of whole milk, and spoonful after spoonful of sugar. She stirred the tinkling, crackling glass laconically, meditatively, and every now and then took a tentative sip. She added more milk, a smidge more sugar, rapt, getting the drink just right. Becka kept a hand on her pleasures. It consoled her to eat Sugar Baby after Sugar Baby while she worked. Butterscotches. Jelly beans. She put herself in the position of choosing exorbitant amounts but then being frustrated when they were exorbitant. A paradox bit at the center of her, just as it bit at the center of me. She was on the verge of disappearing. She hoarded herself. "As if a double hot chocolate weren't enough." Well, of course, it wasn't.

Perhaps I was presumptuous, ascribing my own interpretation to every little thing. But I finally possessed a tool that fetched me back from the antique malaise, the old plunges into invisibility. It let me perceive people when before I would get lost in them as if they were a hotel I'd moved into.

"I'm sure that Becka loves you dearly and she hates you just as much," opined Harriet.

She didn't look more tanned than she had three weeks earlier. She looked precisely the same in her trim white T-shirt and denim skirt over the usual boots. Had she spent her entire London vacation in a library? "This is why a long break is built into therapy," said Harriet. "So clients have an opportunity for breakthroughs. It's why therapists like to see their client every week all year long but then have a number of weeks apart. It allows the clients to consolidate what they learned."

I crossed my ankles. Claws like a cat's were clutching at my chest. "Harriet, I feel like you're taking my achievement away. As if you're saying that it was all your planning, these insights."

"I don't mean to imply that."

"And it feels as if you're trying to circumvent my anger at you for being away. Or any guilt you might have. As if you're trying to persuade us both, 'See, it's all therapeutic.'"

She sat silent. "Were you angry?"

"I was. But then I thought, I have Harriet inside me." I didn't look back.

"You were very excited to share your insights with me."

"Yes."

"And then you felt that somehow I was taking your insights away. Grabbing the glory. Intimacy for you feels burdensome. You want to be very close, thrilled by the intimacy, and to feel we are in complete agreement. But then you must go far away to feel free."

"It's you who went far away," I pointed out.

She was silent. Then said: "Do you see how much you've changed? In the beginning you idealized me and saw yourself as a *nothing*, really groveling. That's how you experienced *everyone* else. Then you experienced me as ruining your life, and you saw many mistakes and wondered if I were a good enough therapist for you, and Alice Miller started coming in a lot and you instructed me on Freud. And now you occasionally idealize yourself and me. But I can make mistakes without being a spoiler."

"What do you mean by idealize?"

"Well, the way a child thinks its mother is the most beautiful woman in the world. And she discovers she isn't. But in a way often she appears to be so, nonetheless."

I looked back at her and she smiled, and I no longer knew if she was beautiful or not. She was simply mine.

I was seeing more and more—and my greatest delight was to bring these observations to Harriet. The pleasure of the observations reached its climax at a writing conference in Madison, Wisconsin. I'd been invited to lead a workshop on Saturday afternoon. A woman named Nora led a workshop on Saturday night.

"You are everything in your dreams as well as everyone," said Nora. She was a pretty, pixieish woman with hair cut like a scalloped black bathing cap, resembling the Tropicana girl.

"For instance, if you dreamed that you were driving a car that was out of control, you would be the car as well as the driver. You might ask yourself, 'What does it feel like to be a car out of control?' It might be terrifying. And thrilling."

She lifted her slim arms, which rang with bangles. "There might be something in that fear you enjoyed. When I first became interested in dreams," she continued, "I was living in Cambridge. I went to the Harvard library to see what others had discovered. The only people who seem to have looked seriously at dreams were psychoanalysts. But they saw penises everywhere. Penises, penises! It was absurd!"

We laughed, forty-five women at big round tables. We sipped from tumblers of water and by now tepid coffee, and before we said good night, we were told: Ask yourself a question as you drift to sleep, and tell yourself you will wake up in the morning with a dream that holds the answer.

Next morning a woman named Tracy raised her hand. She said, "When I woke up I thought, oh, I wish I had Georgette's light pen. Then I could really describe this dream!" The light pen was something Georgette wore around her neck; light streamed out of its tip. She used it if she woke during the night, she'd explained to us, so that she didn't have to wake her husband. Tracy said she'd dreamt of a woman at a podium, and the following sentence was in her head when she awoke: "I have to ＿＿＿ to move forward." But what? What did she need to do? She'd dreamt a sentence with a blank in it, and awoke with the acute sensation of something missing.

"I dreamed about a finger being stored in a freezer," said Georgette. This finger, she somehow understood, was meant for her. It had belonged to a man she knew. A third woman interrupted: "I want my old nose back!" She'd had skin cancer and the surgeon had to remove much of her nose. Her new nose was much smaller than the old one had been, and although it was prettier, she missed her old one. "I want my old nose back," she said again, regretfully.

Is it Freud's fault all us women are dreaming about penises? I thought with a smile. In fact, I had to bite my cheeks to keep from laughing. But I didn't dare speak up: I didn't want to seem rivalrous with the leader. Still, I felt tickled inside. Wait till I tell Harriet! I thought. I myself had dreamt I was coming up through a lake but heard Paul's desperate voice roar, "Stay down!" A boat with a propeller overhead would chop my head off wherever I surfaced. Over coffee I wondered: When may I safely come up? Then I recalled Nora's words, and thought: When I realize I'm the powerboat as well as the woman holding her breath. And perhaps when I realize I'm Paul as well.

"Those dreams do seem phallic," Harriet agreed with a smile. She held her pen against her cheek and nodded. We were now in a private club; we saw things the same way. I murmured, "I might even write an essay about this workshop. I'd call it: 'A Penis of One's Own.'"

"Have you done a search of the psychoanalytic literature?"

"Why?" A queasy, sick sensation passed through me. "Is there something I ought to know?"

"Just wondered." And she vanished behind a cloud of analytic mystery.

But how smug she seemed! The inner smile was no longer ours, but hers. "Tell me what you're thinking about," I pressed.

"You tell me."

"Well, I'm thinking that you know something you think I should know. It's something that would actually make my insights seem puny, crude, and childish. But even knowing you possess that power, Harriet, I still want to write my piece, even if it's flawed and imperfect."

"Can you see how much stronger you are? How much more you can tolerate?"

I gazed slit-eyed at the scarlet lamp. "Yes." My eyes shut and then opened. "But I don't like you to point it out."

"Why?"

"In the very act of pointing it out, you reduce it. You make it yours." The warning in the dream rang in my ears: Stay down.

She was silent. Then asked: "Is there a way we can both be strong?"

"I don't know," I said. "It feels like I can be strong only with your permission."

"You don't want to need my permission."

"No."

"You want to take it into yourself."

"Yes."

"I want that for you, too. I want to give you that."

"But I don't want to take it from you." I turned to her with a smile. "I want to already have it."

"We wish to avoid the trap that already lies concealed in the appeal . . . that the patient addresses to us," wrote Lacan. "It carries a secret within itself. 'Take upon yourself,' the patient is telling us, 'the evil that weighs me down; but if you remain smug, self-satisfied, unruffled as you are now, you won't be worthy of bearing it.'

"What appears here as the proud revenge of suffering will show its true face—sometimes at a moment decisive enough to enter the 'negative therapeutic reaction' that interested Freud so much—in the form of that resistance of *amour-propre*, to use the term in all the depth given it by La Rochefoucauld, and which is often expressed thus: 'I can't bear the thought of being freed by anyone other than myself.'"

I copied these paragraphs into my notebook.

A trio of triumphant dreams arrived a few days later and I scribbled them into my notebook, too. They signaled a high-water mark. In the first dream I saw a mouse that had been scaring me for years in dreams. For once, I wasn't frightened.

I'd been in a room. Through a hole in the wall came the sound of scratching. Oh no, a mouse! Stay in, mouse! Out it ran, though — and was revealed, to my surprise, to be a gray cute unobjectionable thing, frightening only in its hasty, scrambling, desperate movements. It ran under some clothes bunched on the floor. In an instant, back it dashed. I threw a boot at it and chased it into its original hiding place in the next room. And awoke proud that I was no longer frightened by the mouse. I didn't want it, but its presence was really okay.

I fell asleep again, and saw dirt falling in Anita's room. She was being slowly buried. She couldn't help herself. The soil fell onto Anita's bed and in my father's room, too. We lived in some kind of rooming house, and Anita's room lay just below the attic, from where open sacks and yards of soil were sifting between the floorboards in steady streams. I resolved to clean this up. I would get my black plastic garbage bag and pack the bag full and dump it outside, working steadily, going in and out and up and down for as long as it took. Or perhaps when I got up there I'd find a broom. Then I'd brush the soil away from the cracks, aligning it neatly down the floorboards so it couldn't spill.

My method is absurd, I thought in the dream. A more efficient way would involve a bulldozer. But at least it was something. I'd clear the soil in my own way and feel how I was making a difference. In fact, I *was* making a difference.

In the last dream I walked into my parents' building—although it was far older than theirs really is—and stepped into the elevator with frightening, skinny men of various sorts. The elevator didn't go in the direction we wanted. It plunged, and we all thought, But there's nothing down there! Then I got it going upward merely by a strong thought of *up*, reassuring myself as I watched the old gray fabric-covered wires and pulley system (exposed in that antiquated compartment) that the elevator was safe. My parents rode it every day. It hadn't killed anyone. It was fine. I rode in the direction I wanted, with the scary people actually behaving themselves.

I felt quite happy when I awoke. Combating death, plunging into the blank ("The unconscious is that chapter of my history that is marked by a blank or occupied by a falsehood: it is the censored chapter."—Lacan), the dreams portrayed what was above, below, and to the side, like a tarot reading. In the last dream I didn't just plan to ascend, as in the powerboat dream, but actually did. The fabric-covered wires corresponded in real life to the cord of an archaic appliance my parents owned: an electric grill with red burning coils. It's a grill that's no longer manufactured, being such a fire hazard. Still, my parents use it several times a week. Because they are my parents and innocent, the grill poses no threat to them. Such is the absurd logic that seems to ensure their safety. Similarly, in the dream, if you believe the elevator cord will function, it magically will. One will be lifted on a frayed umbilicus.

The presence of the cord, I felt sure, indicated a nostalgia for my own old innocence, the time before I noticed ambivalence toward loved ones. It was an innocence my parents still seemed to occupy. It works for them, why does it no longer work for me? I wondered. And yet I was seeing more than I ever saw (the cage of the elevator is open; I see inner greasy workings).

There's nothing down there, we all think. I paused, rereading the notebook. Who is this "we"? Aspects of the personality, saprophytic, mummyesque. We slip a horrible instant—but then the mechanism works, one is hauled up, toward the parents and life. The bogeymen do not rebel. (Each is skinny because just a shred of a person, an aspect, drained, soulless, the color of soaked skin.) I am bringing my complete self to my parents, even the ruffians in me, even the sullen exhumed hoboes, and it's okay. They will behave themselves because I exhibit confidence. It's a marvelous sensation, this confidence! You can loft up simply by discovering you have more control than you realized. It is tremendously satisfying, like teaching oneself to fly. It is all about belief.

"These are all dreams about men," said Harriet, to my surprise. "Even the mouse goes running into your clothes. You're interested in phallic imagery right now for a reason. Many analysts think the phallus is an emblem of being an integrated individual."

"Sexist as that sounds."

"Yes. You're getting in touch with the whole subject of men. You've been avoiding it for years. But in your dreams you're hoisting up men from below, you're talking about erections. Even though you would prefer them not to, men are coming into your treatment more and more."

"Oh, do you think so?" I felt like saying. I was thinking of Nora's remark: penises, penises, that's all these shrinks ever see! But I remained silent. Inside myself I was smiling, and I didn't want to risk my good feeling by saying a word.

"You look amused!"

"I am," I said to Harriet, and reclined in silence, for the first time ever merely waiting for the clock to say our time had ended.

CHAPTER FIFTEEN

Learning to Think

It began in Florida and scorched a path across my life. Granted, I hadn't really wanted to come with Paul on this business trip; my work was going well. And the grass down here spiked stiff as Scotch tape. Light collapsed as if from an opened sluice. A distant turquoise rental van eventuated toward the horizon ahead of us as we drove to our hotel—the only other traffic. Green signs the size of trailer homes swung overhead. The sky itself was like something you could vanish into, white and boiling.

Mornings Paul and I ate in a Perkins, wagon-wheel pancakes topped with fruit goo. The coffee blanched when I added milk and immediately established a film, like vanilla pudding. "Anything else I can get you folks?" asked the waitress, balancing breakfast platters the size of turkeys on her inner elbows. Voices smashed off the walls. "Just the check," said Paul.

Standing near the counter while he paid, I gazed at the carousel of cream pies, which rotated like those old solar perpetual-motion devices in lightbulbs, spinning mesmerically as if to Morse-code a message deep into the brain: You are happy, you are happy.

Afternoons we swam in lakes the blue of antibacterial beakers and which, viewed from above, would reveal you'd been swimming in Goofy's shoe or the frill of a cupcake. Anywhere you stood the water rose no higher than your chest. After a while we emerged to stretch our bodies on plastic chaise longues, eyes shut. Marimba music bounced through the air. The sun avalanched. It should have sounded like a mountain crashing down but of course sounded like nothing. It simply subsumed. An eternity later, we drifted into the hotel, T-shirts and shorts pulled over swimsuits.

The arrangements of couches seemed funny for no reason we could name. It was just, it was just, the mahogany-veneered vapidity

of this furniture, the surfaces to which no personality could adhere
—laughter simmered in us. The air conditioning slathered like men-
tholated cream. I drifted to the gift shop's candy racks. Such miraculous organization! Orange and yellow and red shiny packages arranged with not so much as a thumbnail's-width empty. "Can I help
you?" The clerk gazed above her outsized newspaper, which was
printed in candy colors. In fact, she herself seemed assembled from
those same candy colors with her teal eye shadow and sprayed yellow
hair, as if the newspaper had been Silly Puttied and stretched.

"No. Thank you."

Yet when I stepped out of the shop, I couldn't remember what
had been so funny. Paul sat on a dusty-rose couch, gazing at an
empty coffee table. The very air exuded a gloss of well-being, a waxy
ample jelly-donut glaze that coated my veins.

On Monday at seven A.M. Paul took a brisk shower, singing the
Toreador song, then kissed my cheek and strode off to his meeting. I
sat in the hotel room swinging my legs off the edge of the bed and
staring at the time bannered across the bottom of the TV screen until it was the instant to make my call.

"I didn't want to be here," I said. "I took this trip because Paul
wanted to."

I crossed my arms to force some clarity. "He really wanted to. I
didn't. My work was finally going well. I'd built up a head of steam."
Suddenly, I was close to tears. "Paul says I always turn a good thing
into a bad thing."

"Interesting!" said Harriet. "What you do with Paul parallels what
you do inside yourself."

"In what way?"

"You take away the good feeling—the excitement—from your
writing and blame it on Paul. You've got an oppressor inside yourself, and a giver. You became excited to write again, and if it weren't
Florida threatening your writing, it would have been something
else."

"Yes!" I exclaimed. "I was already becoming anxious about the
house construction across the street!"

When I set the phone back in the receiver, I felt infinitely better.

How lucky I was to have come to this resort! How much Paul had to put up with from me! Paul jumped when he saw me in the lobby. "Hi! Weren't you catching a noon flight?"

"I'm so sorry I make a good thing into a bad thing, honey."

"That's okay. Come to lunch." He swung an arm over my shoulder, and off we trooped.

Other conferees in the dining room wore chino shorts and pink, green, and yellow golf shirts accessorized with expensive watches. "My wife!" said Paul with a flourish.

"Glad you could join us," people hallooed.

The buffet had a Hawaiian theme. The table wore a fringed green plastic skirt and a majority of the dishes featured pineapple — an ingredient that, I recalled, used to constitute a "surprise" in itself: Stuffed Tomato Surprise, Surprise Cake. I speared a leg of barbecue chicken and a clump of salad sprinkled with coconut, although I couldn't remember the last time I'd actually been hungry.

Paul and I sat alone at a corner table. We smiled at one another, and then it was time for his next meeting. "You sure you want to go home?" asked Paul. "Why not vacation another few days? You're in a resort, after all."

I shook my head. And as I took my seat on the shuttle bus and gazed at the facade of the hotel, which looked like a giant dripped sandcastle, an operatic sorrow engulfed me on behalf of Paul, victim of my temperament. Yet seated on the plane, a shift began.

"If it wasn't Florida, it would have been something else," she'd said.

Well, actually, no.

I was not really as fucked up as all that. I disliked the fatality of her words, their predictive, jinxy, undermining quality. "Too quick to agree," I scrawled on a square tan cocktail napkin that I stuffed in my pocket.

I stared out the egg-cup window at the tarmac and crossed my legs in their pink shorts and sneakers. I tapped my foot. It occurred to me that I was simply transferring my irritation from Paul to Harriet. This thought pleased me since I expected it would obviate my anger, which blazed like kerosene.

But no. It made no difference. I opened up my small green note-book and filled the margins beside the session notes with refuta-tions.

"Bonnie," said Harriet early the next morning, "I didn't mean to deny your feelings about your self-attack," by which she meant Flor-ida. "And when I said that you made a good thing bad, I didn't mean to imply that Florida was necessarily good. Nor did I mean that you would immediately attack your writing, but that eventually you probably would."

Well, "eventually" is a long time, and "probably" a morass. I let the issue go; we were close again. I smiled and sighed, and glanced at my calendar to see my next appointment.

But the joy didn't last. Soon we disagreed over a subject where no explanation made any difference. The subject was the physical world and the disagreement was over the question: Is it real? Does it actually exist?

I'd become sick with an intestinal ailment on a trip to Germany. Back home, I was still not well enough to drive to Harriet. She didn't believe the illness was caused by salmonella, as the physician who'd examined me in Köln diagnosed. It was a symptom of rage, Harriet said. It didn't matter to her that I hadn't been aware of feeling the least bit angry or even vaguely miffed while in Germany. In fact, I'd quite enjoyed my trip. I recalled that the evening before my illness I'd dined on fish chock full of yellow mayonnaise at a restaurant along the Rhine.

"When children are constipated, it's often because they're angry," suggested Harriet.

"I wasn't angry. I ate bad fish!"

"I'm sure there was a physical component," she agreed. "That you did eat something that tasted good when you ate it but then, in-side you, poisoned you. And your body wanted to get rid of it."

Suspiciously metaphoric-sounding, all that.

"Every illness has a psychological component," she said.

"Even the Ebola virus?"

"I haven't examined the psychology of the population struck by it."

Nor did she believe that the sieges of flu that often occurred after my ten-hour trips from Connecticut (it was four hours each way, plus two hours for the session itself) were caused by these trips. She thought my sickness was psychological. She urged me to come north for my next appointment as soon as I was better.

That winter I careened from flu to flu, November, December, January, February: hunched on my living room couch nearly weeping with frustration as the sunlight waned from the brightness of morning to the violet of dusk, and it was Wednesday, Thursday, with still no work done, my hand curled around a sticky glass of OJ, a headache lodged behind my eyes. My doctor prescribed erythromycin and then Biaxin. Clumps of weeks fell away, a hemorrhage of time. Eleven or twelve days after the last trip I was energetic enough to drive to the CVS, and then it was time to drive north again.

"Don't you dare go up there!" shouted my mother. "Do you want to end up in a sanatorium? If you go up there this Friday, I don't want to talk to you again!"

I laughed. "It's all right, Ma."

"She's got you under her control! She's a monster!" said my mother.

"She wants what's best for me," I said gently, and hung up.

This was the second year of driving four hours north. I'd been in treatment for six years. Last fall I'd been so tired for so long I'd finally dragged myself to a specialist up in Danbury. "You've had Epstein-Barr," he said, setting aside my blood work. He stared at me with probing brown eyes, setting the earpiece of his glasses in his mouth. "How did you ever stay on your feet?"

Harriet's diagnosis had been "resistance" and I'd kept driving.

"Your fatigue is a way of punishing yourself from all you get from being in this therapy," she'd said.

"Yes, my illness does feel like a punishment." Hope dazzled me. Yet this interpretation, like the others, didn't stop the fatigue.

Mired in yet another flu, and remembering all the time I'd lost from driving north despite Epstein-Barr, I was irate. So much missed work! So much time spent turning the pages of Peter Gay's 808-page *Freud: A Life for Our Time* while sitting in my pink nightgown beneath the deck umbrella, the emerald grass sparkling below, listlessly waiting for energy. Odd details of Freud's life had haunted: the matching rings worn by the seven men in his psychoanalytic circle as if they were boys in a secret club. The piano his sister was forced to part with when Freud was a child since it interfered with Freud's studying.

I decided to fix on paper the sensation of the particular illness I was in the midst of. Perhaps this would force into consciousness the right way to understand it:

I'm not 100%. I keep vigil for the missing percentage in a nest of paperbacks, tissues, cats, and orange peels, afflicted by an acute awareness of the dust on the rug and the lolling yellow spiders of the unwatered spider plant. Is it because I touched my nose after accepting that five-dollar bill from the Stop & Shop cashier? Because I drank only one bottle of water on my long drive north?

"Deepak Choprah says people die only because they believe they will," says my friend Lucy.

But when I got sick with this last illness, I chomped garlic, swallowed C's, napped, strode the treadmill to alert my immune system, and really believed I'd get better.

"Yes, but maybe you didn't really, really believe it," Lucy answers. She's afraid my wrong thinking will get her sick.

"Your fatigue is resistance," my therapist says.

I nod. I think I know what motivates them: It's alarming, even repulsive, to believe certain things are beyond control. Lucy turns 40 tomorrow. My therapist doesn't like to know her treatment ever contributes to ill health. Or that there is anything immune to interpretation. The world is meaningful for her because she can interpret it, permeate it, make it succumb to her voracious logic. The part she can't infiltrate, wed, master—she refuses to know exists. But this part is a bell in my ears. I sit on the couch hearing it. I wish it would stop—this ringing like our family Zenith shrilled when the picture collapsed to just a white fading dot. Normally that ringing is a background sound subtle as my own breath. But now even when I'm asleep I hear it, piercing my dreams. The ears themselves sing, seashells glued to one's head. The body strikes its note, presses into visibility, rushes us toward who knows where.

My first terror coalesced during a childhood illness. My limbs glass tubes, I studied the dusk, which studied me. From the depths of the house behind me came the clatter of my mother cooking supper. Past my feet rose the Venetian blinds, which flashed with UFO beams sliding from right to left, right to left. Pitiless lights scanned the earth, feeding on us, a giant Xerox perpetually shooting. How innocent my mother seemed, clattering her spoons. And my father, out in the world, whistling as he strolled. At long last his key turned: "Hello, everybody!"

Wild relief! Which lasted just an instant, because the aliens, I recalled, lived in the house too, sucking electricity from lightbulbs that went dead, stealing my father's other shoe which, when it was found wedged sideways between the bed leg and the wall, blue with dust, merely confirmed that we were all prone to this jokester presence, even parents, even old people.

What is alien is what can't be appealed to, I always felt. No tuning fork exists inside to ring in sympathetic harmony. No information is ever enough for it; it scans and scans. I was an alien observing my parents, sometimes. My capacity for coldness dismayed me. I called "coldness" every unseemly emotion and compensated for it by a sweaty eagerness, an urge to infuse with closeness the air of any room I entered that contained somebody else.

To be ill is to be separate. Everyone is sick in his own way, sealed in his own skin. My husband drives off, the serviceman at Copp's Hill Shell palms the key to the Prizm (the belts need changing), my mother phones, and since they are healthy, they are rich as pashas, productive as Puritans. On the couch, watching the bellies of my two tabbies rise and fall, the big cat's rhythm slow, the little one's quick, I'm useless.

"I can't believe you're even thinking of going up there again this week!" cries my mother. "She needs you more than you need her. I'm begging you. Don't go even if you feel better by then."

"If you're not sick, you should be here," says the therapist.

My ears ringing like travel alarms, I watch those old enemies, the
cats, yawn, stretch, reposition so they are incredibly poised yin and
yang, their twined paws a bundle of fuzz. I've left my body and am
that missing percentage hovering, scanning the weary woman on the
couch. How hungry she is for me! How anxiously she awaits my pres-
ence, so eager to return where she left off! But even slaves—especially
slaves—dream of being masters and the invisible craves to appear.

I set down my pen. "She needs you more than you need her."
Could that be true? Surely I clicked with Harriet like a flashbulb in
its socket. Surely she instantly felt so right precisely because she resembled those best friends I've split with: the bossy ones, the willful
ones. Lost one after another until just she remained. What did she
scan off of my face?

Still, the thoughts I had with which she disagreed seemed unreal.
Anesthetized, fallen-asleep places. How to believe in myself when
she didn't? She *was* my belief in myself. Even six years into the
treatment.

My friend Juliet had once pointed out that to learn certain important things requires immersion, inculcation, the surrender of queru-
lous objection. Learning about love was like this, and (Juliet would
say) pre-med organic chemistry. "Let Jesus into your heart," say the
novitiates, meaning this same responsible surrender. I considered it
a strength that I could allow this immersion. My friend Becka could
not. She wore a silver watch and consulted it during her therapy session. Fifteen minutes before the end of her session, she liked to begin "closing up." She didn't like the sensation of free-fall, of diving
into an emotion so deep one is then left gasping. It was my capacity
to let the clock be sunk behind a Himalaya of pillows, I believed,
that had allowed therapy to alter me, the ability to let Harriet's words
shake me like a mobile.

But now I was vexed by the thoughts I had with which she disagreed. These thoughts existed in an etiolated way, resembling the
jellyfishlike lobes of an underwater plant, bloated, pallid. And this
sensation of unreality goaded. I couldn't leave our differences alone,
yet they seemed repugnant, the way I imagined the body's independence, its illness, seemed to Lucy. Nevertheless it seemed pure

stubbornness on Harriet's part that she refused to grant relief. Why wouldn't she concede what any sane scientist would?

"But do you actually believe your treatment with me makes you sick?" she answered.

"The drive does."

"Why do you think you are choosing this issue around which to organize your aggression?"

"Because it makes me angry."

"I think perhaps you're really angry at me for not objecting to you going to Florida and to Germany. Perhaps you wished I'd advocated more strongly for you not to interrupt your treatment by going on these trips."

"No."

"Fatigue is how you commonly express a psychological state," she hinted.

"I don't get fatigued when I'm depressed; I get sleepy. There's a difference. I can feel it in my body."

It felt almost willful of me not to collapse back into our old intimacy. I maintained a new rigid posture on the couch, back stiff, hands clasped protectively over my stomach.

"You've been in treatment so many years," said Harriet meditatively. "Only now do you find something about which to disagree. Don't you think it would be useful to understand why? And why you are using the body as a way of organizing your anger?"

For a moment, I could almost see a new possibility, a gauzy shape suspended in midair, a sugar-glittering architecture. Yes, I was thinking. What is it?

But she added, "What *exactly* about this conviction of mine about illness makes you so angry?"

"Ah! So you admit it's a 'conviction'!" I cried. "You admit it's a religious belief!"

She was silent.

"Paul studied philosophy," I continued heatedly, "and he once explained that something is defined as a religious belief if you can't think of a test that could possibly disprove it. Such a belief is called a 'blick.' It's neither provable nor disprovable. It inhabits the realm of religion. Harriet, can you think of a test that would disprove your conviction that every ailment is psychological?"

She said nothing.

"Even the Ebola virus, in your mind, has a psychological component, right?" I asked. "And by 'component' you don't mean an emotional reaction to being sick, you mean the stricken person's thinking causes the illness. You believe a mind-body connection exists but that it works only one way, that the mind determines the body, and never the other way around. But this conviction of yours is a blick, a superstition."

I stopped. Her question whispered itself in my ears. "I'm angry," I said slowly, shutting my eyes, hands still clutching each other, "because I know you're wrong but I don't believe it. You've given me proof. But apparently no proof is sufficient. You are a blick for me." After a moment I added: "I'm also angry because you won't help me set a date to terminate. And I want to terminate. I can't go on being sick like this."

"I think it makes you feel out of control to be angry. I think that's why you want to terminate."

"Yes!" I cried. "Oh, I do feel out of control. But it's because I want to look forward to a time when all this getting sick will be over, Harriet. The furthest away I can imagine would be in three or four months."

"Would you like to stop treatment at the end of April?"

My heart throbbed with joy. "If I had your blessing on it, yes. Oh, certainly! If you think I'd be ready."

But she replied, "Well, if you want that, then the work we do together would change. It would be the work of termination."

My stomach tightened with anxiety over losing my current connection with her. "When do you think I should terminate?"

"I can't predict that."

I gazed at the nonsensical shapes in the Picasso room.

"But let me ask you," she said, "how would you feel if we set the date?"

I smiled. "I would immediately be happier with you. More appreciative."

"You see?" she said. "You see what you would lose? The opportunity to be angry with me. To work through this 'negative transference'!"

"I just want to stop getting sick!" I screamed. Worry immediately sank into me like a claw. Was she estranged? Hurt? "I feel like apologizing," a leaden voice announced. And then, annoyed at beholding my old familiar tone of defeat, I said, mockingly, "This reminds me of what would happen after I said something truthful but hard to Janice. I would just pelt myself with apologies."

"As if to cancel out your criticisms. But isn't it a sign of how safe you feel with me that you can tell me all these things?" she suggested gently.

"Yes!" I cried. "Oh yes, it is! This is hard work," I said, to encourage her.

She nodded, considering.

Bliss wrapped me like a fur coat by the time I departed Harriet. At the convenience store I chose a carrot-cucumber-cheddar sandwich with honey mustard, along with a packet of Oreos and a Diet Pepsi. A merry feast! Yet as soon as I swung back on Route 95 South an objection sprang up. Why had she said our work together would have to change?

And then: Who exactly would change it? Why make this prediction now? Did she mean it to sound like a threat?

Fire blazed through me again.

The same thing happened two weeks later. I left Harriet's attic smiling, but an objection that had just obscurely shifted under me on the couch leapt up and filled the car with blades. She was reduced, damaged; just a sorry stump of her remained. Or she was a trick-of-the-eye painting and I'd approached too close; here was the grain of her, the sloppy brushstrokes. The long ride home and the entire weekend were surrendered to sick dismay and an oppressive fury. Watching *Masterpiece Theater* I rotated my aching jaw. On the walking machine at the gym I stepped faster and faster, my eyes locked on the gaze of the girl in the mirror opposite who strode more and more briskly in my direction until she was running.

On Sunday night, anger glued me awake. Nite-Nite tablets at midnight did nothing. Nor did two Michelobs desperately glugged after three A.M. At five I was glaring at the sky out the living room windows growing lighter, and shivering with frustration at the sloppiness of Harriet's remarks and their exquisite power over me. At ten she explained how I'd misconstrued her. She amplified her meaning to convey what she'd meant. I crammed the phone hard against my ear.

In just a month I'd become used to sessions in which I raced through my objections one after the other, scouring myself to make sure not even the tiniest cell of an objection remained. But now—oh, it was bound to happen!—I saw this pattern. And so her reassurance became impossible to receive. After all, I didn't want her to drown my objections like cats in a bath. They were attached to me, or perhaps I was attached to them. I did not want her to interpret away my thinking.

What bothered me most was that she almost never admitted she was mistaken and she never backed down. "Don't you see, Bonnie . . ." she'd say. It made me feel I saw her own raw personality gouging through. The elm out my window flashed silvery leaves like scissors. A thousand steel ballerinas twirled on one spiked foot.

Where before Harriet's meaning always seemed beneficent, now it seemed suspicious. Where before her words seemed static, something lambent and nice to carry home, now they seemed slithery, curling, rife with edges, silverfish, X-Acto knives. I was angry all the time. I understood this must be the way many people live their entire lives, hearts walloping in their chests, sandpaper rubbing under their skin. I needed it to stop. "How dare she?" I muttered, measuring Clorox for the laundry. "How dare she?"—walking down the aisles of the Stop & Shop. I craved a new kind of reassurance, only I didn't know what it would be.

"You're in a critical mood now, aren't you?" said Harriet.

I shrugged.

"You're being like an adolescent."

"Harriet, it's as if you think sticking labels on my behavior is going to finesse the accuracy of my perceptions."

"Did you ever rebel against your mother?"

I glanced at her through narrowed eyes. She knew full well I hadn't. Although I suddenly remembered, "Cleft in tush, devil likes mush," a shameful chant in my head when I was eleven.

"In other words," said Harriet, "she was full of shit."

My mother had stood at my brothers' closet, hanging shirts. She'd rapped once hard on the door with her knuckles and strode in. Her sudden presence in my brothers' room while we were watching *Hogan's Heroes* annoyed me. She seemed to be saying, as she clacked shirt hangers onto the rod, "I'm doing something worthwhile that you lazy people scarcely deserve, especially you, Bonnie, who ought to be up helping."

"Cleft in tush, devil likes mush," chanted a secret mocking voice in my head—put there by the devil himself. Hubert Humphrey gazed with his lunar, dolorous face from a poster on the wall, my brothers did mechanical drawings with number 3.0 pencils and four gradations of sandpaper, and I sat near them, an enthralled visitor in their club. Then my mother entered. It shocked me now to realize I'd been mocking her in my head. "How petty!" I murmured to Harriet.

"Some people feel a sense of power when they have a ridiculing thought."

"I don't. It seems childish."

"But the thought was there."

"Nothing to feel proud of."

"You're eliminating the reasons for staying in therapy."

"Am I? What do you mean? Eliminating as in excreting? Getting rid of?"

"No. I said illuminating," said Harriet.

"Do you remember when you first came to therapy with me again, I said 'If you commit yourself to this treatment, you will overcome this problem?' Well, I'm saying that to you again."

I worked my jaw. Her eternal solution: "Recommit! Get more treatment!" Besides, those *hadn't* been her exact words. Was it adolescent to notice? "You know, for once your invitation to get closer seems frightening instead of reassuring, Harriet. It's like the open black mouth of a devouring whale.

She laughed.

"Why did you laugh?"

"It's not very flattering, Bonnie."

"No. I suppose not," I agreed.

"Eight inches of snow by late afternoon," the weather service predicted. I'd called the long-distance number up in Maine.

Well, I could probably make it to Harriet before the storm, but snow would pile up fast all during my session. Then I'd have to battle to get to my friend Maggie's twenty miles away, and the next morning there would be the slog home, my fatigue exacerbated by the knowledge that Harriet was already snug in her own house. Instead of going up, I phoned.

"Leave aside the storm," she said. "Let's just talk about your resistance to coming up here."

I smiled as if she'd granted permission to have stayed home. Yet in a moment, as I tried to remain focused on my emotional "resistance," I realized her instructions just accentuated my guilt.

"See what a hard time you had not referring to the storm in discussing your resistance?" she commented.

"That's because the storm is *real*. And so was my sickness last week. So many others—my parents, friends, Paul—immediately see the punishingness and insanity of making this trip. I wonder why you can't?"

I also said, "I'd like to have a child, or at least to know if I want a child. I can't tell, while I'm in treatment. My energy is absorbed in being the child myself. I want to end treatment while I still have some fertility left."

"Have you and Paul considered adoption?" she replied.

Yet during the next session she surprised me. "The guilt-blame dance is one I've entered into," she offered. "Although you set the pace."

My head spun. So she admitted she'd been blaming! Yet in an instant, I was even more incensed: What right had she to be blaming? How dare she make me suffer for her neurotic needs! Wasn't it enough to suffer for my own? And why claim that I 'set the pace'? Wasn't this just another smoke screen to make it seem my therapy was always therapeutic? The scariest thought, though, was that I'd been right. I'd seen one mistake clearly. So what else had I noticed that she still refused to acknowledge?

I remained furious to my bones.

"I know from my own personal experience how useful it is to work through the negative transference," she said. "Once you work it through you will feel great relief."

I lifted an eyebrow, turning over her words like the dummy hand in bridge.

"I hope this has been one of the most honest experiences of your life," she said. "I am always honest with you."

Well, I didn't know the point of my therapy was for her always to be honest. I believed the point was for her to act with my best interests in mind. And why was she telling me about her own experience in psychotherapy? Until now she'd practiced abstinence. Why change the rules? And look how seductively she still appealed to my old weakness for a transformation. "How useful it is!"—why, the very vagueness of that phrase was an invitation to construe all sorts of benefits! It pandered to my old sweet tooth for a fabulous alteration.

"Are you waiting for me to announce that I'm leaving, Harriet?" I asked one day. "It's occurred to me that that's what you're doing: waiting for when I no longer require your approval. Then you'll give it. Is that right? Is that your strategy?"

"I'm not playing games," she replied dryly. "I'm certainly not waiting for you to say 'I'm leaving, I've decided'—so I can congratulate you. My question for you is two-pronged. The first is, do you have a feeling for what I mean when I talk about working through the negative transference? And secondly . . ."

But I couldn't hear any more. I was too busy wondering why she aimed a two-pronged implement at me. And a few minutes later when she spoke about "assertion—slash—aggression—slash—power," all I could think was: Why is her mind full of slashes? She's never expressed herself in slashes before. Why, she seems to be mirroring me, returning hostility with hostility. Yet hadn't she promised to return my anger as something else?

But even now I half-hoped she would dissolve all my objections!

"Even if you lived five minutes away," she said, "and therapy were not expensive, I think you'd have a hard time staying in now. Because you want to take something from me, you now have the experience of me removing something from you—this coming week. But it's all turned around. In fact, you want to take something from me—what you call 'permission' or 'approval,' what you called up and asked for when you were anxious that it wasn't 'okay' with me to argue. This is the phallus. You want to know how you can have it."

"It's true that you have something I want." I nodded. "Approval about my choice of when to leave. I feel like if I have it, then I won't have to suffer so much from missing you after we say good-bye. I won't have to worry I made a mistake. Whatever you call this sensation of benediction, it's true I want it."

My insurer no longer paid 80 percent but just 50 percent of her fee. Recently I'd been sitting at the kitchen table rolling loose pennies and nickels from the heavy wicker basket in which Paul dropped his change at night. In fact, I could afford this month's bill only because Paul had loaned me the money, which he'd done because I was so anxious. After that, I'd have to wait for a check due from a magazine. I told Harriet that at my next session I'd like to discuss the new economic situation. And on the drive up I thought and thought about the issue of payment. In an uncharacteristic surge of decision, I resolved to tell her the unpleasant facts without begging or mewling.

The instant I lay down on the vanilla couch I said: "I'm sorry, but I'll be paying next month's bill three weeks late."

Many interesting and disturbing behaviors followed this unprecedented announcement, which I later inscribed in my notebook:

1. *"What makes you think I can afford for you not to pay me on time?"* she inquired in an emphatic, steely tone.

I observed in retrospect that she employed a therapeutic locution to cloak a punitive comment.

2. *Her phone rang during my session.*

In seven years of treatment this had never happened. It wasn't the sort of event I'd usually inquire into, yet it was precisely the sort of thing she would, insisting "there are no accidents." So I asked.

"You were a little late," she said, "so I turned on the phone and when you came in, I forgot to turn it off."

As if this explained anything! Why did she "forget"? "I've come late many times before," I said, "yet the phone's never rung. I think you were angry at me even before I walked in because I'd said on Monday that I wanted to talk about money. You are all stirred up." (This last being a favorite phrase of hers to describe my state of mind.) "You unconsciously planned a way to let my session be interrupted." Which was remarkable only because this therapy was predicated on the presumption that she brought a calm, thoroughly analyzed self to my treatment. This presumption constituted the entire basis of her many cool perceptions of me.

3. *"You are trying to figure out,"* she said, *"what would keep me from being withholding."*

Certainly she meant "generous"? Was she herself trying to figure out what kept her from letting me perceive her as withholding?

4. *When I brought up the subject of noise from the construction across the street from my house, she announced, "I'm going to break the frame."*

She gave me a piece of advice, something she'd told me therapists do only at the expense of their patients. "Why don't you get a sound machine?" she said. "I'll look it up in a catalogue." As if I couldn't have thought of this practical solution. As if she herself now despaired of relief through interpretation! And after the session, while I squatted in her colleague's corridor and examined the chimney of a sound machine she'd directed me toward, and which emanated a steady *shhhhhh shhhhhhh*—Harriet's voice exclaimed: "Oh good! You found it."

I looked up, amazed. There she stood, in her glossy boots and shining white shirt. In all my years of treatment, this was just the second time she'd emerged from her office after a session. The first was the session before, when she appeared at the top of her stairs to accept the loan of a book rather than await me in her office. All this "breaking" of "frames" conveyed the sense that she was out of control, jumpy, and eager to have an impact that exceeded the conventional bounds. She seemed in fact to want to break out of the therapeutic frame in which she'd confined herself, to crack out and walk into my life.

The next session, she said, "I think I am uncomfortable with you experiencing me as withholding."

Aha! But my heart sank. What did it imply about our past work together that she needed me to view her as generous? And didn't it follow that she had not actually encouraged me to work through the "negative transference" despite her best intentions?

"It's not really about money," she said, "I don't like you to make decisions concerning us both on your own. Even if it's wrong of me, that is why I was angry when you said when you'd pay me."

Jackpot! She doesn't like me to make decisions? Not on my own? Not if they concern us both? But how revelatory! The very reason I initially came to her years ago was to help me learn to make decisions. She'd immediately said, "I think you need to be in treatment twice a week." Right now, with our identities so merged, won't my most important decisions concern us both? Yet I still want to make them independently.

This new impulse of hers to "break the frame" and enter my life reminded me of the mesmerizing Florida sun, the sense of being helpless before a force that bleaches the mind. Now when she provided an interpretation, I didn't feel hopeful; I felt insulted. She seemed to be forever saying, "What you think is going on is not what's going on. I know better. All you can do—pathetic human!—is act out, a puppet of unconscious conflicts. I see what you can't: the constellation of your sickness. I scan you, lying on this couch. And because you will never have my privileged vantage point, you will never be as healthy as I. You will always need me."

One March afternoon speaking on the phone from my kitchen, I suddenly said to Harriet, "I don't want any more interpretations. I want you to accept what I say at face value, as being exactly what I mean, not just what I think I mean. And, oh, I don't want you to react to my words with arguments, either, as if you're some kind of fractious equal. As if you're so insecure you have to justify yourself." I shook my head, staring at the weave of the peach-colored table-cloth. "And yet, if you spend the whole hour just listening and saying nothing at all, I'll feel as if my words have vanished. Oh, I don't know what sort of a response I want from you!" I concluded in despair.

We were both silent. Then she said: "Maybe you just want me to hear you."

I nodded. And after a moment said, "Yes."

"You are trying to diminish the transference," she said. "It ought to be strong up until the very end."

Then I could never leave! I said: "My friend Franklin tells me that at the end of analysis one ought to be able to sit up on the couch and talk to one's analyst as if he or she were just another person."

Just another person! Even I was forced to smile. Years ago I'd read in a book that after terminating one should be able to pass one's analyst on the street and not have a tide of emotions well up. How sad, I'd confided to Harriet. What pity I'd felt for the poor dull people who didn't rejoice in their hearts when they set eyes on their analyst! I'd never be like that.

But now disenchantment was precisely what I craved.

"You don't want disappointment to be part of my treatment," I said. "You always want to convert it into hope. But I think disappointment is an aspect of maturity. Parents grow old. Children get sick. Anita has multiple sclerosis. You believe every disappointment can be 'worked through' and transformed, that all hay can be spun into gold. I disagree. Some hay stays hay and it's reality to recognize it."

"Why do you believe that?" she asked.

But for once, I didn't answer.

I was thinking that what had disturbed me in Florida was hearing the truth: I was making a good thing bad, and she was the good thing. Yet I didn't know how to stop. Nor did I want to. Her flaws proliferated like the arms on Shiva, that god as blue as an iron file. These flaws were no longer ugly to me. I needed them. Each flaw was a myriad cold blue hand helping me step across to new ground. They were reality itself breaking through.

"You needed to idealize me," she once told me.

True. Goodness had to exist someplace where I could have access to it, I had such an unsteady connection with it myself. I needed a goddess so I could be in touch with something sacred. Oh, to make the balky gritty mechanism of life flow, a big stained glass!

Yet now the particulars of my life needed no beam of interpretive light to strike them into beauty. I no longer wanted a sacred transformation. I wanted this life, just as it was: this husband, this house, this mortality, which, deny it as I might, kept poking through. There was little enough of it left! I was tired of rejecting this life, of trying to spin it into something else.

Once, to perceive myself as good, she must be a goddess to whom I could entrust myself. Now, to perceive myself as good, she must no longer be perfect, nor could I entrust myself. Illness separated me from her. To be separate is to be ill—an interpretation Harriet never offered. Yet even it would have done no good. It was the end of all that.

At this very time, to my surprise, I turned into a person who could think judiciously. Now while aspects of my friend Catherine's new novel seemed superb, flaws floated up, yellow lily blossoms above the water. Plot dragged here, language cloyed there, and I could see the exact places where the tops had been chopped off the novel's Everests.

Similarly, when I received criticism, it no longer reduced me to ashes. I found myself able to learn from artists who would once have simply dazzled. This woman's use of crude sentences that seem childishly true and open the way to sentences full of nuance. That man's use of physical description so precise it verges on poetry, infusing the mundane world of his novels with excitement. I no longer lived in a world of giants.

When I considered what had brought me to Harriet in the first place, I recalled the contract encrusted with crests, which had conjured a fairy-tale invitation to appear, a summons to make sense, but an unassailable, double-blind, public sense. At the same time it represented an invitation to at last dive deeper into the wilds and set my thorns and sunken shoes and lacquered woven white pocketbooks upon the page. And Harriet somehow imparted the feeling that I made authoritative sense and thicket sense spontaneously.

And so I became the man who paid a gypsy thousands of dollars to release him from a curse. Here came the chicken feathers and blood, the quantities of dollars and the interpretation that arouses a gasp, the satisfaction of the fantasy of being truly known. The prone position of the analysand on the couch is the last vestige of Freud's mesmerism, of which he said, "There was something positively seductive in working with hypnotism. For the first time there was a sense of having overcome one's helplessness; and it was highly flattering to enjoy the reputation of being a miracle-worker." I'd sought mysterious aid because what blocked me was mysterious, since the thing I'd craved (permission) was precisely what I'd just received.

It was the body itself that finally gave me my mind. It got too sick, it got too tired, it demanded that I assume responsibility for it despite the fact that my therapist denied its persistent voice, the bell in my ears. A chorus of "outsiders"—my parents, neighbors, casual friends—encouraged me to leave. My friend Veronica said, "She'll never let you go." My mother said, "She needs you. She's just brainwashing you." And many people, Paul chief among them, pointed out that Harriet continued to make money from my treatment, a substantial sum over the years. I was, to put it crassly, an ongoing income stream. I now paid attention to these opinions.

Through Harriet I'd become acquainted with my own obsessive, fanatic temperament. So now I listened to my father and mother, my neighbors and friends. I didn't tell myself, "They don't understand," as I had when my involvement with Harriet was at its height, long before it seemed just she, by herself, trying to maintain a position of privilege. I wanted to break my appetite for a marvelous change. I wanted to stop my ears to the spangled Pied Piper leading me out of my town. Home, please, home, I thought, trying to find what would enable me to stay put.

Harriet called my new way of seeing negative transference. Yet I knew the flaws were real, despite my reasons for seeing them now. My reasons did not create them. Clearly she was correct about negative transference. And yet I no longer cared that she was correct. I wanted to be correct.

Now when she asked a question like, "Why, neurotically, would you want to see me as having all the power?" I couldn't rule out that in fact she really wanted to have it. She said that I painted her in the colors of my nightmare and that I would be better off if I could hold on to a positive feeling about her, even while admitting anger.

I was sure that was true. But I didn't want to take the time. I wanted to be through with this treatment. It was a decision. Time is real, I knew. It is not a delusion or a symptom. Mortality is a flashing frame which throws all our days into relief. The longer I dwelt in my Xanadu, my groggy Florida where the clocks were hidden, the more restless I became. Time is a moth, devouring. Some instinct had stilled my hand years ago when I found under my desk a moth the size of a paperback. Although it horrified me I didn't throw it out. I hid it where I always knew it was, behind a Chagall postcard. I did not want to pretend that moth did not exist.

Harriet's Xanadu was so enthralling that her staircase afterward seemed accordioned from a cloud, and the sidewalks that struck my feet an illusion, an evil mirage, unmetaphoric, crassly themselves, and the long ride home a stupid messy denouement. It was an insult my life itself could not accept. I fed on illness after illness. "If she hadn't been so far away, do you think you'd still be in it?" asked a friend two years after I ended treatment.

"Without a doubt," I said.

Only illness gave me the strength to leave. Of course we're sick with life; we're dying all the time. Mortality itself had spoken to me—the physical realities that would not succumb to metaphor, that did not alter with interpretation. That alien, my body, sought my advocacy, sought my protection. My body taught me to think.

It was true that I pounced on Harriet's imperfections. Each error was a place on which I could gain purchase to push away. As long as she remained ethereal and perfect, I could not leave. Omniscient, and I could not leave. Endlessly openhearted, and I could not leave. Each of her flaws was a revelation, deeply exciting and disturbing, garish, something new on the face of the earth, scarcely to be believed, unanticipated, and of extraordinary beauty.

CHAPTER SIXTEEN

Leaving My Goddess

I was figuring out how to say good-bye. "You're fleeing," said Harriet. "You're running away from working through your feelings about men. You don't know what you're missing."

I'd been rather hopeful about my decision up until then, munching toasted baguettes with butter and raspberry jam on the deck with Melanie and Sally (new friends with whom I was getting closer), watering the pink petunias with their drooping, plush skirts. But Harriet's words made me frantic. Not because of men, but because Harriet didn't approve. And it felt as though I was leaving the source of all goodness or a lover on whom I had a wild, endless crush, or even, at times, some thwarting wicked witch who might unwittingly curse me by holding back something crucial at the last instant. I'd been in treatment seven years.

What would it mean to leave? I recalled last August when for three weeks I sweated into my blue living room couch writing sentences that frayed and split and tasseled, pointing in a dozen directions at once until even I couldn't tell what they meant, waiting for the clock to say it was late enough to swim laps.

At the town pond, ladies on legless chairs tilted on the sand, gossiping, their eyes filled with sun, and I swam between them and the raft where boys cannonballed, smashing the water with the bright bats of their shins. Weeds caressed my arms and snagged my fingers, swarming out of the giant yellow clumps that flourished late in the season. At last I was exhausted and dragged myself out of the water, and my soul exclaimed, When will she come back? Why can't I make myself feel better? Could I be *meant* to feel this way? What purpose does it serve?

Oddly, leaving Harriet feels most like being left. I recall the scalding emptiness of the house last August. Because she was gone, I

■ 234

wanted her constantly. And that first day she was back I phoned from my ramshackle vacation cabin. There I sat on the blue plastic rug gazing at the square phone that bore no number, at last hearing her voice, knowing she heard me ("Hello, Bonnie," intoned in her even cello tone. At last!), spilling forth my experience breathlessly, paradoxically like a child drinking too fast. After fifty minutes her entire interpretation was: "You see, you are not yet ready to leave."
Finis.

Rage tornadoed through me. And afterward—what exhausted depression, what bewildered disappointment as I trailed my hand through the water of Lake George off the side of my canoe. Still, she was back. That was the important thing. And soon I was merely happy, lying on a cool black rock in the center of the lake, brushing ants off, seeing, when I opened my eyes, the yellow fans of an unlikely ginkgo tree against the watered-silk blue of the sky, as if the heavens themselves were a patterned lamp in someone's consulting room. I tucked my unhappiness at her words into the greater happiness of her presence. Soon the smaller unhappiness dissolved into my greater happiness. Yet eventually it returned and swallowed up everything else.

I slip off my shoes and set them side by side. I look at the ceiling with its pinprick holes, a thousand tiny sockets. Her pen is scratching before I open my mouth. I say: "I'm already angry, knowing how tired I'll be later."

She remains mute.

"No interpretation of yours has ever modified my fatigue. Has that ever occurred to you?"

Her pen rubs. Then stops.

"What are you thinking?" I ask.

A moment's pause. "I'm listening to you very carefully, Bonnie."

The door to the Picasso room swings open: the sea and a flutter of wings. Delirium. It's as if she's said: Everything you experience is important. This therapy is important, and it is for you, to enhance the pleasure of your life. I am sorry you are suffering so much. I'm listening to you very carefully, Bonnie.

"How will I ever leave you?" I ask. "I tell myself; 'If only she'd let me go! If only she'd give me what I need: permission.' Or if you would give me a talisman that would stand for your permission, Harriet, so I know you want me to go out into the world and do well."

"You don't feel that?"

"No, I don't. My friend Juliet knows a woman who believes her soul was stolen," I tell her. "This woman was in therapy—she's a Jungian analyst herself—and she fell in love with her therapist and he fell in love with her, too. So they stopped the treatment and waited six months, and then they began a relationship. It was wonderful. Eventually, though, he broke it off. That was when she felt that he stole her soul. After a few months, she called him up. 'What can I do?' he asked. She told him certain sentences to say which she thought would make all the difference. He said them, but they made no difference. The two of them went back to a beautiful reddish meadow that had been special to them when they were a couple. That didn't do it, either. She still felt like he had her soul.

"So now she's living as if she has a soul. She eats supper with her housemates as if she has a soul. She does therapy with her patients as if she has a soul. It's been two years."

Harriet has stopped writing. I turn, and she lifts her head and gazes steadily at me with her dark blue eyes. "Maybe she isn't ready to feel that this man doesn't own the best part of her. Don't you think," she asks in her low, meditative voice, "that there is a phase of development when the child is ready to leave the mother, and is happy about it?"

"Oh, 'phase of development'! I don't want to wait for another phase of development! Besides, I don't agree with you. You believe that independence comes out of dependence."

"And you?"

"I believe dependence leads to more dependence, Harriet."

Her face looks battered, the off-color of gristle on a veal chop. This work fatigues her, I think. I scribble my check, gather my possessions. At the door I turn back. She smiles, and the room goes bright.

* * *

In the diner on the highway, I sip coffee with half-and-half, and eat egg salad on anadama bread with potato chips and pickle spears (more food! more food!—these Fridays, I eat all day), and scribble notes. The green tabletop floats, I'm so tired, and the white tile corridor between booths angles up, rising like an adding machine tape.

How often Harriet has said something that makes incandescent sense then later makes no sense at all! I like to be able to look up just what it was that I found so life-altering yesterday. Although over time I've come to believe that the therapy doesn't lie in the sentences she's said to me or the ones I've said to her; it resides in this sensation of incandescence.

A group of Scandinavians affiliated with Bowdoin crowds into a booth: one person speaks English and negotiates with the waitress for three-berry pie all around, although for herself she specifies she wants just a scone, a currant scone. At dusk I drive to my friend Maggie's. She lives with her husband, Hank, in an eighteenth-century farmhouse on a mountaintop.

When I step in the door, the first thing I see is Fleecy, the longhaired marmalade cat, curled on the sofa. "Tea?" asks Maggie. She eats dinner with Hank at five, goes to sleep at eight, and wakes up quite early, when she does chores and then prepares a tomato-and-lettuce sandwich for her job at the town library. She never asks about my sessions and I never tell her. Her life seems so reasonable, her two blond, athletic sons grown and away, her afternoons dedicated to writing her novel, her evenings with Hank telling him stories about the people who visited the library that day and watching the six P.M. local news after supper. She says, "I don't go to book group in winter. I don't like to go out on winter nights." How smart she is.

Around 7:30 she yawns. She collects an Anita Brookner novel and goes off to draw a hot bath. I climb the stairs to the big room with the four-poster piled with quilts and pillows. I crank the knob on my box travel alarm with the light green numerals, then settle in with the galleys of my friend Melanie's first novel. It's a book of girlhood and reminds me of the one I attempted. My own spread and spread. I never realized that at some point I had to decide what my novel was about. I thought, discover! I maintained a receptive curiosity toward the sentences and chapters and hundreds of pages emerging from my pen, and at last the inertia of the great sprawling body of my novel overcame me: I set it aside.

I never said good-bye to it, though. I simply shifted it onto the floor and began nonfiction. That novel, from which I'd never parted, became coated with dust, bleached with sun, a jab in my heart when my eyes fell on it, as if, despite everything, it were still possible to fix.

Once upon a time I loved my therapist's authority, it occurs to me, sitting in Maggie's high bed. Harriet helped me when no one else could. She was knowledgeable; she was definitive; she did not doubt herself.

In fact, she never doubted herself in my entire experience of her. She was supremely confident, usually without seeming smug. I'd borrowed her confidence — rented it from week to week — and wrote the book I craved. She favored "deep" interpretations: analytic, intrapsychic. "When you receive a compliment, it stirs up your envy." "The airplane noise makes you anxious because you project your aggression into it. Your split-off anger is actually what makes you anxious." Baroque interpretations that struck me as startling, brilliant, and because they were often just beyond my intuitive grasp (my mind occasionally grasped them, but never my soul), infinitely consoling.

The very mystery of her interpretations reassured me. Her mysterious interpretations made me feel she could help me when I could not help myself, that she could understand me better than I understood myself. They made me feel cared for in part because they were beyond me. I felt awe when her mysterious interpretations arrived, and enlivened — they were convincing in the manner of poetry — and it seemed as if she'd set in my hand a round-the-corner telescope like the kind my brother possessed growing up, constructed of trick mirrors and paper corridors, and enabling a privileged perspective.

"Do you realize how few people ever get to this point?" she'd asked two years ago, when I'd expressed a desire to terminate. "You've come so far in your treatment! So few people ever reach this point. At last you are in a position to really explore things most people never explore."

Ah, the slave-mentality people are left in the desert while she and I enter the promised land. How marvelous I'd felt then, lying on her vanilla couch! Hopeful. Exalted. She and I were doing important cultural work; my energy once more renewed itself for the task ahead. She was a sort of stalwart prophet and I trod behind, thinking: How safe people feel from the lure of a leader simply because they haven't met the Pied Piper meant for them. They think, "Those kooks in Waco!"—astonished by what is so very commonplace. If only they possessed a round-the-corner telescope such as I have!

Years were powerless to impinge on her attic room. New leaves swam greenish shadows on the wall or the blue dusk of winter gathered while I lay on the couch, or it was high summer and the room careened with light. It was always between 1:30 and 3:20. My face carried wrinkles it hadn't when I began and my hair was now streaked with gray, but still it was between 1:30 and 3:20. Must all our yesterdays light fools the way to dusty death? Can't some light fools toward life? I held up the candle of my yesterdays until, when I shut my eyes, a thousand flashbulbs flared, formed a constellation, became for an instant an exquisite shape I could almost, almost discern. Oh, I was so close to something! Quite close! I turned, and it was my therapist wreathed in window light, beautiful beyond all clarity, and if I could only touch her, wouldn't the beauty be mine?

"Are you going to make your therapist into a composite?" my agent had asked.

"But I already am a composite," observed Harriet in the voice of a certain smug ex-friend.

Harriet could mimic perfectly, as well, my domineering, delicate, and utterly destroyed sister, my fragile, beneficent mother, even the G-d whose very name, out of respect, harbors a span of mystery, two picas of infinity. Walking down her flimsy steps, I was descending from a fortunate height, and it was my own fault if my life after so strongly resembled my life before, if by the time I reached my door after a four-hour drive I was merely exhausted, empty, incensed, craving to cut this treatment off, to cut it off—

What I'd wanted to be transferred to me had not yet been trans-ferred. We both kept it safely in the therapist's hands. Expertise, authority—I'd wanted a goddess and I found one. Yet every angel is terrible and every goddess two-faced; even the good witch in *The Wizard of Oz* is smug, saccharine, withholding, with a laugh like a mosquito in your brain.

"Sometimes my interpretations are better, sometimes they're less better," Harriet said.

"Superior, either way," I scrawled in my notebook now, then set the book beside the travel alarm and plummeted into an uneasy sleep in which the old pounding trucks of Salem roared all night up and down innumerable highways, although Maggie's mountaintop was perfectly silent.

Sitting at my Formica kitchen table on Monday morning, I contem-plated the sweet passivity that crept over me late in a session when Harriet commenced to speak. I always froze, wishing not to distract her by so much as a breath. I wanted her to think about me so strongly that I wasn't there. An ideal me hovered in the air: the one she was thinking of. Then I tried to join it, to pour myself into it. While she spoke, I refused to stir: no itches got scratched, no crick soothed. It was a mood of aching receptivity. I yearned to be helped, to be shown yet again the tungsten blazing through the clouded bulb of my life, to be reminded I made sense, the journey was worth it, my mind was worthwhile. I craved to be the person she had in mind as she thought about me. I was good insofar as I was that woman. It seemed ingratitude, or dispiritingly obtuse, to be anyone else.

And if she gave an interpretation that aroused no resonance, I didn't think it was wrong. I thought, I will grow to see its truth. She perceives me where I cannot. Sometimes I drove home confused, turning over words that didn't yet seem right. I held them this way, I held them that, like a little shrunk backwards-buttoned sweater whose arms have crept into itself. How could I make it fit?

I'd needed magic authority. Yet believing Harriet was the author of my powers, how depart without her approval? I was terrified to leave my goddess. I needed, I realized, to find a way to change her into a human. She did not necessarily want to change.

Harriet said again, "Why are you trying to diminish the transference? We ought to keep it strong up until the very end."

My husband, witnessing my terror, said: "You're in a cult! You need to be deprogrammed. I've held my tongue for years, but it's just insane—incredible!—that you've been driving four hours to see a therapist."

I stared at him, astonished. "A cult!" I said. "How did you guess?"

It was the exact term I'd used so many years ago—my very first month of therapy, driving home through the freezing January night, the steering wheel creaking on the turns, while listening to reports of Iraqi SCUDs falling on Israel, families locked in sealed rooms with plastic over the windows and doors—to describe this therapy to myself. So, it's a cult, I'd thought. The therapist and patient develop a secret language. Only they can understand precisely what they mean when they speak. Everything the therapist says possesses enormous significance. One is so grateful. A cult! But why didn't anyone just say so!

And when, two years later, my friend Janice, also a therapist, declared, "But why does she say you ought to bring your anger toward me to her? What does it have to do with her? You ought to bring your annoyance with me to me!" I merely sat in my rocking chair and smiled. I was looking up and to the side, at a row of Janice's old books. We were sitting in the nursery she'd just decorated. She was holding her brand-new baby. She said, "The point of therapy is to have better relationships with other people."

Again I smiled. Such a simpleton, I thought. Your kind of therapy I understand. So plodding, so rational. I want the kind of therapy I do not understand. Besides, my goal is not to have better relationships with other people. It is to function better. To quit being so anxious. I'm not in treatment for your benefit, Janice.

But by then, of course, she was already half-metamorphosed into an enemy.

The first step in making the therapist human, I decide, is to make her acknowledge that she exists. "I realized that you will never give me permission to leave you," I say.

"Your mother would never give you permission to leave her."

"That's true," I concede. "But you, Harriet, I think you have a real issue with distance."

"What makes you say that?"

"Well, the first mistake you ever made in this treatment, the first statement of yours you ever acknowledged as a mistake, was when I phoned for my session when I was on vacation in New York that time, and I said, 'I feel so far from you!' and you answered, 'I feel far from you, too!' Remember how that upset me?"

"And we discussed at that time," she responds, "how you unconsciously signaled me to take that role with you. Remember? I was duplicating an old pattern of yours for you."

"That may be. I have no way of knowing."

"You know your own history."

"But I don't know yours. Although in a way I do. I know your history with me. And my experience of you has been that you dislike distance between us." I remembered a trip Harriet had disapproved of—to a small town in Southern France. I'd gone anyway, with my friend Mark and his boyfriend Daniel. "Remember how strongly you opposed that trip with Daniel and Mark because it meant missing a session?" I asked now. "You gave me such a hard time about it! You even wondered if perhaps I'd have an affair with one of them! I was shocked. You know they're gay. Now I wonder why you'd wonder if I'd have an affair. Were you insecure? My point is, I'm not alone in this room."

"We create a psychic reality."

"Yes, your psyche has scripted mine just as mine scripts yours. It's got to be! Oh, when I think of the ways I've had to suffer because of your emotional needs! The agony I went through over that trip to France! I'm so glad I went!" The blue-green trees had formed an arched colonnade into the town where we lived for a week, Mark and Daniel and I. My stone bedroom had casement windows that opened onto a crooked street stalked by cats. One night Daniel cooked chicken in the closet-sized kitchen on the one scorched, battered frying pan, and the chicken emerged succulent. Mark cut tomatoes that were a dark, ripe, brooding red, and we ate roasted potatoes, and salad and bread from the corner market, and drank wine made from the grapes that grew on the mountains rising around us. If I hadn't gone! But this was life! Harriet would have kept me from life! And Daniel was very kind to me, though mean, perhaps, to Mark. I was, in my own way, it's true, in love with Daniel.

"You are fleeing this treatment because you want to avoid exploring your feelings about men," she says at that very moment, as if reading my thoughts—although this is also her recent theme.

"That may be," I say softly. "It no longer matters. Three years ago you said I'd be ready to leave when I could self-analyze. Then you said I'd be ready to leave when I'd consolidated a positive sense of you within myself, since it meant a positive sense of me as well. I accomplished that last year. Then you said I'd be ready to leave when I'd worked through my adolescent anger at you—last winter. Now you say I'll be ready to leave when I explore with you my feelings about men."

"Don't you think those are all, in a way, the same thing?"

My head swirls. The old anesthetized delirium.

Don't I think.

Those are all.

In a way.

The same thing.

I have a sort of dreamy physical sensation of how they might be. All good goals are really the same thing, aren't they? In a way? She can certainly explain how they are. I've merely to ask.

"They may be true," I say. "All I know is, I'm going. That is my goal. And I want to talk about disappointment. Because I know I'll feel it, and if we don't talk about it, I'll be alone with it, and it will be worse. I'm disappointed because my life in many ways is the same despite therapy. I still wake up sometimes at dawn and feel such melancholy. And I recall you saying, 'Wouldn't you like that to change?'—holding out the clear promise that therapy would bring that change. Now my treatment is ending and the melancholy is still with me. It's not horrible, but I feel in a way you used that melancholy to keep me coming. And now I believe that melancholy might even be merely a physiological response to waking up quite early. Isn't that why armies attack at dawn?" I stopped. "Oh, it's so disappointing to think of the hopes you fostered!

"The whole time I've been in therapy—until now—I held out messianic hopes. My life would be different, I couldn't say how. I didn't think how. My mother used to have a phrase: 'You have no idea.' 'I love you so much, you have no idea.' I never liked that phrase but I believed it was true, that there were certain things that existed about which I couldn't even have an idea. That's what kept me in treatment so long. The belief that I could get something in return better than I could even conceive."

I fall silent. It's true I did get something better than I could even conceive. Once upon a time I envied other people even their suffering (although I wasn't quite aware of this; no means were available to distinguish my sensations, which glued together in a mass like a packet of glassine stamp hinges that's fallen in a puddle). My friend Becka said, "When I first got to college, there was a day of excruciating pain, a feeling that everything was falling apart. Ever since that day, I've had the feeling that I mustn't ever really let go. A black vortex." I secretly envied my friend even her black vortex, because it was dramatic, and it was being intensely alive, and it was hers. In high school she'd danced to the lyric, "Go ask Alice when she's ten feet tall," eyes closed, the red lights from lamps draped with scarves throwing shadows as she danced before a candle, away from it and back, as if in a form of worship, and I thought, Oh, to be Becka!—because she, with her eyes shut, however stoned and miserable and even momentarily berserk she felt, was clearly inside her experi-

ence, whereas I was outside, looking at her. She was like the butterfly whose tender body is always to be found between its two lumi-
nous wings, even if she's not aware of it. Whereas I had no wings,
and was in a state of gazing, like a child watching a mother who sits
before a mirror brushing her own hair, the mother's face framed by
the lovely hair she keeps brushing and brushing as she gazes forever
into the glass.

My mother did not actually do this. But when the door shut behind the older children when they trooped off to school, she wanted
not to be bothered. She seemed to be groping for something lost
deep inside herself, and which she might glimpse as she flipped a
page of *McCall's*. I sat near her ankles, inside her mood like being
in a tent. I looked up at her often. She was so beautiful, with her
arched black eyebrows, her upswept burnished hair, her blue-gray
eyes. She turned the page. She took a sip of her black coffee, leaving
a lipstick scallop.

Harriet helped extract me from invisibility. Through her, I
showed up. And yet, though something crucial had changed, I still
hadn't entered the beautiful life my therapy had promised (and it
did promise this, in a dozen suggestive ways). The texture of my
days—as was true of the texture of most people's days, for all I
knew—was tatters and rags, steel wool and old diapers and a swatch
of antique chiffon curtain all twisted on a spinning wheel, and life
didn't make sense as it went, you kept having to pull some sort of
meaning out of it until your arms ached. The texture was still catch-
as-catch-can, smooth and then horribly grainy. One woke up and
discovered who one was that day.

"I always thought that at the end of treatment my life would run
as smooth as glass," I told Harriet. "It seems silly to admit. But one
works and works in a session and arrives at that moment of ecstasy—
and I assumed that was the whole point, that ecstasy. It seemed that
when I was all done with the therapy, it would somehow be the state
in which I lived.

"Now, of course, I see it won't. My life after treatment will be
almost exactly what it is right now. And I won't get back the seven
years I've been in treatment, either. I suppose I believed that at the

end of the treatment I would be handed back the years I put into it. Or the novel I would have written—that you'd set that book in my hands."

The book written in milk! I thought. The words that surface only over a flame. The book discovered in a bottom drawer, composed during an unrecollected fever when the soul left its imprint like a vow on the page, something magical caught in the snares and monocles of the serif type, something one couldn't plan on but craved to appear. "That won't happen," I said.

"You're disappointed," she said, "because you don't know what would happen if you continued in the treatment."

"No, that's why you're disappointed," I replied. "And there are those messianic hopes! 'You don't know what would happen!' Even if I stayed in, I'd be largely the same woman."

But perhaps not! Perhaps I'd be the woman Daniel looked at so intently, so shockingly in France, when he acted the part of Henry. For that evening, when we pushed the plates away, we began jointly to compose a novel, each assuming the role of a character we found especially delicious. Mark recorded our words on a notebook computer, his fingers tapping. Daniel was my dear old friend Henry, successful, sardonic, enamored of a pretty and self-serving boyfriend played by Mark. Henry and my character fought, lightly. Henry liked to fight. He said clever words that hacked to the bone. He stared at me suddenly with a dark, enraged, ravishing intensity—I blushed, then he jumped up. "You always do the writing!" he said to Mark, who gazed at him with an innocent look that said, "You are a madman." Daniel strode from the room. A door banged. Mark slowly turned his gaze toward me. "A madman!" his face utterly expressed. After a moment, he too stood up and left. Blood thumped in my ears. Was I still blushing? Late that night their murmuring voices approached in the street below my window as they returned from a walk. The front door clanked. Their whispering voices fell to silence as they creaked past my bedroom.

Perhaps it's true, I thought, that if I stay in treatment I would find the Henry I desired. The man glimpsed once in a character in a novel, and who'd stared for an instant with absolutely serious desire as if in my very flesh and bones I was wanted, teeth and talk and reek and the shadow of a thought as it approaches edged in cobalt, while I'm still confused, before it's legible—all these things. Perhaps it's true I'd find this man if I stayed; Harriet's been right before. Oh, but it's the old seduction! Follow me! Oh, follow me!

"I didn't used to be able to make a decision," I said slowly. "Now I'm making one. I am turning away from some good things to get other good things. That's what making a decision is, it seems to me. Otherwise it would be easy, and there would be no decision."

Must leaving be betrayal? Must one take the telescope and spin it, and behold the thimble monarch, the thumbnail empress, the tyrannical sister dancing on the head of a pin, the therapist no bigger than a molecule, past the horizon, up in Maine?

"Let's work through your anger," proposes Harriet.

"You're scaring me," I say. "I want my anger. I have no other way of going." Recalling how uncloaked and needy I felt last August.

"What makes you think that being angry is the way to go about separating from me?"

"It's not about thinking. I *didn't* think this up. I simply found, emotionally, that it works. I've been in an underground tomb with no way out. It's been pitch dark. At last I've found the crack of light that indicates a door. And now you want to cover it over and caulk it and leave me in darkness! Even if it's not the best way to leave, at least it is *a* way to leave without feeling stricken."

"I'm sure you can quote me better than I can quote myself," she says wryly, "but earlier I asked you why you felt that anger was the way to separate from me, and I said we could look at this."

"You're absolutely right!" I cry triumphantly. "Oh, I'm so glad, Harriet! You know, I can quote you better. How many times in the past have I questioned you about some interpretation only to have you say I'd misremembered. In fact, you asked me earlier: 'Why do you *think* . . . ?' And I told you it wasn't a matter of thinking. I've felt my way to something that works. You seem unable to supply me something that works." Although she certainly had unwittingly just given me something in giving me her error. "I don't want you to take my anger away."

"I'm actually suggesting for us to get more into it."

I glance back. Is that really what she'd been suggesting?

"You see," she says, "I think you're concerned that you haven't yet consolidated a strong enough sense of yourself. I'm concerned about that, too."

I squint past my blue-socked toes toward the birds painted in place. And realize that Harriet has transformed into a father whose concern makes me sag inside. I refuse it. Even though I know that her mind fathoms geometries far more complex than mine ever could (isosceles Oedipals, the self bisected and refracted into the least suspected nook). I'll have to rely on something incalculable. Something that races away down the highway, a mad thing, an imp, something to which the red fingers point in their continual circuit, this minute, this. The clock is the one thing repressed in therapy, the one object purposely positioned so I can't see it. I've delegated my temporal existence in order to enter a holding pattern, a miasma of time, an amniotic embrace. Yet those fingers that forever sign across me to her mean something—pulsing, urgent.

No, I refuse for once to feel daunted by Harriet's worry. Even if it means a stupider life than the one she planned, even if it means a messier, incomplete, inferior life—so be it, it's my own.

To free my goddess, I must give up my worship. Just as, to leave my father, I had to choose my own mistakes—I had to allow the swamp, the marsh, the primordial soup craving its lightning bolt, the palms smudged with pencil rubbings, the sundry muddy shades of my thought. This idea occurs to me one spring morning as my glance falls on the spines of the cloth-bound notebooks in which I've kept a running history of this relationship.

To leave Harriet I must give up the rapture of interpretations. I must surrender my training in being neurotic—for I was never half so crazy as when I was in treatment, never half so touchy, spooky, savage, squirrelly, cynical, selfish, all of which convinced me I needed more treatment. In fact, I now viewed the tumult of those years sometimes as merely an attempt to purge myself of the foreign body I'd embedded in my psyche: Harriet.

My dependence, too, I must give up. For years I'd lived like a child driven home at midnight, the streetlights extending long white arms and whisking my car from one lamp to another, one session to another. However haunted my week, the session glowed ahead. What splendors the future might possess! Why, this might be Eden, with enough therapy. And Harriet implied that I was sick if I experienced her interpretations not as a benefit but as a tax. Since therapy to her was by definition good, she was blind to the ways it was harmful. Authoritative interpretations, though, I suddenly understood, are always acts of violence.

The morning of what I didn't know was to be the third-to-last session, I woke, brewed coffee, and sat in the green vinyl kitchen chair.

An hour later, at nine A.M., I was still there. My body was supposed to get up and walk down to the garage and sit in the wine-colored Camry, and drive. It knew that. That's what it had always done. But my body did not move. How much time and energy I'd have if I didn't go, I thought as I sat down. Yet even this thought didn't seem sufficient to account for the unbudging presence of my body in the chair. Ten o'clock. Now it was too late. There was no way I could make my session. I dialed Harriet and informed her machine I would do the session by phone.

I did not open a magazine. I did not turn on the radio. I did not eat. For the next three hours I simply sat in that hard green vinyl chair.

"Hello, Bonnie," she said in a clipped, irritated tone when she answered her phone.

"You sound angry. Are you angry?"

"Yes," she replied. "I am."

Fury overtook me. I'd wanted reassurance! I stared at the peach-checked tablecloth, unable to utter a word.

"You see, Bonnie—"

"But I'm incensed!" I interrupt. "Your anger has no place in my treatment. Work it out with your own therapist! I'm so mad I feel like hanging up right now! If you kept an attendance sheet I'd have a perfect record. I think it's good I didn't come up. I think it's growth."

"You see, Bonnie," she says again, a supremely irritating phrase, "your not coming up is provocative."

"My not coming up is because it's exhausting, and because I'm trying to figure out how to leave you. And because, frankly, I don't feel the need to come up. It's about me, not you."

"We have an agreement. I'm angry because it's difficult to save these two-hour time slots for you, and I do it because you drive up."

I nearly hold the phone away from my ear and stare at it. "Are you the martyr now?" I ask. "Are we in some competition about who suffers more? You've been giving me two-hour sessions for seven years! And now you tell me how difficult it is for you? Are you trying to make me feel guilty?"

"I'm explaining why I'm angry."

"I'm happy to hear you're angry," I suddenly declare, realizing it's true. "It's a relief. Perhaps I did want to provoke your anger into the open."

I sit a moment, thinking. "Because it's inflected my entire treatment. I've felt your will—your anger—as a presence in my treatment for years. When I called you racked with guilt because I didn't want to drive from New York to Brunswick and back to Framingham in one day, when I pled with you to let me drop my sessions back to every other week—so often I've felt the need to get your permission! I always thought it was just my problem. I couldn't see how in fact blaming you were. Your will has warped my treatment in a way I couldn't see clearly until now. Your anger was present, but hidden by my fear of it."

"You want me to become an ogre. Then you can feel permission to leave."

My heart stops. I shut my eyes. "Yes," I say, softly. "If you're a monster, then I don't need to feel guilty about leaving you. Then you deserve to be left."

"Why must I be a monster for you to leave?" she inquires in a new tone. All anger has vanished from her voice, replaced by empathetic interest.

"Because then you are not my old sad mother who I am leaving," I say slowly.

"You see, Bonnie," she says, "for you the whole process of separation was turned around: your mother left you when you were too young. Then, when you were old enough to leave, she discouraged you from going."

I am so happy that my therapist no longer sounds angry!

"Yes. It got turned around," I agree.

"Unfortunately it is not only beginners who are obsessed with the need to feel superior in therapeutic skill and who literally live on the unexplored and unchanging dependency needs of their patients. More than anything else, this subtle exploitation of the relationship for one's own reassurance, even self-aggrandizement, is probably the basis for those cases of seemingly interminable therapy. Like an overprotective and possessive parent, such a therapist keeps a patient from moving toward maturity and independence, the legitimate goals of psychotherapy." (Hilde Bruch, 1974)

I happen upon this in an old textbook at Borders a few days later and copy it down. Could I get angrier?

It looks as if Harriet is moving to a new office. Her attic room gives the impression she's transferred some pieces of furniture out already, although in fact I can't say exactly what's missing. I'm on the couch for the first time in ten weeks. The windows admit a dull midafternoon sunshine. Her little figure of Athena is gone, replaced by a Buddha.

"I've been thinking about how you encouraged me—trained me, even—to be dependent," I say. "Your advice that I have my session by phone even when I was away on vacations, your suggestion that I might be anxious if I didn't. You didn't encourage my independence."

"Do you want to drive up in September or would you like to just do a phone session?" she replies.

And something within me sags. She is good; I am wrong. She loves me; I am wrong. She is not a monster, not a machine, not a cruel, self-serving alien. She's given me so incredibly much. I was wrong, my vision was distorted.

"My criticisms dissolve as I'm talking to you," I say slowly. "And yet they are real. I will think them again when I leave. But I can't share them with you. You argue. Or else you seem to alter, as you did just now. You show a new, unexpected sensitivity. I feel again as if I don't know you. I mistrust my own perceptions. But I'm not crazy. I know what I'm saying is valid. Aren't you curious? Wouldn't you like to know what it's like to be in treatment with you?

"I'd like you to learn from my experience," I continue. "Shouldn't the end of treatment be like the debriefing at the end of a job, when the employee gives feedback? Wouldn't you like to know what it's like to be your patient? I'd like to make a contribution to you, Harriet, and to your other clients. I think there are things you could learn from me. I don't feel you've allowed me to have an impact on you."

"How would you feel if I gave you an emblem," she replies, "of how you've had an impact on me?"

Fear clenches me. Is she going to write about me? "What are you thinking about?" I ask, wheeling around.

"I was thinking of giving you my Athena."

"Oh."

That replica of Freud's own Greek warrior in a helmet and spear, tall as my hand. Why, it's always seemed an emblem of Harriet herself! I'm lying extremely still. My leg is rigidly stiff, wood from hip to toe. What a glorious present. And yet—

"Think about it," she says. "You don't have to only feel happy. Do you think you'd feel inhibited if you were given it?"

"I might not feel free to express all my feelings."

"But all your feelings are what I accept you for. They are all— even the negative ones—part of what makes you up."

I tell her about a Sabbath candlestick that once slid from my arms to fall into a lump of mangled silver under the number 1 train and about a patient of the analyst Winnicott who shattered a precious vase in his office. "Perhaps I'd better wait."

"Why don't you take it now," she presses. "If you want to, you can send it back. We can see how my experiment goes. I never did this with a patient before."

The molecules in the room swell to the size of basketballs bouncing and jostling. I breathe shallowly. After a few more minutes the session ends. I stand.

"Well, here it is, Bonnie," she says, standing up, too. She sets the Athena (unwrapped! Not even a box! Now if she really and truly loved me, couldn't she have at least bought a bow?) straight into my hand.

But—what a shock! The thing's light as a hollow Easter egg! *Plastic!* Why, all these years I'd assumed she was bronze, even knowing she was a replica.

I unzip my pocketbook.

"You don't have to do that now," she says for the first time in seven years.

"That's okay." I shrug awkwardly, the open pocketbook looped over my arm, and scribble the check.

"Good-bye," I say in the doorway, and she replies, "Good-bye, Bonnie," restored to her old, remote, abstemious incarnation.

I drive. Skip session notes. Get in stale car. Go. Why, the figure seems like a bribe, a gag. The goddess sticks in my throat. Harriet should not gratify my fantasy of being the favorite client. She should not poke her reality through the protective envelope of the therapeutic rules. And if she loves me in a unique way, doesn't it prove she's overinvolved, has been acting on her own needs and not my best interests? I've wanted to terminate for the past three years. Always she found a reason why not. I feel ill.

It's she who's sabotaged the transference, it occurs to me. She's exposed her real feelings (special love, anger when I don't appear) and to that extent I can no longer project onto her. She seems, frankly, out of control. Over the phone last week she asked me to send her a story I'd just written ("But why do you want it?" I asked. "To analyze," she replied, a most chilling answer, as if any art I might produce could be reduced by her, collapsed). She also gave me a list of questions to ask my mother — unprecedented ways to extend our contact into the outside world. As I increase control over my actions, she forfeits control over hers.

So, she has become fully human, after all. I'm hunched over the wheel, unable to go fast enough although the speedometer says 83 and the car is thrumming. She's peeled away from the shimmering person who was reassuring and magical, and who understood me, I sometimes felt, before I opened my mouth.

"You will always exist in my mind," she'd said. A shiver of terror rang through me: she'd never let me leave. I would exist forever in her head, Dorothy trapped in the witch's globe. It was a frisson of her old supernatural power, the sensation that she'd made my unconscious her domain, an eerie imperialism.

Ultimately it was her very insistence on worship that transformed her into a human, I saw now, the road flinging itself underneath me so fast it almost mesmerized. It was her insistence on her own perfection. When at last I rebelled against this, she sprang into a messy, rule-breaking, shocking humanity. She responded to my moves to leave by reaching out, and the more she reached, the easier it was to step away.

"The mother's eventual task is gradually to disillusion the infant," Winnicott wrote. I looked the passage up as soon as I got home, pacing across my kitchen as I read it. "But she has no hope of success unless at first she has been able to give sufficient opportunity for illusion."

Harriet did not seem to want my disenchantment. She wanted me to remain in the world of magic, the primal omnipotence that newborns with good-enough mothers supposedly feel. Harriet granted me what she could of that omnipotence, which was far more than I'd ever had. Yet she seemed unable to tolerate my disappointment. Winnicott noted "the infant can be disturbed by a close adaptation to need that is continued too long, not allowed its natural decrease, since exact adaptation resembles magic and the object that behaves perfectly becomes no better than a hallucination."

He added that a person "can actually come to gain from the experience of frustration, since incomplete adaptation to need makes objects real." Disappointment was the one emotion that seemed to have no home in Harriet's office, and it was the emotion I feared would assail me once the therapy stopped. She always wanted to spin my disappointment back into hope. Once I'd said, "Some hay stays hay and it's reality to recognize it." "Why do you believe that?" she answered. I should have questioned why ever she didn't. She seemed addicted to our mutual fantasy of her. It was as if she wanted to float up and merge with the idealized view of her that hovered in the air between us (and whose fetish was the knockoff goddess she set in my hand), to remain the floating green head between gusting smoking salvers in Oz and not the woman with her own problems behind the couch.

The goddess got tucked into a pocket of my satchel. She was both too much and too little. When Harriet placed her in my hand I'd been shocked—mere plastic! Yet the goddess was even more beautiful up close than across the room. Her face was attenuated as a Giacometti with deep-gouged powerful eyes; her gown hung in colossal folds. She wore a tall helmet and breastplate and carried a shield—Wisdom, she is a warrior—and her raised left hand clasped an invisible spear. Time had removed the original from her grasp.

No, I decided, I wouldn't return her. She was precisely what I craved. An emblem that all this really happened. The talisman of her permission, for which I'd asked. A Freudian symbol I could hold in my hand. True authority, the invisible spear, suggested more than seen, never belonging irrevocably to someone else.

CHAPTER SEVENTEEN

The Spectral Palace

The last day dawned—a radiant morning in October shaken by a towering wind. I poured coffee in a mug hand-painted with yellow pears and apples, and smiled as if remembering a particularly pleasant dream. But I was remembering no dream. Rather, I seemed to inhabit one whose source of pleasantness resided everywhere, as if I were the bride on top of a cake and everything I set my eyes on was frosting. The bunch of bananas: frosting. The ripped green vinyl chair: frosting. Suddenly the walls boomed and a shiver ran through them. I raced to the window and saw that the green iron table—heavy as a sofa—lay on its side, shoved against the deck's railing. It had been lifted up and flung a clear four feet. Its umbrella top gouged the floorboards, a gigantic spindle. In the distance, treetops plunged in the wild October wind.

I stepped out barefoot and hoisted the table aright. The umbrella immediately tugged like a sail, as if the table too had places it wanted to see, appointments to keep. I had to crank the thing shut to keep it from flying off. Then stood with arms raised so that that tumultuous wind could riffle me, resorting me like a deck of cards.

What would come next in my life? Oh, I couldn't wait to find out. Paul and I were moving to Brooklyn, to a block of brownstones. The Verrazano Bridge laced across the living room windows, surprisingly picturesque, and if I stuck my head out the window I could watch the crayon-orange barge of the Staten Island ferry gliding back and forth. The R train would set me on Prince Street in twenty minutes to visit Sally with her glorious blond hair in her tiny art studio and to step around the corner with her to Café Gitane to sip bowls of café au lait. In thirty minutes the 2 would bring me to Times Square to watch a play for fourteen dollars apiece on mailed-in TDF tickets. It would have been impossible to move here while still in treatment;

the drive each way would take six hours. But now I simply couldn't wait to live among people who jangled *vegalahs* up the street, sometimes with little dogs riding inside, and who complained at a Donnell Library concert while turning the pages of the *Daily News*, "I've heard better Debussy"—devotees, novitiates, immigrants, poets, a man swiveling silver Magic-8 balls in his giant hands while he sits on the number 4 subway, a woman across the jolting aisle calmly crocheting a pink baby blanket with a hook the size of a toothpick, and the whole city jostling at dusk like a stageful of dancers attempting pirouettes. Delirium, after the sedate society of trees.

I looked forward, too, to the extra days and energy I'd have—and the money—when my treatment was through, and to the time with Paul. I wouldn't always be rushing away or toward him. Time together made us happier and happier with each other, I'd found, afternoons of pawing through old music books at the Danbury library, eating together at the cheap, good Ecuadorian restaurant, creeping into bed while he was still asleep to surprise him with kisses on his mouth. Silver glinted in the stubble of his beard, and I longed to just have hours to stroke and hold him. Time together was the best aphrodisiac.

I was also looking forward to something else, although I couldn't say quite what. A baby? A new book? Maybe, but it seemed this good thing would be something else, too, something which I couldn't know as long as I remained in treatment.

In the kitchen, tap water overflowed my bottles for the very last time. I pulled on my favorite T-shirt, dark blue, with the word YAN-KEES curling off, and changed into a pair of snug Levi's. And instead of listening to a book on tape during the ride, I left the radio on, sexy songs that called to mind bars and dancing. Purplish blue mountains jolted up beneath a monumental sky. Here was the bend where the green land suddenly opened out far below. In my mind I'd already left.

The radio in her waiting room effused classical music, and I didn't touch the radio to turn it down or up, and I didn't open a magazine to root out a face to envy, and when I set my crumpled paper bag into the white wicker trashcan the size of a flowerpot, I felt fine,

I didn't wonder what Harriet would think when she emptied her trash. I didn't expect anything to change today. All the changes between us seemed to have already happened.

"Hello." She stood framed in the doorway, smiling. Her hair, draped to her shoulders, held its myriad shades of black.

The room seemed even emptier. The hook on which Harriet hung her coat in winter jutted more nakedly from the wall. I half-expected to see dust tracing the ghosts of moving boxes like the boxes that hid behind the furniture in my parents' apartment: flattened dish-barrels behind the bookcase, wardrobes squeezed behind the upright piano. But Harriet's walls were pristine. Still, her office possessed a desultory, exhausted look. I was thinking how I knew everything in this room so well I'd never forget it when—

"Harriet! Your lamp isn't poppy red!" I exclaimed. "I've always described it as poppy red in my notes." It was bottle green. A familiar worry stabbed me: I'd been wrong. I'd misapprehended everything. Then I smiled. "I won't change it," I said. "There's bound to be some differences between the facts and what I remember. Whenever I read about your poppy-red lamp it can be a sort of reminder, a lighthouse to signal the boundary of unsuspected fantasy."

She said nothing.

"You are always smarter than I remember," I said. "In my thoughts of you, you become more two-dimensional. I'm constantly shocked at the things you say which I couldn't predict. I'm going to remember this, too," I promised. "That you are surprising."

There were things about which I was still angry, I told her, but I no longer wanted to fight. Her question, "Have you ever contemplated your mother's ambivalence toward you?"—which she'd asked in the session before—still struck me as retaliatory, as the curse I'd been dreading. In all the years of our treatment she hadn't seen fit to draw my attention to the idea of my mother's—and Harriet's own—ambivalence toward me. Why now, at the very end, raise this question? It struck me as punitive.

To Harriet's credit, she said nothing. She listened and wrote.

I couldn't think why. What would she do with these last notes? Did she imagine that even now it might be appropriate for her to chart the constellation of my thought and spring it upon me? Her note-taking seemed idle, ritual, an EKG that hasn't been disconnected although the patient is walking out the door, or a bit of stage business so the actress isn't left facing the audience empty-handed.

Yet even now a mad hope clung to me and I was prepared to believe that some virtue resided in her note-taking beyond anything I'd imagined. Even now, I had an impulse to cast my vote with my own ignorance and to endow her with a surpassing intelligence.

It was not the conclusion I'd anticipated. For the past three or four years I'd imagined a good-bye during which I'd recall crucial moments we'd shared. How often I'd driven along Old West Mountain Road fantasizing about the day I'd leave Harriet. The song about thanking someone "who has taken you from crayons to perfume" played in my ears. But, again to Harriet's credit, reminiscence now seemed moot. "I've been here, too," she said tartly. "I also have a memory."

I smiled. "Recently," I said, "with more time available since I've been coming up only once a month, I've been writing up a storm. I'm at it for longer hours than ever. I've found that writing itself calms me when I'm tense."

"Writing is your interpretation."

"What do you mean?"

"It's how you resolve things."

"Oh, you nitwit!" I felt like crying out. "Of course! I was writing for years before I met you. Why did you ever try to replace my writing with your psychotherapy?"

Yet I said nothing.

"I must be one of your longest patients," I reflected, "if not the longest." The Picasso room still seemed full of elliptical, untranslatable objects, birds organized like files, branches writhing before a block of sea. "After all, I came to you for the first time when you were still a student."

Her pen had fallen silent a long time ago, I realized. At some point she'd quit taking notes. This marks a new beginning in our treatment, I thought: the time past her writing. "This must be a big day for you, too."

She seemed to nod, although I didn't look.

A film had formed between me and the Picasso as if a dusty window had dropped.

Then it was over. I sat up and laced my shoes. The few paces to where she'd risen were crossed in an instant. I had an impulse to hug her. My eyes suddenly filled with tears—at last! the melancholy I'd anticipated—but she shot out her arm. She gave a stiff handshake, a resolute smile on her face.

"Good-bye," she announced.

I drove. Felt as if I'd stripped off a heavy, waterlogged sweatshirt, and fresh skin was exposed to the air. So clean my body almost stung. My foot pressed hard all the way to the state liquor store at the Massachusetts border. Go. Go. I'd never actually stopped at this store before. But now the thought possessed me that a special bottle of wine —an "important" bottle—would be just the thing to commemorate this day.

Inside, I wandered aisles past people with miniature carts the size of baby carriages filled with bottles. A certain seven-year-old burgundy kept luring me. Seven years! That was how long I'd been in treatment! How would that many years taste? The little white sticker said $39.99. Far more than any wine had ever cost me. But something extraordinary was called for tonight.

When I arrived at Juliet's big green house on Centre Street in Somerville, another idea seized me. "Can you afford the insurance on two cars?" I asked when her door swung open. "Because if you can, I'd like you to have my Camry."

Juliet's Maxima had over 200,000 miles and was a source of constant concern.

"White smoke gusts out the tailpipe in the very beginning," I said, "but let it run five minutes, and it drives smooth as can be. It's a terrific car."

"Let's just think about it," she said, smiling already.

"One car in New York will be hard. Two's impossible."

"Just see if you really want to, later."

I nodded, and pictured dropping the key in her hand.

We rushed off into Juliet's kitchen—a vast room with dark walnut paneling hung with Greek Orthodox saints. Haloes shimmered, and the cathedralesque robes looked hammered out of wood. A friend of Juliet's was an ikon painter. I handed her the wine.

"Oh, my gosh! Seven years."

"Should taste good. Hmm . . . you baked." Two crusty round loaves lay in special willow baskets. The only ingredients in these loaves, I knew, were flour and water; the baskets left spiral patterns of flour around the rims.

"You don't have to like them," she said.

"But I do!"

So we sat and slathered hunks of the bread with butter and sea salt from a tall canister. The crystals sparkled in the candlelight and scintillated on our tongues, bright asterisks. Juliet had draped her table with a sky-blue and russet cloth. The border leapt out in the candlelight, a lambent blue band that seemed to hover over the fabric. She set out a bowl of salad with a homemade raspberry vinaigrette and pasta in a bright-tasting simmered sauce. We lifted our glasses and inhaled the wine's dark bouquet. Then sipped. Our eyes met. We burst out laughing.

The wine had stuffed our mouths with sand! We shook our heads. Then sipped once more, tentatively. Again it did it!—instantly sucking up all the moisture as if a dentist had wedged our mouths with cottonballs.

"Is it supposed to taste like this?" I said. "I'm no expert, but this can't be right."

"Hmm. I actually sort of like it," said Juliet.

I smiled. I was feeling quite happy that my treatment was over. Despite this, Juliet kept reassuring me that my face looked sad. She insisted, in fact, that I seemed about to burst into tears. I raised my eyebrows, wondering if it reassured Juliet to believe I was sad I'd left Harriet and sorry to have such a big part of my life end.

"Hey, why don't I set out the Athena?" I said. "Guest of honor!" I'd been carrying her around in the inner pocket of my tote for a month.

Now I reached inside and set the Athena on the table. But my heart seized. Her right arm was gone! And where was her round shield? White nicks scored the green surface all down the lovely folds in her dress.

"I had no idea she was so fragile," I murmured.

Juliet nodded. "I know."

"I shouldn't have kept her in my bag!"

I hadn't wanted her power to dissipate and for the figure to become ordinary. And I hadn't known if seeing the Athena on my desk would make me happy or angry. Now, though, I was possessed of the feeling that Harriet had given me something valuable that I hadn't appreciated.

And yet I *had* appreciated her. I did. And in a funny way, the fact that the goddess was damaged made her easier to accept. She was transformed. She was mine.

The next morning Juliet rode to Connecticut with me, and drove her new car home. And within two weeks I was ensconced in a sunny apartment in Brooklyn with a view of brownstones out the front windows and around the corner a store selling bagels so fresh the butter melted in. HOT BAGELS the store was called. It was open twenty-four hours a day. The names of the sandwiches were posted on index cards. Da Gooch was the name of one. Smokin' Joe was another. People actually used these names when they ordered. Sometimes I stood on the line just to hear.

A few months after we moved in, I opened my mailbox with its little tin key and spied her familiar stationery. My stomach plunged. A bright yellow forwarding sticker lay glued crooked alongside my old address, written in her hand. What did I expect—a curse, a harangue? Did I still suspect that even now she had the power to banish me from myself?

She drew my attention to my outstanding balance. She asked me to please "handle the matter." And she expressed, "on another note," the hope that I was doing well. This paper drifted into the nest of laundromat coupons and magazine-renewal notices in the corner of my desk. And in the months that followed, whenever appreciation for Harriet arose, my mind found that bill—a simple paper machine that turned gratitude to guilt. Yet still I did not pay.

She'd enriched herself at my expense, I felt. She'd held me too long. She confined me unwittingly in an eternal maze. A lamp blazes at the end of a corridor and you pursue it, caressed now by dangling worms (spaghetti?) while friends swivel Satan faces (papier-mâché?) and you hurry toward the lamp's warmth only to smash your nose—on glass! What? But the lamp hovers behind you now, directly over your shoulder. It hangs there. No, there! Until at last in one headlong rush you plunge straight into midafternoon. Sun bleaches the grass. Scent of hot, pulverized earth. Families stroll past in the drowning brightness, and a voice murmurs in your ear, "Here is your final bill."

Do you pay? You turn and there sways a pavilion of blankets! An antique, moth-eaten tent! Flocks of people stride past without giving it a glance. Some, though, cross themselves and grab their children from straying in. Why, it's an all but discredited sideshow, you gather! Psychoanalysis. A miserable-looking person, eyes glowing like ball bearings, stumbles in, is swallowed whole. Two worried-looking aristocrats step daintily out of a limousine. They too vanish. My insurance company transformed me into an aristocrat, right before the days of managed care. A loophole in history; my pockets stuffed with cash.

Gazing in amazement at the dark pavilion, one notices a corner lift in a billow of air. A sneaker flashes past; someone is racing. There's a turmoil of limbs and then the empty blanket hangs straight. To think that one can actually duck out at any time! It just hadn't seemed possible. Besides, the floating lamp entranced. And the world outside had appeared so dull and disjointed.

Naturally I could not pay.

To pay would be to disavow the very last bit of her mystery. It would be to dispose of her like the razors of the Bronx. A hole gaped right in our apartment's construction, between shelves of medicine. When my father finished a shave, he pushed the disposable blade into this slot. All those Bronx walls, spiked! But why hadn't the builders foreseen the day the razors would grow up to us on the third story and beyond, a metal beanstalk, and the hole glinting, unable to swallow even one more blade?

The secret of the razor wall compelled me as a girl. I pulled open the mirror often to see the hidden mouth, which was like the narrow backstairs near the incinerator or the gold medallions on the corridor walls or the blue gas haloes my mother showed me behind the dryers in the basement near the milk machine, or even the skittering hard-shelled waterbugs that wandered fat as stopwatches over the painted green floor, part of an empire I'd inherited with a checkerboard lobby and murky chandelier.

An old pianist gave lessons in an apartment off the lobby. The daughter of a certain trim white couple gave birth to four lovely polite children by three different black men, and the children and mother all lived with the white grandparents, who kept fit by striding the dim gold corridors back and forth from the A apartment to the N. I myself wandered those same corridors as Cassandra in Anita's school-play costume, blue ribbons crisscrossing up my calves and a pattern of rigid gold waves lapping at my knee, shouting, "Trick or treat!" at each door, too timid to do a trick and knowing I was too old for this, being twelve, but lingering in these halls just one last year since I didn't yet know anything as good as childhood and I liked an excuse to knock on doors, to glimpse the lives within.

An unbreathing infant was found in the incinerator closet on the fourth floor, nestled on the stacks of newspapers, but the policemen who arrived—looming blue and sweaty in the suddenly tiny apartments—shifted their weight and declined to make an arrest. On the top floor a millionaire's son sold all the air conditioners out of the windows for drugs, and in the apartment beside my parents' a black cat named Baby waits at the door, declawed, fat as a pillow, remembering perhaps his life as a gaunt mouser consigned to the basement of a liquor store, now cream-fed, with a heap of toys, whining out of sheer satiation. My own ex-brother-in-law this very month is installing his new wife, a plump doctor, into the apartment where Anita used to live, and, through the ceiling of my parents' apartment late on Friday night comes the voice of the man upstairs singing tomor-row's Torah portion, a medieval minor-noted melody across which heaves the 100 bus as it thrusts itself from the curb at 238th Street.

I dream of Anita all the time. The 100 bus was hers, of course, pulling away from the curb beyond the terrace door, open on its chain. In my dreams she just needs to be immersed in water for her to be able to swim, and Oh, she says, the movement feels so good! Or she is in a room that's run out of gas. We need only to have the gas company come and they'll add fuel and she'll be better. Often I don't remember these dreams until midmorning, pouring milk into my second cup of coffee, when suddenly I realize I've dreamt about Anita.

The 100 bus still seems hers, hauling away into the night, as if Anita were really aboard it, just obscured behind all the strangers stepping on after, like a snapshot she once glued into the family scrapbook. "But you're not even in the picture!" we other children complained. "But I should have been," she responded, and the photo stayed. It was a snapshot documenting the first time she rode a bus by herself. First was a photo of Anita standing on line in a round blue hat with trailing ribbons, and then came a photo of men and women surging up the stairs. "I'm sitting behind these people," Anita said, and we stared at the strangers. I remember the time we phoned her in Israel. "Tell her don't run!" we asked the person who raced across the kibbutz to tell "Aneetah" she had a phone call from home. The international operator had explained that we wouldn't be billed until Anita picked up and actually started to speak. "Tell her to walk!" we pled. But Anita ran across the entire kibbutz, and although we were craving to hear her voice, for the first three or four minutes of the call she could only listen as we heard her panting. Her illness feels like that. She is panting, trying to reach us, and we are desperate to hear her voice.

All this was mine, as was Harriet, who had erected in me her own balustrades and crenellations, her own weedy passageways: a spec-tral palace. Settling her last bill would end it, I feared. The wool rugs would roll up, the chandelier flicker out, and what had been real would resolve itself into the flatness of cardboard, a fever dream.

In decamping, Harriet might just pack up my insides, too. And even if she didn't, even if she simply made off with her own tent and fluttering pennants, her own doily staircase and encyclopedias of Melanie Klein, something in me would vanish—seven years and a skein of belief, the sewn binding that kept my own self together, year folded into year.

As long as I held on to this bill, Harriet and I were not done. The last symphonic chord had not been struck. It lay before us, waiting to resolve everything. I shut the glass, sealed her up in me and kept her final bill as a love letter: Oct. 11, 12 . . . . . $180.

Adam Phillips writes, "To analyse a transference, of course, is to analyse a person's need for belief, their craving for experts." Harriet was a slot in which I could press my razors. Envy, terror. Because she fixed my writer's block so fast—two weeks!—I assumed she was magic. I wanted to assume that. The quick cure could have as easily provided reason to quit; instead it announced to me her power and furnished proof I should stay.

I never looked up Harriet's publications, as Janice did with her therapist. This reassured Janice, just as it reassured me to leave Harriet's outlines indistinct, for her presence in the real world to remain indeterminate. I wanted an experience of magic and that's what I received. But I seem to fear she herself was a packing box that lurked behind the furniture the whole time, behind the couch, behind her desk: a folded shadow. Or that behind me stretches an empty crate, and everything I thought was something amounts to nothing. From time to time I even thought of phoning Princeton to ask about her dissertation but was afraid I'd be told: "We never had a Harriet Sing study here. We have no record of such a person."

The first three months after I stopped, while I was taping up a Poetry in Motion poster from the subway museum on Schermerhorn and discovering how good the pizza was at the corner joint, I was in fact sure Harriet was a species of vampire: the real thief of happiness, after all. Now, though, over two years later, I'm amazed by how much of value remains.

"You are not a hundred percent different from how you were before treatment," says Paul. "The main difference is you didn't clearly have your own things. Now you do."

The unexpected gift that arrived immediately upon leaving treatment was the discovery of my own powers. Without Harriet to resort to, I learned to find my own peace. I took to setting goals and, despite how I felt, advancing toward them. My relation to noise altered as well. Even when the brownstone to our left was gutted, I could write. And a month later, when the facade of the building on our right was jackhammered I told myself: I want New York and this is an aspect of living here. I choose this situation, which entails noise. With that thought, words flowed again.

Walking down Montague Street recently, it occurred to me that if I simply thought about it now, I could finally understand why anxiety electrified me the entire time I was in therapy.

The answer came at once. Therapy created in me the feeling of being alone in the house with my mother, being alone with the fabulous mother and quite intimate with her and happy, and yet lacking in all defenses, as a little child is. No boundaries. The entire world was the warm room in which I lived with my mother. And so the least conflict with friends was disturbing because they were in the house with me, they were in the room with me. I was frantic they would ruin my connection with this mother. Their very presence distracted from her and thus from well-being. I needed to be alone with this source of goodness, who had reverted me to a childlike but frustratingly helpless state.

Naturally Dr. Sing would say that the anxieties I wanted to defend against were simply parts of me. Still, the dependence that therapy induced was in itself, I could see now, a maddening stress. Once I ended the treatment, my fears stopped galloping over the walls. They became smaller, and smaller yet, and I was normal again.

I'd been searching for a goddess for years—someone who would allow me to feel the joy I imagined Kate felt tracking before me in her doeskin jacket, or Anita pasting stamps in her Master Global stamp album, or a bold friend striding through a door proclaiming that she wanted to be a star and by that utterance snatching the heavens into a shawl that trailed behind her.

I didn't know how to let anything of my own be good. The value of my own things always eroded until they seemed like dirt, debris. Nor was I able to make decisions, because I disregarded so many of my own reactions, while at the same time holding out for a perfect solution, something unassailable. Now I'm able to feel pleasure in a way I couldn't before the therapy. I was a bucket with a hole, and Harriet plugged it. I no longer leak out all over the place.

I'm also able to perceive other people with greater clarity. I take in with delight my Uncle Julie's prudent black rubber boots as we walk to the Union Square station for his trip back to Long Island City, and Franklin's need to keep his house perfectly clean, so clean that he must mail me back my scarf rather than wait for me to collect it, and Paul's parents, those very forgiving people—my adventurous father-in-law handing me a lichee nut to try, my mother-in-law pulling herself up straight in her chair and braving back pain with more grace than I ever could, and my friend Claire's slow, deliberate style of conversation, as if carefully assembling the beams of an erector set, a style of conversation that makes you wait and wait for her whole idea to be complete so that you can see what it is, and Claire's own resistance to this. I'm able to see other people in a way I couldn't in the days when I wore my cheerfulness like a big hoop skirt, keeping others at a distance. The world is more complicated, and near.

Two weeks ago I called Princeton. It had been two and a half years since I'd last seen Harriet. It occurred to me that it was about time to read her dissertation. I smiled. It would be good to immerse again in the old Kleinian terms, that brutal poetry. Perhaps I'd even stumble across some keys to her approach to me.

"Just a moment," said the librarian in New Jersey.

She put me on hold and I sat, jiggling my leg. "The alumni files don't list any Harriet Sing," she said.

"What?" It was exactly like my nightmare!

"Oh, excuse me. Wait. Yes. Harriet Eileen Sing?"

Eileen! "Yes."

"She received her doctorate from the University of Wyoming."

A wave of nausea overcame me. "*Wyoming?*"

"In Laramie."

But she'd let me believe she'd studied at Princeton all those years!

"Her dissertation is called *Effect of a Leader's Direction on the Focus Group.*"

Not even about Kleinian psychology! "Are you sure?"

"That's what it says here."

"Thank you." I hung up. Then, after a few minutes, dialed Wyoming.

Harriet Sing earned her doctorate from the University of Wyoming in 1990, a woman in the alumni office informed me.

"Thank you very much," I whispered, and replaced the receiver. I stared at the phone for several minutes as if it were something alive, explosive. Then dialed again. "I'm so sorry to bother you, but could you possibly please tell me where Harriet Sing did her undergraduate work? The name of the college?"

More computer clicking. "Arts and Sciences."

"Is that at the University of Wyoming?"

"Why yes, ma'am."

"Thank you. Oh, please—one last thing. Could you possibly tell me what year she earned her undergraduate degree?"

My heart banged. I'd always assumed that Harriet had taken several years off before pursuing her doctorate. After all, she was at least a decade older than I.

"Let me check," said the woman. More clicking. "1983."

She was five years younger! A strange feeling of melting in the center overtook me, as if I were a watercolor, running—as if everything we'd done together were a fraud, I'd wasted a decade. And the issue of children—why, I assumed her attitude was based on seasoned wisdom, that she understood more than I! "Thank you for your trouble," I murmured.

"Okey-doke."

☼ ☼ ☼

So she was the Wizard of Oz after all. Riding in, like him, in a hot-air balloon from some Kansas State Fair. Sprung from out West and self-invented in the East, the Great Gatsby of Psychoanalysis. How often had she allowed me to declare what supreme confidence I had in her because of her Princeton training? Of course, she didn't correct me: why interfere with the transference? But hadn't she felt the least bit fraudulent?

Why, it seemed like the end of a *Star Trek* episode when the beautiful woman dissolves into a mass of lava, or the mask is removed and one realizes—yes, oh it was a "composite portrait" all along, elements you'd projected unconsciously onto an alien being.

In reality, she was just a cocky young woman from a big state school, holing up with her tomes of Kleinian analysis the way others pore over texts on divination, alchemy, Morse code, the top tier of orange and yellow kabalistic angels, numerologies, charts of nightshade vegetables, self-invented periodic charts.

Of course, people receive excellent educations at western state universities all the time and reasons abound for why Harriet Sing might have studied at one. Still, she wasn't who she'd allowed me to believe she was. "Give me a place to stand and a lever, and I can move the world," said Archimedes. But what if the place you're standing on dissolves?

"Your big issue in life was always being overdeferring," said my friend Mark. "So you played it out with her. The benefits you got are real."

"Yes," I said. "But I keep thinking of that line from the book *The Wonderful Wizard of Oz*, 'How can I help being a humbug when all these people make me do things that everybody knows can't be done?'"

"She's the last humbug," he said.

I smiled. Realizing how young she'd been made me see her in retrospect as short, shrunken, doughy-faced, dyspeptic, full of her own ego strivings of which I'd been oblivious—a sort of Janice, in fact. How old had she been when she soberly advised that I have sessions twice a week? Twenty-six? Perhaps she hadn't felt the press of time the way I did, the years tearing away. How she must have savored being told: "This therapy is one of the great experiences in my life! This is my Paris. I'm enjoying the prime of Miss Harriet Sing."

A glittery white AV screen seemed to have been sprung shut, swiveled, its tripod legs collapsed—until just a tall thin can with a blank scroll inside remained. There was no more Dr. Sing.

In the days that followed, I kept having the sensation of the ground spinning, no matter what I was doing. Sitting at my computer, rushing down Pell Street past fishmarkets, peeling an orange with my back against the silver ribs of the tepid radiator, stepping down the winding flights of my building, the world spun and spun as if I'd been turning in place.

And yet, when my eyes opened early one morning a few weeks later, it occurred to me that I'd had a true encounter with someone who had a distinct mental brilliance, profound empathy, and even wisdom. Despite the trappings, I'd had a real encounter with a real person. The rest is inkblots, stage settings. I'd wanted magic, and I found it, and it was good and powerful magic. Since Harriet provided a doorway to the spectral palace, I assumed it belonged to her. But the echoey empire with its checkerboard lobby and murky chandelier, the painted-over mezuzahs and the super's wife who calls everybody "Love"—all this was an inheritance I'd locked away like the blue valentine. Harriet helped me recapture it, but my name was inscribed on the deed.

A person who's alive is constantly getting lost. The big thing, it seems to me, is to realize that this is one's own adventure, and that all the field guides and oracles and shamans, the whole caravansary of people holding up mirrors, can only flash you at best a glimpse of your own story, a brilliant glimpse, perhaps, but it's yours to savor and spend. It belongs to no one else. Only you can be its expert.

Harriet taught me to value what's mine, even with its imperfections, its razor mouths and Attic nymphs dressed as their sisters wandering from A to N, knocking on doors, remembering the day when the lightbulbs seemed too weak to illuminate so much beauty. It was all a spectral palace, but real.

✳ ✳ ✳

Harriet's bill crept away. It vanished into a packing box or a heap of papers dusty as silt. How much did I owe her? I dreaded to think. Certainly thousands of dollars. Three years had passed since we'd said good-bye.

During that time it had come to seem unfortunate to me that in order to leave Dr. Sing I'd become the scandalized, outraged daughter I never was to my own parents, gloating at her errors, fixated on her blind spots, deflecting her observations, enumerating her flaws like a perverse catechism, praying her voodoo power would stop the instant I slammed the door shut behind me.

How triumphant I'd felt when I located something that seemed hypocritical in Harriet! The world went topsy-turvy for an instant, as if she'd tricked me into believing that a chess queen was actually the Statue of Liberty (she'd shrunk me that small!) and a cardboard skyline was every bit as wonderful as the honking, panting, sidewalk-flung city itself—but that now, at last, I could see the truth. I was leaving the checkerboard world, the red plastic queen with her prickly crown, the patterned paper that impersonated real avenues, the mesmerizing mirrors at our ankles that projected us many stories high, the entire world of fantasy. Hadn't she meant to hold me there forever? Or was that really my own wish pasted onto her, my own terror of leaving?

At last, impulsively, sitting in my Brooklyn kitchen, I wrote a letter. Could she tell me the size of my debt? Perhaps I'd pay it off on an installment plan.

The envelope arrived shortly after—her familiar yellow linen stationery, with her neat handwriting spelling out my name. Even this surprised me. She was so intimate to me that there lingered the faint conviction that I'd made her up. But no—here came her envelope, addressed in her own hand. I clasped it a moment, then opened it carefully. She'd locked my records away in storage. But she estimated that I hadn't paid her for the last four sessions, a total of $360.

What a relief! In my mind the debt had swelled to an impossible sum, and I was long past being able to get my old insurance to pay for it.

I scribbled out the check, licked shut the envelope, and sent it forth to Harriet. I no longer needed the paper machine that converted gratitude into resentment. I could afford to be grateful now. I could afford to assess the many riches our therapy had brought me—the freedom from envy and from the melancholy in which I'd obliviously lived while assuming that sadness was the true nature of existence. I'd gained, too, an ability to think independently, to perceive others' internal struggles, and to believe in the validity of my own experience. I simply vanished less now than I used to. These benefits hadn't evaporated upon terminating the treatment. I could now tolerate Harriet Sing and me being through.

And then, last week, a phone call:

"Bonnie? Hello. It's Harriet." The room jolted. My palm pressed hard on the kitchen counter as I straightened myself. Her southern-inflected voice was playing on my machine. What a sweet, confidential tone she had!

"I received your book and I'm anxious and excited to read it," she continued.

I'd mailed the manuscript for this book the afternoon before, and invited her to tell me anything she wished changed. I wanted her to feel her privacy was protected. I didn't want her to feel harmed by my book. And I wanted to make sure she wouldn't sue me.

"I want you to know," she said, "your experience of therapy is yours, and what you do with your experience is also your decision. I don't have a right to alter your experience in any way. I don't feel like it's in my purview to ask you to change anything of your experience because your experience is so personal, and so yours."

The old remorse washed over me. I sat down. She was good—marvelously good—after all. I'd been so afraid of her disapproval! For years I'd woken up worried about her reaction. What if she tried to prevent the book's publication? What if she hated how I'd described her? What if she wanted to punish me?

Now I thought: She was as good as I knew her to be from the very beginning. As good as I felt her to be those first years! Why had I ever decided to leave?

Then I shook my head. Up to my old ways, was I? Again trying to make Harriet's goodness into evidence that I was bad? That I ought to lapse back into dependence, into a conviction of my own error?

I smiled. She was as good as I'd known her to be, which was truly quite wonderful. That didn't make me wrong or mistaken. I nodded, and collected my heap of books to return to the Brooklyn Public Library, where the checkout women have fingernails painted with sunsets and you frequently open a hardcover to discover commentary penciled in the margin. Books are respected here, but even they aren't treated with too much reverence. I passed my landlady's apartment and heard her piano lessons through the wall—a child laboring through "Frère Jacques"—and pushed open the front door and stepped out onto the sunny, bustling city street.

Acknowledgments

Deepest gratitude to Malaga Baldi, agent extraordinaire, and Amy Caldwell, my insightful and inspiring editor at Beacon Press, for their faith and encouragement.

Patricia Foster, Rachel Basch, and Gary Glickman read early drafts of this book and gave astute feedback. Priscilla Sneff, Meryl Cohen, John Kane, Elissa Altman, Darrell Rosenbluth, Peggy Merrill, and Melanie Braverman provided much wisdom and good cheer during the events described in these pages. And Sally Randolph shared with me innumerable café au laits, Short Wave margaritas at Mexican Radio, and pink things.

Thanks also to my parents, for being the big-hearted, tolerant, supportive, and generous people they are. And to my husband, Paul, for putting up with me despite everything and always believing in me.

07/03

LOWER MILLS